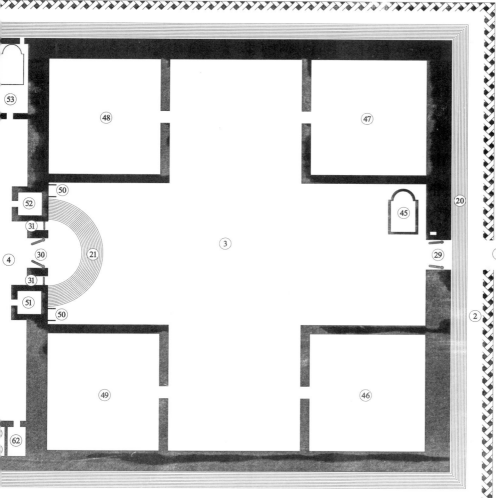

Seven
Special
Weeks

Seven Special Weeks

Naftali
in the
BEIS HAMIKDASH
BOOK SERIES

The adventures
of a young boy
and his classmates
during the time of
the Second Temple

A historical tale detailing
the layout and halachos
of the Beis HaMikdash
and the laws of korbanos

---

by **Yaakov Meir Strauss**

FELDHEIM PUBLISHERS
JERUSALEM   NEW YORK

Originally published in Hebrew as *Mul Kisei HaKavod* (5763)

Translated from the Hebrew by Rabbi Boruch Kalinsky
Edited by Rabbi David Kahn and Deena Nataf
Illustrated by Tova Katz

Yaakov Meir Strauss
18 Ravina
Bnei Brak, Israel

FELDHEIM PUBLISHERS
POB 43163 / Jerusalem, Israel

208 Airport Executive Park
Nanuet, NY 10954

www.feldheim.com

Printed in Israel

לציון נפש חיה

In loving memory of a righteous woman

Yaffa Miriam Strauss ע״ה

daughter of ילב״ט Rav Meir Snyder הי״ו

*She raised and educated her children
to love of Torah and pure fear of Hashem
with much self-sacrifice and devotion.*

She passed on to the World of Truth
on 22 Kislev 5758.

תנצב״ה

Memorialized by her children שיחיו

Contents

On pages 321 to 325, you will find a complete list of every item in the Beis HaMikdash, and at the very end of the book, on the inside back cover, there is a map showing the Women's Courtyard and the *Azarah*.

Key to Charts and Maps

*...I will heal you from your wounds...for they called you
"Rejected"! [saying,] "This is Zion – there is none who seeks
her!"*

(YIRMEYAHU 30:17)

*From the words "There is none who seeks her" we learn that
she requires seeking.*

(ROSH HASHANAH 30A)

*When the Jews cried out in their anguish, Hashem responded
through the words of Yirmeyahu the Prophet, saying: I can
bring you salvation, but what can I do when "This is Zion
— there is none who seeks her"? Zion herself cries out to me:
The Jews don't remember me [even] with a remembrance of the
Holy Temple!*

*Thus, our Redemption requires that the Jewish People re-
member and yearn for the Beis HaMikdash.*

(SEFER YOM TERUAH ON TRACTATE ROSH HASHANAH)

Dear Reader

SEVEN SPECIAL WEEKS IS A work of historical fiction. The book takes us through the seven wondrous weeks between Pesach and Shavuos that our hero, Naftali, spends in Yerushalayim studying the *halachos* of the Beis HaMikdash and its sacrifices. The story takes place during the end of the Second Temple period.

Much thought and care has gone into making sure that the details are accurate and based on Torah sources. However, because the author has tried to bring to life the experiences of a boy and his family in ancient times, many of the happenings and the people in this story are fiction.

The *halachos* have been checked and re-checked for accuracy. You will find their sources in the footnotes and can look them up yourself. Because, to our sorrow, today we don't have the Beis HaMikdash, some of the *halachos* mentioned in the book are applied differently in our times. Therefore, no ruling in this book should be seen as a definitive *p'sak*.

The numbers in parentheses in the text correspond to the charts and maps that are included throughout the book. In this way, you will be able to see for yourself where the different structures and objects in the Beis HaMikdash were situated.

It is our hope that young readers will benefit greatly from having a glimpse of our glorious past, and life in the Holy Land when the Beis HaMikdash stood. May it be rebuilt speedily in our days, Amen.

The BeChatzros Beis Hashem Institute

WITH HASHEM'S HELP WE FOUNDED the BeChatzros Beis Hashem Institute. Our goal is to acquaint young readers with the laws concerning the Beis HaMikdash and the Divine Service in an innovative way that we hope will capture and thrill their hearts and minds. We sincerely hope to be among the privileged to see the Beis HaMikdash rebuilt speedily in our days, and to witness the Divine Service being carried out by the Kohanim.

It was also our aim to make it easier and more interesting for children and youth to learn the *halachos* connected with the Beis HaMikdash and, in this way, to attract them to the concepts discussed in *Seder Kodashim* and to encourage them to study this *seder* in detail.

We humbly thank Hashem Yisbarach for blessing our first book, *HaZechiyah HaGedolah*, with great success. It deals with the *halachos* of *korban Pesach* and was enthusiastically welcomed and accepted in all religious circles. It has been translated into English under the title *Three Special Days* (Jerusalem: Feldheim Publishers, 2003), and into Yiddish as *Ashrei Ayin Ra'asa Zos*, published by the *Et Sofer* Institute.

Seven Special Weeks (*Mul Kisei HaKavod* in Hebrew) is our second book. It presents a concise anthology of the *halachos* discussed in *Masechtos Middos* and *Tamid*, interwoven with the laws of purification of a *metzora* and the burning of the *Parah Adumah* (red heifer).

The third volume in this series, dealing with Yom Kippur issues, is currently in progress.

Introduction

A PRINCE WAS ONCE EXILED from his father's home to a far-away country, because his behavior was not fitting for a prince. Later, the king wished to bring back his son to his palace, but he wanted the request to come from his son. He hoped that the son would feel a strong yearning to return. The son, however, had only a hazy memory of the splendor of his father's house, because a long time had passed since he was exiled. Even when he asked his father to allow him to return, the request did not come from the depths of his heart.

A long time afterwards, the son received a letter describing the palace and its activity. While reading the letter, forgotten memories from days past filled the thoughts of the son. He felt great pain that he could not live in that wonderful palace and enjoy its delights. Finally, he pleaded with his father, saying that his greatest desire was to return to his father's house and to witness its glory.

And we too, want to return to our Father's House — to the Holy Temple, God's House. As we say in our prayers, "Because of our sins, we were exiled from our country and we are far from our land. We cannot go up and appear and bow down to You, and perform our duties in Your chosen House, the great and holy House, on which You placed Your Name." It is true that we request every day: "And to Yerushalayim, Your city, return

with mercy ... build it speedily in our days, an eternal building."
Three times a day we pray: "And may our eyes see when You return to Zion with mercy." But the Holy One Blessed be He wants
us to sincerely desire it. He wants us to *feel* the loss of the Beis
HaMikdash.

It is our prayer that this book succeed in stirring the readers to ask from the depths of their hearts: "Merciful Father, have
mercy on us ... build Your House as it was originally, and estab-
lish Your Beis HaMikdash on its foundation. May we look upon
it when it is built, and rejoice in its establishment. And return
the Kohanim to their service and the Leviyim to their songs and
music."

Seven
Special
Weeks

Chapter One

Naftali Stays in Yerushalayim

A pleasant breeze stirred the barley in the field. The brightly lit houses of Yerushalayim appeared on the horizon. Ten-year-old Naftali stood with his father squeezed among the huge crowd of the thousands of Jews who came to watch *ketziras haOmer* — the reaping of barley used for the *Omer*-offering (*korban haOmer*).

They had left Yerushalayim as soon as the stars appeared in the sky and had traveled to the fields south of the city. These sun-drenched fields produced the best grain, and it was from them that the *omer*-measure was taken for an offering.[1] Naftali was so eager to see the reaping of the first harvest that their short trip seemed to him like an endless journey. The sight of so many other Jews who were making their way to the south with keen anticipation compelled Naftali to wonder:

"Abba, why is the reaping of the first crop carried out with such great pomp and ceremony?"

"Well, it's done on purpose," his father replied, "in order to publicize the correct date on which the *Omer*-offering must be brought. This is so that people do not make a mistake[2] by letting

1. *Menachos* 85a.
2. *Menachos* 65a.

themselves be duped into accepting the erroneous opinion of the heretic Tzedokim. The Tzedokim do not believe that Hashem gave Moshe Rabbeinu the Oral Torah, in which He explained to him exactly how to interpret the Written Torah and all its laws. Thus, they distort the true meaning of all the Torah's verses by misinterpreting them.

"In the case of the *korban haOmer*, they misinterpret the verse, 'From the day after the rest day (*"ha-shabbos"*), from the day you bring the *omer*-measure for the wave-offering, you shall count for yourselves seven weeks.'[3] According to their opinion, 'the rest day' refers to the seventh day of the week, and one must therefore begin to count the seven weeks from the day after Shabbos — that is to say, from the Sunday following the first day of Pesach. According to this wrong opinion, the *korban haOmer* will always be brought on the first day of the week, which means that the Yom Tov of Shavuos will also occur on a Sunday, every year.[4]

"We are part of the group known as the Perushim, who do not accept the false notions of the Tzedokim. We interpret the Written Torah the way Hashem explained it in the Oral Torah, and this is the only true interpretation. The term 'rest day' or '*ha-shabbos*' in the verse does not denote the seventh day of the week. Rather, it denotes a 'rest day' similar to Shabbos, a day on which *melachah* may not be done — in other words, the Yom Tov day at the beginning of Pesach. So the correct meaning of the verse is 'from the day after the first day of Pesach.' That's when the *Omer*-offering is brought."

Naftali's father added, "Our Sages quote many other verses[5] to prove that this interpretation is correct, but we won't discuss

---

3. *Vayikra* 23:15.

4. *Menachos* 65a.

5. *Menachos* 65b.

it now. The main reason that we harvest the grain for the *korban haOmer* tonight is because this is how we received the tradition via the *Torah she-be'al peh* — the Oral Torah.[6] This is how it was done by the prophets and the Sanhedrin throughout every generation. Even if we could not prove that we're right from verses of the Written Torah, we would still act according to the tradition of our Sages.

"By the way, our *Chachamim* publicly debated the Tzedokim on this issue and defeated them. The debate lasted from the 8th of Nisan until Pesach, and those days were therefore proclaimed as festive days, during which fasting is prohibited."[7]

*   *   *

An all-encompassing silence ensued in the open field, and only the whisper of the barley stalks was heard stirring in the breeze.

"Has the sun set?" the three reapers asked in a loud voice.[8]

"*Hein*! Yes!" the public answered.

"Has the sun set?" the reapers inquired again.

"*Hein!*" was the answer.

"Has the sun set?" they asked a third time, as if they were still in doubt.

"*Hein!*" was the prompt reply.

"The reapers are asking if the sun has already set, which means that the time to reap the *omer*-measure of barley has come," Naftali's father explained to him in a whisper.

The reapers lifted up their sickles, and asked:

"*Magal zo*? With this sickle?"

"*Hein!*" the people who surrounded them replied.

---

6. Rambam, *Hilchos Temidin u'Musafin* 7:11.

7. *Menachos* 65a.

8. Ibid.

The question was repeated twice more, followed by the prompt replies of the public. The father explained to his son that the reapers must ask many questions, repeating each one three times. This gave the event great publicity, eliminating any possibility of making a mistake concerning the correct date of the reaping. It appeared to Naftali that a distinguished-looking older man, who was standing next to them, was listening to their conversation.

"*Kuppah zo?* This basket?" the reapers asked, which meant: "Shall we reap into these baskets?" To which the public answered: "*Hein!*" Again they repeated the question twice and were answered twice by the people who surrounded them.

"*Ektzor?* Shall I reap?" the reapers asked.

"*Ktzor!* Reap!" they were commanded.

"*Ektzor?*" they asked again.

"*Ktzor!*" everybody replied.

And after they had received a positive answer for the third time, the three reapers,[9] who were holding sickles in their hands, started reaping. Each one of the reapers reaped the barley with his sickle and put it into his basket. When the three baskets were full, each one containing the measure of a *se'ah*,[10] the messengers of the *Beis Din* brought them to Yerushalayim, whereupon the public dispersed, impressed by the exciting scene.

*   *   *

On their way back to Yerushalayim they were joined by the older man who had been observing Naftali talking with his father in the field. They had greeted him politely and offered him a ride in their wagon. Naftali turned to his father, who had embarked on a very interesting, detailed discourse:

---

9. *Menachos* 63b.

10. *Se'ah* — a grain measure equaling 8.2 liters, slightly less than ¼ bushel.

"If you have the choice, it is always better to reap from a field that is close to Yerushalayim.[11] There are two reasons for this. First, there is a principle in halachah not to pass up an immediate opportunity for performing a mitzvah. Therefore, it's best to bring the *Omer*-offering from a closer field, rather than from one that is farther away.

"Secondly, the verse[12] says that the barley used for the *Omer*-offering must be '*karmel.*' This means that its kernels must be fresh, tender and soft, so that you can still rub and crush them with your fingers. If they are brought from a remote area, they may get dry and hard on the way to Yerushalayim.

"It happened once," his father related, "that it was necessary to bring the *Omer*-offering from a place called Gaggos Tzerifin,[13] which is far from Yerushalayim. That year the two rival Chashmonai brothers, Horkenus and Aristobulus, were at war with each other over who would control Yerushalayim. Aristobulus ruled in Yerushalayim, and Horkenus and his army laid siege to the city in order to capture it.

"Every day the citizens of Yerushalayim lowered a container full of gold coins over the wall. Their Jewish brethren who were besieging the city took the coins and replaced them with sheep for the regular daily sacrifice [*korban Tamid*].

"Once, the besiegers saw an old man on top of the wall, signaling to them with his hand. The old man wanted to help the army of Horkenus, so he sent secret messages to them in a special coded language that was based on Greek wisdom. The messages said that as long as the Jews inside the city walls continued to

---

11. *Menachos* 64b.

12. *Vayikra* 2:14: "…you shall bring the first, fresh kernels of the [barley] harvest, parched in fire and coarsely ground, as the meal-offering of your first ripening grain."

13. *Menachos* 64b.

sacrifice the *korban Tamid* in the Beis HaMikdash, the besiegers had no chance of defeating them.

"Horkenus and his army were very happy to receive those messages, and they thought of quite an odious idea. The next day they put a pig into the container instead of sheep. In the middle of its ascent, the pig stuck the nails of its impure hooves into the wall of Yerushalayim. Then, something shocking happened: the Land of Israel quaked. Tremors were felt throughout four hundred square *parsah*[14] of its territory. Because of that, the *Chachamim* issued a decree: 'Cursed is the man who breeds pigs, and cursed is the man who teaches his son Greek wisdom.'"

Naftali's father stopped for a moment to breathe in the pure air of the holy city's environs, and then remarked sadly, "You see, my son, how grave the sin of brotherly hatred is, if it leads to such terrible consequences?! That year the soldiers, who had laid siege to Yerushalayim, destroyed all the surrounding fields, and the messengers of the *Beis Din*, therefore, had to reap the *omer*-measure in Gaggos Tzerifin."

Naftali noticed that the old man who was traveling with them kept looking at him closely. He turned his eyes away confusedly. After they reached the city gate, the old man asked to speak with his father privately. His father got out of the wagon, and they talked together in low voices. Naftali was very curious to know what the subject of their conversation was, and hoped that he would eventually find out. But when he heard his own name suddenly mentioned, he pricked up his ears. He wondered what made them talk about *him* of all people.

At that very moment, his father parted with the old man and got back into the wagon with a smile that obviously hid a secret. They drove on until they reached the house of their host, Reb

---

14. *Parsah* — a parasang, a measure of length equaling 2.68 miles (4.32 kilometers).

The old man and Naftali's father spoke privately in low voices

Asher. There, Naftali's curiosity grew even more when he saw his father exchange whispers with his mother. He jumped from his seat when he heard his father call him, and ran to his parents' side.

"Tell me, Naftali, would you be interested in staying Yerushalayim until Shavuos?"

"To stay in Yerushalayim?! Wow, of course!" Naftali exclaimed, his eyes shining with joy. "But who am I going to stay with? And why am I staying? Where will I learn?"

His father smiled at his excitement and confusion. "I'll explain everything. The older man whom we gave a ride to in our wagon is both very wealthy and a great Torah scholar. He lives in the northern city of Tiveriah. He came to Yerushalayim with a great amount of *ma'aser sheini* money, with which he redeemed his *ma'aser sheini* produce.[15] As you know from the Torah,[16] this money must be spent on food, and it has to be eaten in Yerushalayim.

"Now, this worthy Jew — whose name is Reb Avraham — distributed an ample part of this money among poor people who had come up to Yerushalayim for Pesach as *olei regel*,[17] so that

---

15. *Ma'aser sheini* — Various tithes must be removed from produce. One of them is called *ma'aser sheini*. *Ma'aser sheini* is removed on the first, second, fourth and fifth years of the seven-year *Shemittah* cycle. It must be brought to Yerushalayim and eaten there, or redeemed for money. The money is then brought to Yerushalayim, and food is bought with it.

16. *Devarim* 14:26: "You shall then exchange the money for all that your heart desires — for cattle and sheep, for strong wine, or for all your heart may wish — and eat it before the Eternal, your God, and you and your household shall rejoice."

17. *Olei regel* — The mitzvah of *aliyah le-regel* requires men to make a pilgrimage to Yerushalayim for the three Festivals of Pesach, Shavuos and Sukkos (*Shemos* 23:17): "Three times a year, all menfolk among you shall appear before the Lord, Hashem."

they would be able to purchase some food for themselves for Yom Tov.

"As a reward for performing this mitzvah, Hashem has given Reb Avraham an opportunity to perform yet another one — just as our Sages say, 'One mitzvah brings about another.'[18] Reb Avraham thought of an idea to open a special learning circle in Yerushalayim. It will consist of ten children your age, who live outside Yerushalayim and have come here for Pesach. These children are going to study the *halachos* pertaining to the Beis HaMikdash and its sacrifices. They will stay in Yerushalayim until Shavuos, in a building that belongs to Reb Avraham. Their meals will be cooked from the food bought from his *ma'aser sheini* money.

"Reb Avraham only wants to choose boys who sincerely strive for learning and knowledge. After he listened to our learning together, he came to the conclusion that you are suitable for his special class!"

Naftali gave his father a questioning look, and his father answered his mute question. "Yes, Imma agrees — even though she is reluctant to go back home without you. But she is prepared to sacrifice her feelings for your sake, and for the sake of your growth in Torah. What do you say to this, Naftali? Are you interested?"

Naftali answered on the spot, without any hesitation whatsoever. "Of course I want to stay! I'll probably learn with boys from *chutz la'aretz*, from other countries!" he added excitedly.

"Are you sure you won't miss home, Naftali?" his mother hesitated. "Maybe you want to change your mind and return home together with us?"

"Don't worry, Imma, if I start feeling homesick, I'll think of how much I've gained by staying, and how much I've learned. I'm sure I won't regret it!"

---

18. *Midrash Tanchuma, Parashas Ki Seitzeh*; Mishnah *Avos* 4:2.

Chapter Two

The First Meeting

The next day, Naftali met his classmates. It was Friday of *Chol HaMo'ed* Pesach, Erev Shabbos, so they didn't have too much time at their disposal. The ten students met in a small synagogue next to the eastern gate of Yerushalayim. Naftali was very excited because he got his wish: there were four boys from *chutz la'aretz* in the new group. Yechezkel came from Rome, Bo'az came from Macedonia (Greece), Yonasan came from Persia, and Chananya HaLevi from Babylonia.

"My father will also stay in Eretz Yisrael for a few months," Yechezkel told him, "but Bo'az, Yonasan and Chananya are going to stay in Yerushalayim by themselves. Their fathers will return home immediately after Pesach."

Naftali was really amazed at the self-sacrifice of the parents who were prepared to leave their children in Eretz Yisrael on their own, so that they could study Torah.

The other members of the group were from Eretz Yisrael. Alexander HaKohen arrived from Tzippori, which is in the Galilee. Reuven was from a small village near Acco and Gamliel was from the town of Nov. Yehoshua came from Har Efrayim, Binyamin from Be'er Sheva. Last but not least, the hero of our story, Naftali, came from the village of Moda'is.

"It is a great privilege to form a class of pure-hearted, sweet children to study Torah in Yerusalayim," the elder Reb Avraham began with emotion. "Studying Torah is vitally important all over the world, no matter where one lives. But it acquires special importance when it is studied in Yerushalayim, our Holy City, as the prophet Yeshayahu emphasized in the verse: 'For the Torah shall come forth from Tzion, and the word of Hashem from Yerushalayim.'[1] Torah studied in Yerushalayim is saturated with *yiras Shamayim*. This fear of Heaven is the source of its special value. The sanctity that permeates the very air of Yerushalayim and the sight of the Kohanim[2] performing the holy service of the *korbanos* fill a person with tremendous *yiras Shamayim*."

Now Reb Avraham turned to the practical details of the curriculum. "Your *rebbi* will be Reb Shmuel, a great Torah scholar. His lessons will deal mainly with the Beis HaMikdash and the *korbanos*. He will frequently take you to the Beis HaMikdash, to see in practice what you have learned.

"I own a building that has several rooms," Reb Avraham told the boys. "You will study, eat and sleep there. You will have the building to yourselves, except for a venerable elderly man named Reb Yissachar. He is an old friend of mine and I am privileged to be able to offer him a place to live.

"Your studies will begin only in another week, right after Pesach. That's when the rest of the building will be vacated by the *olei regel*, who are staying there for the Festival. In the meantime, each of you will stay with his family and prepare for your classes.

"You must remember, children," he continued, "that it is your duty to be extremely careful regarding the laws of *tum'ah* and *taharah*, as you will be entering the Beis HaMikdash. As you know, it is strictly forbidden for a *tamei* to enter into the Beis HaMikdash.[3]

---

1. *Yeshayahu* 2:3.
2. *Bava Basra* 21a, Tosafos (ד"ה כי מציון).
3. *Bemidbar* 5:2–3.

During your six-week stay here, you will eat mainly food bought with *ma'aser sheini* money.[4] You will have to be very careful with that food, because it may not be eaten when one is impure."

Reb Avraham stopped for a moment, gazing lovingly at the faces of his young charges, who were listening to him with rapt attention. Then he spoke to them again in a serious tone: "Dear children! I want you to know that although I could have formed a group of fifty pupils, I chose only ten. I have meticulously selected each one of you, having discerned your genuine desire to learn very diligently. I hope you use well the time that is given to you, because you won't always have the opportunity to study Torah undisturbed. May you always be able to study Torah, and may you have the privilege to study it throughout your lifetime."

Naftali nodded instinctively, as if making a solemn promise to study Torah enthusiastically and diligently in order to live up to Reb Avraham's expectations of his success.

*   *   *

The scraping of the chairs roused Naftali from his musings. He hurried to stand up when he saw a venerable-looking Jew enter the room. "This must be Reb Shmuel," he thought, and then heard Reb Avraham saying, "Children, meet HaRav Shmuel! He is going to be your *rebbi*."

Reb Shmuel's voice was deep and mellow: "Welcome to the new class, my dear pupils! I can see an expression of great determination on your faces, and I am confident that with the help of Hashem, our studies together will be fruitful. And now, tell me, which one of you knows of a special event that occurred three hundred and fifty years ago on this day?"

---

4. *Ma'aser sheini* or food bought with *ma'aser sheini* money may be eaten only when one is *tahor*, as it says (*Devarim* 26:14): "I did not eat of it… in a state of impurity."

Yonasan from Persia raised his hand hesitantly. "As far as I know, the wicked Haman was hanged on the 16th of Nisan.[5] I once visited Shushan, the capital of Babylonia, with my parents," he added, "and my father showed me where Haman was hanged. I also visited the tombs of Mordechai and Esther a few times. They are a holy place to pray."

"I mustn't forget to ask Yonasan if the fifty-cubit-high gallows is still standing there," Naftali thought.

"That's correct," Reb Shmuel praised Yonasan, "Haman was indeed hanged then. By the way, it is customary to have an additional meal on that day."[6] Reb Shmuel turned to the entire class. "Today I would like to do what Mordechai *ha-tzaddik* did on this day, three hundred and fifty years ago. Who knows what he did?"

"He surely celebrated the downfall of Haman," Gamliel of Nov said.

"Mordechai also rode on a horse in the main city square of Shushan," said Reuven. "So perhaps we can go horseback riding too?" he suggested smilingly.

"I believe it has something to do with Torah study," proffered Binyamin from Be'er Sheva.

"What is your name?" Reb Shmuel asked.

"Binyamin," was the timid reply.

"Binyamin is exactly right," Reb Shmuel said. "After Achashveirosh had commanded Haman to mount Mordechai on a horse and lead him through the streets of Shushan, Haman went to look for Mordechai. The wicked man found him sitting with students, studying the *halachos* pertaining to the meal-offering. And if you ask me why Mordechai saw fit to learn this particular

---

5. *Megillah* 16a, Rashi (ד"ה הלכות קמיצה).

6. *Mishnah Berurah* 490:1:2.

subject at an hour when the decree of annihilation threatened the Jews, I will remind you that it was the 16th of Nisan. On that day a special type of meal-offering is brought, the *Omer*-offering. That's why Mordechai found it necessary to study the topical issue of the day.

"When Mordechai saw Haman approaching on horseback, he was terribly frightened. He was sure that Haman was coming to kill him. He told his students to run away fast, so that the wicked man would not hurt them. He himself stood and prayed to Hashem, thinking that it was his last prayer. He was amazed when he continued to pray for a long time, and his prayer was not disturbed: Haman sat down and waited patiently nearby. When Mordechai finished, Haman asked him:

"'Tell me, what did you learn with your students?'

"'We learned the *halachos* of the *kemitzah* of a meal-offering,' was the *tzaddik*'s concise reply. 'When the Beis HaMikdash existed, the Kohen grasped [*kamatz*] a fistful of meal, burned it up on the Altar, and the sins of the person who brought it were thereby atoned for.'

"'It looks like your little fistful of a meal-offering has beaten my ten thousand *kikar*[7] of silver,' said Haman grimly.[8]

"Even a villain like Haman understood that it was the merit of Torah study that stood up for the Jews and rescued them from their enemies," Reb Shmuel concluded triumphantly. "So let us also delve into the study of the laws of *korban haOmer*. We don't have too much time before Shabbos, so I'll be brief.

"I am sure that you are aware of the fact that an *omer*-measure of barley from the year's new crop [*chadash*] must be offered be-

---

7. *Esther* 3:9: "If it please the king, let a decree be written to annihilate them; I shall have ten thousand *kikar* of silver weighed out by those who do the work to be brought to the king's treasuries."
8. *Megillah* 16a.

fore any grain from the new crop may be eaten. The *korban ha-Omer* is called 'the first grains of your harvest.'[9] Only after the *omer*-measure has been reaped is it permissible to reap grain from the new crop.[10] And this new crop may be eaten only after the *korban haOmer* has been offered, as it says in *Vayikra*:[11] 'Now you must not eat bread, parched grain flour or fresh kernels [from the new crop] until this very day.'

"Of course, we perform all the *mitzvos* even without understanding their meaning, only because Hashem, the Supreme King of kings, commanded us to perform them, and we are His servants who must do His will. Nevertheless, it is proper for a person to reflect upon the holy Torah's laws and to understand their fundamental meaning as much as he can."[12]

After that, Reb Shmuel turned to the main subject of his lesson.

"The Torah says,[13] 'Yeshurun [the people of Yisrael] grew fat and kicked [rebelliously]; you grew fat, became obese, [and] covered yourself [with fat]. They abandoned Hashem Who made them.' This verse means that sometimes, having too much wealth and owning too much property cause a person to forget the One Who has given it to him, and to neglect the observance of Torah laws.

"Therefore, HaKadosh Baruch Hu endowed us with numerous *mitzvos* that remind us that all our property and wealth are free gifts from Him.[14] They are nothing but additional vehicles

---

9. *Vayikra* 23:10,11.
10. *Menachos* 70b.
11. 23:14.
12. Rambam, *Hilchos Me'ilah* 8:5.
13. *Devarim* 32:15.
14. *Sefer HaChinuch, mitzvos* 18, 302, 606.

for fulfilling Hashem's will — not for disobeying Him, *chas ve-shalom*. Therefore, the Supreme King of all kings commanded us to reap the harvest of our crops for the purpose of a *korban* first. Only afterwards may we eat the produce of the year's new crop. This is so that we may not erroneously imagine that everything we possess is a result of our own effort, and that it all belongs to us.

"And now, who knows more such *mitzvos* whose aim is to re-mind us of HaKadosh Baruch Hu, so that we may not mistakenly think: 'My strength and the power of my hand have amassed this wealth for me'?"[15]

A silence ensued in the room and lasted for a few min-utes — until Chananya HaLevi spoke up:

"The mitzvah of *bikkurim*! The first of all the fruits of the land that grow in the fields, the orchards and the vineyards must be brought up to Yerushalayim to the Beis HaMikdash and given to the Kohanim — the servants of Hashem — who serve there."[16]

"The mitzvah of *pidyon ha-ben*," Reuven said quietly. "The firstborn son is redeemed in exchange for five silver *shekels* given to the Kohen."[17]

Yehoshua was the third one to respond. "The law concern-ing the firstborn of an animal is also in the same category.[18] Two weeks ago a calf was born in our cowshed. It was its mother's firstborn. Abba said that when it is fifty days old,[19] we shall give it to our neighbor the Kohen. He will sacrifice it in the Beis Ha-Mikdash."

---

15. *Devarim* 8:17.
16. *Devarim* 26:1–11.
17. *Bemidbar* 18:16.
18. *Bemidbar* 18:17.
19. *Bechoros* 26b.

Bo'az from Macedonia, who was on his first visit to Eretz Yisrael, presented a vivid description of a scene he had seen on his way from Yaffo to Yerushalayim: "I saw a man transferring thousands of little sheep from one gigantic pen into another. Every tenth sheep that came out, he marked red. In this way they became *ma'aser beheimah* and were to be brought as *korbanos* in the Beis HaMikdash.[20] There were hundreds upon hundreds of them! I'm sure this wealthy man, who has consecrated so many of his sheep for *korbanos*, will never forget his real purpose in life!"

Reb Shmuel analyzed the issue in depth:

"Besides having the privilege of performing the mitzvah of *ma'aser beheimah*, this Jew will gain many more *mitzvos* and merits. He will bring up his animals to Yerushalayim, and will spend a long time there, until he finishes sacrificing and eating them. All this time he will, of course, devote to the study of Torah. And when he returns home, he will teach his children what he has learned, and thus, they will also become knowledgeable.[21] Not to mention the mitzvah of *tzedakah* when he distributes the meat of his sacrifices among the poor people of Yerushalayim!

"My dear pupils!" Reb Shmuel exclaimed smilingly, "You can't imagine how happy I am to find you so very well versed in Torah! However, I must remind you —and myself, too—that it's Friday today, and time is short. Soon the *shofaros* will be blown to stop people from working.[22] Our lesson is finished for today. We shall meet again, *b'ezras Hashem*, on Thursday, right after Yom Tov."

---

20. *Vayikra* 27:32.
21. *Sefer HaChinuch*, mitzvah 360.
22. *Sukkah* 53b.

Chapter Three

Honoring the Beis HaMikdash

At the first lesson that took place after Pesach, Reb Shmuel gave his pupils a pleasant surprise. "This afternoon, I'd like to take you for our first visit to the Beis HaMikdash." Upon hearing the boys' happy shouts, Reb Shmuel hurried to call for quiet in order to make an important announcement.

"Before one enters a holy place such as the Beis HaMikdash — the place where the Shechinah [Hashem's Divine Presence] rests, one must thoroughly learn how to behave there. Have any of you ever visited a king's palace?"

"No!" was the general reply.

"Yes!" Yechezkel said to everybody's surprise.

Yechezkel's friends looked at him in wonder as he began to tell his story.

"My father is one of the leaders of the Jewish community of Rome, you see. Once, on one of his regular visits to the Emperor's palace, he took me with him. Although I was not permitted to be present at his audience with the Emperor, I was granted the privilege of seeing his imperial palace.

"On our way to the Emperor's reception room, we passed through long corridors, foyers, and magnificent halls and galleries. The splendor and grandeur was indescribable. Everything was covered in gold, shiny mirrors stood in every corner, and of

18

course it all sparkled with cleanliness. Servants, dressed in exqui-site apparel, walked around with awe and trepidation.

"After we returned home, greatly impressed, my father told me that he had taken me to the Emperor's palace in order that I would learn how to behave in a synagogue. If a king of flesh and blood is feared so much in his palace — and everybody is ex-tremely careful to honor him — how much more so must a person be careful about behaving respectfully in a synagogue, which is the dwelling place of the Supreme King of kings, HaKadosh Ba-ruch Hu!"

"Beautiful, Yechezkel," Reb Shmuel praised the boy, "and if one must be so careful about appropriate behavior in a syna-gogue, which is a *mikdash me'at*,[1] a 'small Beis HaMikdash,' how much more so must one be in the real Beis HaMikdash.

"The verse in *parashas Kedoshim* says, 'You shall...revere My Holy Temple.'[2] It is, therefore, a *mitzvas asei*, a positive com-mandment, to fear the Beis HaMikdash.[3] I am sure you under-stand that this means to fear HaKadosh Baruch Hu, Who dwells in the Beis HaMikdash, and not to fear the place itself. A person who enters the *Azarah* must remember in front of Whom he is standing.[4] He must walk there with awe, fear and trepidation, as it says,[5] 'In the House of God we shall walk with emotion.'

"Of course," the *rebbi* clarified, "a person must remember at all times and in all places[6] that HaKadosh Baruch Hu watches

---

1. *Yechezkel* 11:16, *Megillah* 29a.

2. *Vayikra* 19:30.

3. Rambam, *Hilchos Beis HaBechirah* 7:1.

4. As the verse says, "My eyes and My heart shall be there always" (*I Mela-chim* 9:3).

5. *Tehillim* 55:15, Rambam, *Hilchos Beis HaBechirah* 7:5.

6. *Shulchan Aruch, Orach Chayim* 1:1.

him and scrutinizes all his deeds. However, a person must be especially careful not to behave frivolously in the Beis HaMikdash, the dwelling place of Hashem. As the Torah says,[7] 'They shall make a sanctuary for Me, so that I may dwell among them.'

"Remember, my dear pupils: Just as there exists a Beis Ha-Mikdash here in our world, so does one exist up in Heaven. The Beis HaMikdash in Heaven is positioned above our earthly Beis HaMikdash. This means that opposite our earthly *Azarah* is a Heavenly *Azarah*; and the same is true for the *Heichal*, and for all the sites in our Holy Temple.

"The verses of the Torah hint at a Heavenly *Kodesh HaKo-dashim* — Hashem's Throne of Glory. It is positioned directly opposite the *Aron* that was in our earthly *Kodesh HaKodashim* [Holy of Holies].[8] As far as *korbanos* are concerned, just like in our earthly Beis HaMikdash we bring *korbanos*, so are they offered in the Heavenly Beis HaMikdash by the angel Michael."[9]

Reb Shmuel finished his discourse. Naftali voiced what all his friends were thinking. "After this explanation, I realize that while I am in the Beis HaMikdash, wherever I move, I'll be standing opposite the same place in Heaven. I'll have to be very careful about behaving with proper seriousness!"

The *rebbi* did not hide his immense satisfaction, and turned to the children again.

"Who knows a few *halachos* about honoring the Beis HaMikdash?"

Five of them answered in chorus, quoting the words of the Mishnah:

---

7. *Shemos* 25:8.

8. *Midrash Tanchuma, Parashas Vayakhel.*

9. *Chagigah* 12b.

"A person may not enter the premises of the Temple Mount wearing his shoes and *pundah*, or with dust on his feet. He must not use the Temple Mount for a *kapandria*, and certainly not spit there."[10]

"Excellent!" Reb Shmuel commended them. "One must take one's shoes off before entering the Temple Mount area, out of respect for the Beis HaMikdash.[11] Remember what Hashem told Moshe Rabbeinu at the burning bush? 'Remove your shoes from your feet, for the place on which you are standing is holy ground.'[12] And seeing that you mentioned a *pundah*, what does it mean?"

Two boys wanted to answer. Gamliel said, "A *pundah* is a hollow belt, where one keeps money.[13] Even if the money is wrapped in a cloth, one may not enter the Temple Mount with it."[14]

"I found a different interpretation of the word *pundah*. It's a garment[15] that a person wears on his body to absorb the sweat, so as not to dirty his clothes. It is considered a disgrace to the Beis HaMikdash to enter its premises wearing this garment only — without another layer of clothing," Yehoshua said.

"Well, both interpretations are correct!" Reb Shmuel confirmed.

"But if it is forbidden to enter with money, how will a person be able to donate money to the Beis HaMikdash if he wants to?" Reuven asked.

---

10. Mishnah *Berachos* 9:5.

11. *Berachos* 62b.

12. *Shemos* 3:5.

13. *Berachos* 54a, Rashi (ד"ה בפונדתו).

14. *Berachos* 62b.

15. *Berachos* 9:5, Bartenura.

"Good question!" Reb Shmuel expressed his satisfaction. "The answer is that entering the Beis HaMikdash with money is only forbidden when it is carried the way merchants carry it.[16] This is because when a person walks in wearing, say, a money belt, it looks as if he has come to the Beis HaMikdash for business.

"Now, a few of you mentioned the law that prohibits using the Temple Mount for a *kapandria*. What does that mean?" Reb Shmuel asked.

"A *kapandria* is a shortcut," Bo'az said. "My father told me that it is also forbidden to use a synagogue for a shortcut.[17] Our synagogue in Macedonia has two entrances. Once, when I was in a hurry, I wanted to take a shortcut. I entered through one door and walked across the synagogue with the intention of getting out through the second door. My father, however, noticed it, and did not let me do it. He explained the halachah to me."

"Quite correct! And the prohibition to use the Beis HaMikdash for a *kapandria* is the source of this halachah. This is because a synagogue is a *mikdash me'at*. Many other laws such as these are learned from the *halachos* pertaining to the Beis HaMikdash.

"Now let's see who can explain the last part of the *mishnah* you quoted: 'and certainly not spit there.' The prohibition of spitting on the Temple Mount is learned from a '*kal va-chomer*.'[18] Can anyone explain this?"

Binyamin's hand shot up, and Reb Shmuel turned to him.

"My *rebbi* said this halachah is learned from the prohibition of wearing shoes in a holy place. If wearing shoes is prohibited in a sacred place, as the verse says, 'Remove your shoes from your

---

16. *Bava Metzia* 26a, Tosafos (ד"ה בהר הבית).

17. *Berachos* 62b.

18. *Kal va-chomer* — One of the thirteen rules for learning *halachos* in the Torah: If a strict law applies to a lenient case, it certainly must apply to a more strict case.

feet,' how much more should spitting, which *is* contemptible, be prohibited on the Temple Mount."[19]

"And my *rebbi* taught that the *kal va-chomer* is based on a verse from *Megillas Esther*," Yonasan from Persia burst into the discussion. "The verse says, '...for one could not enter the king's palace in sackcloth clothing.'[20] Sackcloth may not be honorable clothing, but it is not disgusting, either. Even so, it is forbidden to appear before a king of flesh and blood in it. How much more so must spitting be prohibited, which *is* disgusting — and, especially so, before the Supreme King of all kings!"

"Well said, both of you!" Reb Shmuel rejoiced. "And here's another halachah: just as one doesn't visit the king's palace for no reason, just to take a stroll there, so it is forbidden to enter the premises of the Temple Mount except in order to perform some mitzvah there.[21] Our visit to the Beis HaMikdash will serve the purpose of a mitzvah — to study and see the service of the Kohanim.

"By the way, do you know that the Kohanim were not the first ones to offer sacrifices at the spot where the Beis HaMikdash now stands? *Korbanos* were sacrificed there long before it was built. And the first man who offered *korbanos* there was..."

"Avraham Avinu!" Bo'az shouted. "It was when Hashem asked him to sacrifice Yitzchak on Mount Moriah as a *korban Olah*, but in the end, he sacrificed a ram instead of his son."[22]

"True," Reb Shmuel confirmed, "we know it from tradition that the spot where the ram was sacrificed is the spot of the Altar today.[23] However, Avraham Avinu was *not* the first man who offered *korbanos* there!"

---

19. *Berachos* 62b.
20. *Esther* 4:2.
21. Rambam, *Hilchos Beis HaBechirah* 7:2.
22. *Bereishis* 22:13.
23. Rambam, *Hilchos Beis HaBechirah* 2:2.

Silence ensued in the room. The pupils wrinkled their foreheads in thoughtful concentration.

"Could it be Noach, who offered sacrifices at this spot after he had come out of the Ark?"[24] Chananya said hesitantly. "I think I heard that once."

"Yes, that is correct, but he wasn't the first one. The first man to offer sacrifices at the spot of the Beis Mikdash was Adam Ha-Rishon.[25] Kayin and Hevel, his sons, also offered sacrifices there.

"Back to Avraham Avinu now. Needless to say, the merit of *Akeidas Yitzchak* on Mount Moriah protects *Klal Yisrael* throughout all the generations, even today,"[26] Reb Shmuel added, his face aglow with inspiration. "Our holy *Avos* prayed for us at that holy spot, as we know from *parashas Chayei Sarah*: 'Yitzchak went out toward evening to pray in the field.'[27] Yaakov dreamed his famous dream there,[28] when he was on the way to Lavan's house.[29] There is no other nation in the world like our nation, whose *Avos* prepared such spiritual fruits for their descendants — for me and you, who live thousands of years after them. Only among the Jews can this be found, and this makes us feel very happy to have been born Jewish!"

Reb Shmuel paused for a moment, and then said, "Now I'm going to tell you a story, which I once heard at a Torah *shiur*.

"There once lived a Hellenized Jew named Yosef Meshisa.[30]

---

24. Ibid.

25. Ibid.

26. *Bereishis* 22:14, Rashi (ד"ה היום).

27. *Pesachim* 88a; *Bereishis* 28:17, Rashi (ד"ה כי אם); *Berachos* 34b, Tosafos (ד"ה חציף).

28. *Bereishis* 24:63.

29. *Pesachim* 88a; *Sanhedrin* 95b.

30. *Bereishis Rabbah, Parashah* 65.

He was brought up as a Jew, but became assimilated into the Greek culture.

"When the wicked Greeks got to Yerushalayim and approached the Beis HaMikdash in order to break in, the dread of the place fell upon them. They were afraid to enter the *Heichal*, and wanted a Jew to enter there first. They issued a decree announcing that whoever entered the Beis HaMikdash first would be permitted to choose one of its vessels for himself.

"Yosef Meshisa had sunk to such a low spiritual level that he had the audacity to enter the Beis HaMikdash without any fear or shame. He entered the *Heichal* and came out a few minutes later holding the golden Menorah, which glittered brightly in the sun. However, the Greeks thought it was too much, and did not allow him to take it.

"'You are not worthy to own such a magnificent object,' they said to him. 'Enter again and choose a different vessel!'

"To their great surprise, he refused to obey them.

"'No, I don't agree to enter again,' he said. 'Isn't it enough that I have angered my Creator once? Must I anger Him a second time?'

"The Greek warriors tried to persuade him, promising to give him a great fortune, but he refused. They threatened him with torture and death. But nothing helped. Yosef Meshisa would not budge.

"The Greek villains took a table and laid him on it. They began to cut off his arms and legs. He wept and screamed: 'Woe is me, for I have angered my Creator! Woe is me, for I have angered my Creator!' Thus he died a martyr's death, *al kiddush Hashem*."

Reb Shmuel paused to take a deep breath. He looked at the shocked children and said, "The scholar who told this story asked how it was possible that a wicked man—who desecrated holy objects and stole the golden Menorah—refused to enter the *Heichal* again even when he was threatened with death. He offered the following solution: Yosef Meshisa entered the Beis

HaMikdash with evil intentions. But in spite of that, the sanctity that pervaded the place had such a powerful impact on him that it sparked his Jewish soul to life, and he preferred to die a martyr's death *al kiddush Hashem* out of sincere repentance, rather than to sin again."[31]

---

31. Rav Y.S. Kahaneman *zt"l*, the Ponovezher Rav.

Chapter Four

The Five Gates

The students followed their *rebbi* at a quick pace, trying to keep up with him. Soon the southern gates to the Temple Mount appeared in the distance before their eyes. Another few minutes of walking brought them next to one of the gates. The children took off their shoes and left them there.

"Don't forget to clean the dust of the road off your feet," Binyamin reminded his friends.

"Hey, look! There's no mezuzah on the doorpost of the entrance gate!"[1] the sharp-eyed Yehoshua remarked.

"Only a regular house requires a mezuzah.[2] A sacred house, like the Beis HaMikdash, is exempt," Reb Shmuel reassured the boys. "And don't forget, children, we are now entering the courtyard of the House of HaKadosh Baruch Hu! Beware of light-headed behavior!"[3]

Gamliel was still busy cleaning the dust off his feet, trying to make them spotless so as not to leave even a single speck of dust

---

1. *Yoma* 11a.
2. *Yoma* 11b.
3. *Berachos* 54a.

27

on them. Reb Shmuel signaled to him that there was no need to overdo it.

There were two doors at the big gate,[4] and they were both open. They passed through the gate and entered the Temple Mount [Har HaBayis]. The children had already visited the place during Pesach, but after the lesson that they had heard in the morning, they entered the area with even greater awe, as the verse says, "You shall revere My Holy Temple."[5]

"The Temple Mount(1) occupies an area of five hundred square amos,"[6] Reb Shmuel started to explain. "As you can see, most of this area is not built up. There are five gates[7] leading to the Temple Mount: two on the southern side, which is where we came from; one on the eastern side; one on the northern side; and the last one on the western side. The two southern gates are called the Chuldah Gates(25), named after Chuldah the nevi'ah,[8] who prophesied during the time of the First Beis HaMikdash. Chuldah the nevi'ah uttered her prophecy standing between these two gates."

"I don't quite understand," Binyamin wondered. "The First Beis HaMikdash was destroyed, so how is it possible that these two gates are still standing?"

"When Nevuchadnetzar destroyed the First Temple, he only demolished the ceiling, but the walls, with their gates, remained intact," Reb Shmuel explained. "Thus, these are the original walls that stood in those days."[9]

---

4. Mishnah Middos 2:3.

5. Vayikra 19:30.

6. Mishnah Middos 2:1. An amah, or a cubit, is about 21.25 inches, or 54 centimeters.

7. Mishnah Middos 1:3.

8. Ibid., Tiferes Yisrael #24.

9. Mishnah Parah 3:3, Rabbeinu Shimshon.

Temple Mount and Ezras Nashim

West

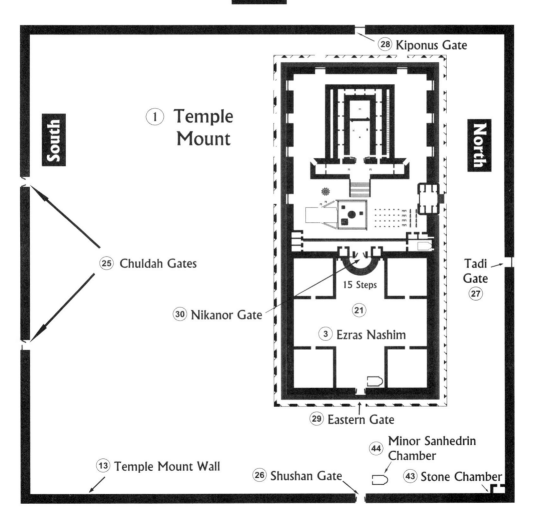

South

North

(1) Temple Mount

(28) Kiponus Gate

15 Steps

(25) Chuldah Gates

(30) Nikanor Gate

(21)

(3) Ezras Nashim

Tadi Gate
(27)

(29) Eastern Gate

(44) Minor Sanhedrin Chamber

(13) Temple Mount Wall

(26) Shushan Gate

(43) Stone Chamber

East

"Why is there only one gate on each of the three sides, and two gates on the southern side?" Alexander asked.

"Yerushalayim is situated to the south of the Temple Mount,[10] so most people enter and exit on the southern side. Therefore, there is a need for two gates," Reb Shmuel answered. "This is also the reason that most of the empty area of *Har HaBayis* is on its southern side, to facilitate the crowds that congregate there — while the Beis HaMikdash is situated on its north."

"Perhaps we could go around *Har HaBayis* and see the other gates?" Yechezkel suggested.

"Why not?" Reb Shmuel agreed. The group turned to the right, toward the eastern gate of the Temple Mount. While they were walking, they encountered a man with an unhappy look on his face, walking toward them southwards from the north.

"Why do you walk around the *Har HaBayis* leftwards?" Reb Shmuel asked him.

"I am a mourner," the man replied sadly.

"May the One Who dwells in this House console you," Reb Shmuel wished him.

The man continued walking in the direction of the Chuldah Gates(25). Reb Shmuel read in the children's eyes a desire to hear an explanation of this strange conversation, and he willingly provided it.

"I asked the man why he was walking toward the left, because the accepted custom is to move rightwards when one enters the Temple Mount(1) area. We also followed this custom: we came in through the Chuldah Gates(25) and turned to the right, toward Shushan Gate(26). However, a person to whom a bad thing happens walks toward the left[11] and, therefore, whoever

---

10. Mishnah *Middos* 2:1, *Tosfos Yom Tov*; Mishnah *Middos.* 1:3, *Tiferes Yisrael* #24.

11. Mishnah *Middos* 2:2: "All those who enter the area of the Temple Mount,

meets him on the way gives him a blessing that his situation may improve.

"The man we saw was a mourner, so I gave him a blessing that HaKadosh Baruch Hu, Who dwells in this House, will console him. A person who is in *cherem* — who is excommunicated by the *Beis Din* — also follows the same leftward route, and the people who meet him give him the following blessing: 'May the One Who dwells in this House influence your heart, to obey the words of your friends, so that they may bring you close once again.'"

After the group reached Shushan Gate(26), Reb Shmuel went out through it and turned to face it. His pupils followed him. He then pointed to the spectacular stone relief on top of the gate.[12] The shape of a walled city with a palace in it was carved on the stone surface.

"Does this engraving remind you of anything?" Reb Shmuel asked Yonasan from Persia. Yonasan studied it for a while, thinking.

"It reminds me of the city of Shushan," he finally said. "The palace looks exactly like the king's palace in Shushan."

"You are not mistaken," Reb Shmuel confirmed. "When our ancestors went out of the Babylonian exile, it was none other than the king of Persia who gave them permission to build the Second Beis HaMikdash. Persia was a powerful empire in those days. The king of Persia ordered the Jews to etch the shape of the city of Shushan on one of the Temple Mount gates, so that the Jews would remember the Persian Empire and not forget to honor it. Therefore, this gate is known as Shushan Gate(26)."

---

enter it through the right side [in the counterclockwise direction], except for a person to whom something [tragic] happens…"

12. Mishnah *Middos* 2:2, Bartenura.

The boys looked at the spectacular stone relief on top of the gate

Reb Shmuel took his pupils to a set of stairs that led to a small room above Shushan Gate.[13] Two sticks, of slightly different lengths, were kept in that room. One of them lay in the northeast corner of the room, and the other one lay in the southeast corner.

Reb Shmuel preceded their questions with his explanation. "With the help of these measuring devices that you see here, the work of craftsmen who build things and fashion vessels for the Beis HaMikdash is measured in order to estimate the amount of their salary."

"But isn't one measure enough? What do they need two for?" Yehoshua queried.

"As a matter of fact, children, there are three measures altogether," Reb Shmuel surprised them.

"Three?" they asked in an impromptu chorus.

"Yes, there are three measures," Reb Shmuel repeated. "One of them is a regular *amah* measure, which is six *tefachim*[14] long. It is not here. The measure that is kept here in the northeastern corner is half an *etzba*[15] longer than the regular one. The measure that lies in the southeastern corner is a whole *etzba* longer than the regular one."

"So why do they need three measures?"

"These measures are used by the treasurer of the *hekdesh*. Hekdesh controls the money and other things donated for holy causes, such as the upkeep of the Beis HaMikdash. When the treasurer makes a deal with artisans to do some work for *hekdesh* — for instance, to manufacture some vessels or to build a building — they agree on a certain price for each *amah* of construction work. The

---

13. Mishnah *Keilim* 17:9.

14. One *tefach*, or a handbreadth, is about 3.5 inches, or 9 centimeters.

15. One *etzba*, or a thumb-width, is about .9 inches, or 2.25 centimeters. There are 4 *etzba'os* in a *tefach* and six *tefachim* in an *amah*.

things that the artisans make are measured with the regular *amah* measure. However, when the job is completed, the treasurer measures their work with the help of one of the longer measures, and the craftsmen get paid according to the new estimation."

Binyamin made a rapid calculation and came to the following conclusion: "In that case, the artisans end up losing money. If an artisan builds a wall twenty-four *amos* high, the treasurer pays him the price of twenty-three *amos* only. How can this be permitted?"

"Well, if the artisan wishes to do work for *hekdesh*, he must willingly accept such conditions beforehand," Reb Shmuel explained. "This arrangement is not made with the purpose of cheating the artisans, God forbid. It's in order to prevent them from ever transgressing the sin of *me'ilah*[16] in case they build less than they are supposed to according to the contract. Only if they are paid a little less than they actually earn can it be taken for granted that they will not commit *me'ilah* by taking extra *hekdesh* money and using it for their own, non-*hekdesh* purposes."

"But why are there *two* different measures that are longer than a regular *amah*?" asked Reuven quietly.

Reb Shmuel answered immediately. "It depends on what type of work is being done. If a craftsman constructs a building for *hekdesh*, his work is measured with the longest measure, the one that is one *etzba* longer than the regular one. But if he manufactures a silver or gold utensil, his work is measured with the measure that is only half an *etzba* longer than the regular one. This is because if it is measured with the longest measure, the artisan will lose too much money, because even a small quantity of silver or gold is very precious.[17]

---

16. *Me'ilah*: using *hekdesh* for one's own purposes.

17. *Pesachim* 86a.

"The northeastern corner was considered proper for the shorter measure on the basis of the verse in *Iyov*: 'Gold comes from the north.'[18] Can you guess why these two measures were placed in this particular room that is above Shushan Gate?" Reb Shmuel asked at the end of his explanation.

Bo'az from Macedonia volunteered to answer and began confidently. "The Sages want the measures to be kept specifically above the gate that bears the stone picture of the city of Shushan. It reminds the Jews of the fear of human kings and their reign. This, in turn, will remind them to fear HaKadosh Baruch Hu when they deal with matters concerning *hekdesh*, and prevent them from committing *me'ilah*."[19]

Reb Shmuel and the other boys were very impressed with Bo'az's excellent answer.

"Wonderful!" the *rebbi* praised Bo'az, who blushed.

The group finally entered the *Har HaBayis*(1) area. Gamliel rubbed his feet again, removing some imaginary specks of dust from them. Reb Shmuel pointed at the building that stood on the right side of the gate(44), and said: "This is the seat of the *Beis Din*."

"Is this where the Sanhedrin, the greatest Torah Sages of the people of Yisrael, sit in judgement?" Chananya HaLevi from Babylonia asked excitedly.

"The Seat of the Sanhedrin is in *Lishkas HaGazis*(53), which is next to the *Ezras Yisrael*(4)," Naftali replied.

"So who sits here?"

Reb Shmuel, who had been following their dialogue with relish, entered the discussion. "There are three courts in the Beis HaMikdash.[20] One of them is located in this building(44) on *Har*

---

18. *Iyov* 37:22.

19. Mishnah *Keilim* 17:9, *Tosfos Anshei Shem*.

20. *Sanhedrin* 86b.

HaBayis, the second one(45) is in the *Ezras Nashim*, and the third one is in *Lishkas HaGazis*(53). In this *Beis Din*, and in the one in the *Ezras Nashim*, there are twenty-three judges [*dayanim*], who are called *Sanhedrin HaKetanah* [Minor Sanhedrin].[21] In *Lishkas HaGazis*, seventy-one *dayanim* sit in judgment, and they are the Great Sanhedrin, or *Sanhedrin HaGedolah*.

"And what is the purpose of the three courts?" the *rebbi* asked, and provided the answer. "When a difficult *she'eilah*, or question in halachah, arrives from anywhere in the world, the *Beis Din* on *Har HaBayis* is given it first. If this *Beis Din* can't solve it, the *she'eilah* is forwarded to the *Beis Din* in the *Ezras Nashim*. If they do not know the answer either, the *she'eilah* is then dispatched to the *Sanhedrin HaGedolah*, which is located in *Lishkas HaGazis*."[22]

"I remember now," Binyamin said, "that one evening my father wrote a difficult *she'eilah* on a piece of parchment and sent it off to Yershalayim with a special messenger." At the sight of his friends' surprised looks, he explained, "My father is a *dayan*."

Reb Shmuel pointed at the northeastern corner of *Har HaBayis* — where *Lishkas Beis HaEhven*(43) was. "This is where the Kohen stays for seven days, away from his house, before burning the *Parah Adumah*.[23] The *Parah Adumah* is a red cow whose ashes are used to purify people who have become *tamei* through contact with a dead body. *Lishkas Beis Ehven* is located specifically in the northeastern corner because the *Parah Adumah* is referred to as a *chatas*, or a sin-offering, in the Torah,[24] and a *chatas* is slaughtered in the north.[25] And what does 'east' have to do

---

21. Rambam, *Hilchos Sanhedrin* 1:3.
22. *Sanhedrin* 86b.
23. Mishnah *Parah* 3:1.
24. *Bemidbar* 19:9.
25. *Yoma* 2a.

with it? The answer is that the cow is burnt on the Mount of Olives, east of the Beis HaMikdash. It is from there that some of its blood is sprinkled toward the entrance to the *Heichal*.[26] And now let's proceed to the next site."

The children continued to walk northwards until they saw Tadi Gate(27).[27] "This gate is called Tadi, which is probably the name of the man who built it," Reb Shmuel revealed.[28] "There are some authorities who maintain that it is called Tadi Gate because it is used for occasions when there is a special need for privacy.[29] *Tadi* is the Aramaic word for secret, or modesty.[30] This northern gate is built differently from all of the other gates.[31] Its lintel is made of two stones placed diagonally, leaning on each other, in the shape of an upside-down 'V.' This serves as a kind of sign for the person, who wants to enter or leave the *Har HaBayis* secretly, to pass through this gate."[32]

They proceeded on their way and reached the western side of *Har HaBayis*, where they saw Kiphonus Gate(28).[33]

Reb Shmuel turned to Bo'az and said, "You must know the meaning of the word *Kiphonus*."

"Yes, of course. *Kiphonus* is a Greek word, and it means 'garden work.'"[34]

---

26. *Bemidbar* 19:4: "Elazar the Kohen shall then ... sprinkle some of its blood seven times directly toward the front of the Tent of Meeting."

27. Mishnah *Middos* 1:3.

28. Ibid., *Tosfos Yom Tov*.

29. Mishnah *Middos* 1:9.

30. Mishnah *Middos* 1:3, *Tiferes Yisrael* #26.

31. Mishnah *Middos* 2:3.

32. Ibid., *Tiferes Yisrael* #28.

33. Mishnah *Middos* 1:3.

34. Ibid., *Tiferes Yisrael*.

"There is a rose garden behind the gate. The roses are used for the preparation of the incense. Kiphonus Gate is named after this rose garden," Reb Shmuel explained.

When the boys returned to the southern side of *Har HaBayis*, they saw a roofed place, with wide stone benches under the roof. Tired people were sitting and resting on them.[35]

"Is it permissible to sit on *Har HaBayis*?" was Reuven's surprised question. "I learned that only the kings of the House of David are permitted to sit in the *Azarah*!"

"That's a good question," Reb Shmuel complemented Reuven, "but you yourself have provided the answer. The *Azarah* is indeed a place where sitting is permissible only for the kings of the House of David,[36] as the verse says, 'King David came and sat before Hashem,'[37] meaning in the *Azarah*(4)(6). But it is permissible to sit on the rest of *Har HaBayis*. Here benches are provided for the *olei regel*, so that they may be able to sit and rest. Let's also sit here for a while, and I'll tell you an interesting story that has to do with this halachah," Reb Shmuel suggested.

"In the time of King Rechav'am, son of King Shlomo, ten tribes [*shevatim*] rebelled against him and proclaimed Yerav'am, son of Nevat, king over them.[38] Yerav'am was a wicked king and a sinner, and what's more, he caused all Yisrael to sin together with him.[39] Our Sages said that his pride led him to this.[40]

"Yerav'am knew that only the kings of the House of David were allowed to sit in the *Azarah*. He thought to himself: 'When

---

35. *Pesachim* 11b, Rashi (ד"ה על גב).

36. *Yoma* 69b.

37. *II Shemuel* 7:18.

38. *I Melachim* 12.

39. Mishnah *Avos* 5:18.

40. *Sanhedrin* 101b.

everybody goes up to Yerushalayim for the Festival, they will see that Rechav'am is sitting and I am standing. They will say that Rechav'am is the king and I am a slave, and they will reject me and accept him as king again.'

"Yerav'am was not prepared to put up with this, and in an outburst of pride he committed a grave sin: he forbade the ten *shevatim* to go up to Yerushalayim as *olei regel* for Yom Tov. Instead of letting the people observe this mitzvah and serve Hashem in the Beis HaMikdash in Yerushalayim, Yerav'am made a substitute. He took two golden calves and set one up in Beis El, and the other one in the territory of the Tribe of Dan, and ordered the people: 'Go up, and worship the golden calves!'[41]

"Yerav'am's ban on pilgrimage to Yerushalayim was in force for many years, until the times of Hoshea, son of Eilah.[42] The new king annulled this terrible decree, and the members of the ten tribes could once again perform *aliyah le-regel* to Yerushalayim. The evil decree was abolished on the 15th of Av, which is one of the reasons why this date was declared a holiday."

---

41. *I Melachim* 12:25–26.
42. *Ta'anis* 30a.

Chapter Five

In the Ezras Nashim

The next morning, Reb Shmuel announced, "Children, today we're going to the Beis HaMikdash again, to learn about the *Cheil*(2) and the *Ezras Nashim*(3)."

They entered *Har HaBayis*(1) through one of the Chuldah Gates(25) and continued without pausing there. They stopped when they reached the *Soreg*(14), which is actually a wall, ten *tefachim* high, separating *Har HaBayis* from the *Cheil*.[1] This wall is not solid, but is made of boards of wood, arranged diagonally in a crisscross pattern, with empty spaces in between, like latticework.[2]

"The *Soreg*(14) surrounds the entire wall that encompasses the *Ezras Nashim*(3), the *Ezras Yisrael*(4) and the *Ezras Kohanim*(6)," Reb Shmuel explained. "The narrow area between the *Soreg* and this wall is called the *Cheil*(2). The *Soreg* serves as a restricting barrier for those who have become *tamei* due to contact with a dead body. Although the Torah actually permits these *teme'ei meis* to enter the *Ezras Nashim* as far as Nikanor Gate(30),[3] our Sages

---

1. Mishnah *Middos* 2:3.
2. Ibid., Bartenura.
3. *Zevachim* 116b; Rambam, *Hilchos Beis HaBechirah* 7:11.

40

wished to protect them from actual transgression, so they forbade them even to go beyond the *Soreg* limits."[4]

The group turned to the right, toward the entrance to the *Ezras Nashim* — the Eastern Gate(29).

"Look at this," Reb Shmuel said suddenly. He drew their attention to the large sign next to the gate. It warned in three languages: "*Teme'ei meis* and Gentiles are forbidden to go beyond the *Soreg*."

This stone, engraved with Greek lettering, was found in an archeological dig on the Temple Mount. It says: "A non-Jew may not enter past the partition that encircles the Beis HaMikdash into the surrounding courtyard. Violators will be put to death."

"Non-Jews are also forbidden to enter the *Cheil*," the *rebbi* made clear.[5] "The *Soreg* made the Greek kings very angry. It stood there as a partition between Gentiles and the people of Yisrael, as a constant reminder that Yisrael is the chosen nation.

---

4. Mishnah *Keilim* 1:8.

5. Ibid.

Only they can enter the Temple and offer sacrifices to Hashem, their God, whereas other nations can only send their *korbanos* to be offered by Jews.[6] This is what caused the Greeks to breach thirteen holes in the *Soreg*, when they captured the Beis HaMikdash before to the rise of the Chashmonaim.[7]

"By the way," Reb Shmuel wanted to know, "are all of you sure you are not *teme'ei meis*?"

"Yes," the boys answered together.

"Okay then," the *rebbi* smiled, "let's go in!" The boys hurried to enter the *Cheil*, which was ten *amos* wide,[8] and climb the Twelve Steps(20), each of which was half an *amah* high and half an *amah* wide. When they reached the Eastern Gate(29), Reb Shmuel said, "There are many more gates leading to the Beis HaMikdash, but the main entrance is through this gate. The other gates lead to the *Ezras Kohanim*(6) and only Kohanim usually enter through them."[9]

Naftali said, "That's because Yisraelim are forbidden to enter the Kohanim's Courtyard unless there's a specific need for it."

"Exactly," Reb Shmuel agreed. "By the way," he asked, "do you know why this courtyard is called *Ezras Nashim*, or 'the Women's Courtyard?'"

"Is it because women stand there?" someone guessed hesitantly.

"In that case, what are *we* doing here?" Reb Shmuel feigned surprise. "Do men enter the women's section of a synagogue?!"

"I know the difference!" Binyamin answered. "This particular *Ezras Nashim*(3) is not designated for women only. It is called by

---

6. *Menachos* 73b.

7. Mishnah *Middos* 2:3, *Tosfos Yom Tov*.

8. Mishnah *Middos* 2:3.

9. Mishnah *Keilim* 1:8.

this name because women are not permitted *beyond* this court-yard, in order to enter the adjacent *Ezras Yisrael*(4) — if there's no special need for it."[10]

"I have already visited the Beis HaMikdash many times," Yehoshua said. "During Sukkos, at the *Simchas Beis HaSho'eivah*,[11] the *Ezras Nashim* is very densely packed. People stand squeezed together in the crowd in order to watch the Torah Sages dance and rejoice before Hashem. During these hours the women oc-cupy the balconies upstairs, and the men stand downstairs, so they won't mingle."[12]

Reb Shmuel continued his lecture. "You know of course that a person who is a *tevul yom* may not enter the *Ezras Nashim*.[13] This is a man who was *tamei* and has begun the purification process by immersing himself in the *mikveh*. This makes him *tahor* for some things, but he must wait until after nightfall, when enough stars appear in the sky [*tzeis ha-kochavim*], to become more com-pletely *tahor*.[14] And now, boys, I'm going to give you a little test:

"Who is not allowed to enter *Har HaBayis*?"

"A man or a woman whose *tum'ah* came from something dis-charged from their body, such as a woman after childbirth."[15]

"And who is not allowed to enter the *Cheil*?"

"*Teme'ei meisim* and Gentiles."

"Who is not allowed to enter the *Ezras Nashim*?"

"Even a *tevul yom* is not allowed there," one of the boys an-swered to Reb Shmuel's satisfaction.

---

10. *Kiddushin* 52b, Rashi (ד"ה וכי אשה).

11. The joyous procession to and from the spring, from which water was drawn to pour on the *Mizbeach* each day of Sukkos.

12. *Sukkah* 51a; Mishnah *Middos* 2:5.

13. Mishnah *Keilim* 1:8.

14. *Vayikra* 22:7.

15. Mishnah *Keilim* 1:8.

Reb Shmuel summed it up. "As one enters deeper into the Beis HaMikdash, he comes to progressively holier areas. The higher the degree of holiness a place has, the more restricted the entrance to it is. The holiest place on earth is the *Kodesh HaKodashim*(12), and the only one permitted to enter it is the *Kohen Gadol* on Yom Kippur!"[16]

Trembling in awe, the children entered the *Ezras Nashim*. They saw a large area in front of them, occupying 135 square *amos*.[17] In each of its four corners stood a building. There was another building on the right side of the entrance.

"The seat of the *Sanhedrin HaKetanah*(45), which we discussed yesterday, is in this building," Reb Shmuel said.[18]

"Oh, please, Reb Shmuel, could we go and see the Sanhedrin?" Yechezkel pleaded with the *rebbi*.

"Yes, yes, please, Reb Shmuel!" all the others joined Yechezkel's refrain.

"How can I refuse when you ask so nicely!" Reb Shmuel smiled in agreement. "But," he warned, "you must behave with proper respect here. Don't talk so as to disturb the *dayanim*. They need to concentrate in order to determine the halachah properly, which is a most holy task."

The children entered the room in total silence. They stopped and looked at the twenty-three *dayanim* with great reverence. The *dayanim* were seated in a large semicircle, so that they could see one another when they debated each case. Three rows of disciples were sitting meekly on the ground in front of the *dayanim*. The litigants involved in the dispute were standing between the *dayanim* and their disciples. The boys stood and gazed silently at

---

16. Mishnah *Keilim* 1:9.
17. Mishnah *Middos* 2:5.
18. *Sanhedrin* 86b.

Ezras Nashim

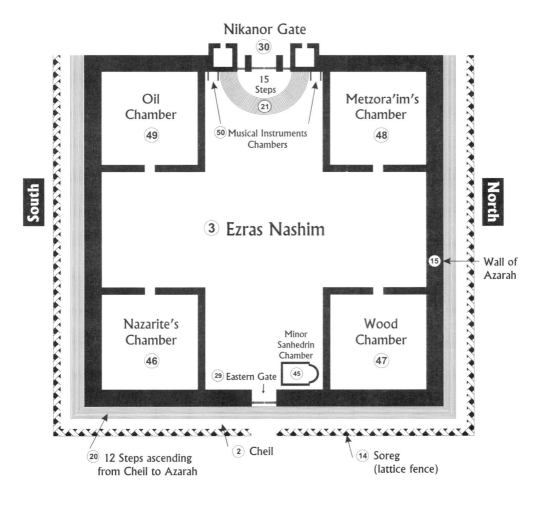

West

Nikanor Gate
(30)

15 Steps
(21)

Oil Chamber
(49)

(50) Musical Instruments Chambers

Metzora'im's Chamber
(48)

South

(3) Ezras Nashim

North

(15) Wall of Azarah

Nazarite's Chamber
(46)

Minor Sanhedrin Chamber

Wood Chamber
(47)

(29) Eastern Gate
(45)

(20) 12 Steps ascending from Cheil to Azarah

(2) Cheil

(14) Soreg (lattice fence)

East

the *dayanim*. After a few minutes, Reb Shmuel motioned for them to follow him.

After they left the *Beis Din*, the *rebbi* said: "One of the main reasons why the *dayanim* sit in a semicircle, and not in a full circle, is because if they sat in a full circle, the witnesses and litigants would have to stand in the middle of the circle. The *dayanim* who couldn't see the faces of the witnesses would find it difficult to analyze their testimony with precision.

"Another reason for the half-circle is that it represents the following idea: the *dayanim* perform half of the needed work and Hashem takes care of the rest. Hashem is present when the *dayanim* judge, as it says, "God stands in the council of judges."[19] He crowns their efforts with success. This is similar to the half-*shekel* donated for the service and upkeep of the Beis haMikdash; each adult male does his part and Hashem, as it were, finishes the work."[20]

"What is the purpose of the four buildings in the corners of the *Ezras Nashim*?" Gamliel remembered to ask.

"They are not real buildings," Reb Shmuel surprised them. "They only look like buildings, but they have no roofs. Each such chamber occupies an area of forty square *amos*, and each one serves a different purpose."[21]

The group came closer to the chamber situated in the northeastern corner, and peeped through the doorway. People were busy inspecting logs of wood inside.

"All these people are Kohanim," Reb Shmuel explained, "and they are preparing the wood that is to be used for burning *korbanos* on the *Mizbeach*. Each piece of wood must be inspected to

---

19. *Sanhedrin* 36b, Rashi (ד"ה כחצי גורן).
20. *Oheiv Yisrael al HaTorah, Parashas Shekalim*.
21. Mishnah *Middos* 2:5, *Tiferes Yisrael* #41.

Kohanim were busy inspecting logs of wood inside Lishkas HaEitzim

make sure that it doesn't have worms. If it does, it is *pasul* for use upon the *Mizbeach*. That's the reason why this chamber is called *Lishkas HaEitzim*(47) [Wood Chamber]."

"But this is such a simple job!" Binyamin exclaimed. "Why aren't these Kohanim given more important and more honorable tasks?"

"This task is also very important and very honorable," Reb Shmuel chided him gently. "The Kohanim who work here cannot be involved in the service of offering *korbanos*, because each one of them has some kind of bodily defect.[22] Nevertheless, they still wish to be involved in at least some kind of service in the Beis HaMikdash. Therefore, they busy themselves with the preparation of the wood for the burning of the *korbanos*."

While listening to their *rebbi's* explanation, the boys watched the Kohanim fulfill their task with great seriousness and concentration.

*   *   *

"Once there was a Kohen," Reb Shmuel began to relate a new story, "who worked in *Lishkas HaEitzim*. He fiddled with his ax and walked along the *Lishkah* with it. All of a sudden he noticed that one of the marble blocks of the flooring protruded from the flat surface of the floor and was higher than all the rest. He understood that this block must have once been removed from its place, and then returned afterwards. The Kohen was amazed with his discovery, and started to tell his friend about it. But he had hardly uttered a few words when he collapsed on the floor and breathed his last! That's when the Sages came to the conclusion that the *Aron Ha-*

---

22. *Vayikra* 21:16–24: "Speak to Aharon… any man of your descendants… who has a deformity must not draw near to offer up the food to his God, since it is not fitting that a man who has a deformity draw near to serve: a man who is blind or lame or has a sunken nose-bridge, etc."

Kodesh [Holy Ark] was hidden underneath *Lishkas HaEitzim*."[23]

The children listened with gaping mouths, incredulous.

"The *Aron HaKodesh*? But isn't it in the *Kodesh HaKodashim*(12)?" Naftali asked in surprise.

"Don't you know that there is no *Aron* in the *Kodesh HaKodashim* of the Second Beis HaMikdash?" Alexander asked in surprise. Naftali blushed.

"Listen, I don't know everything either," Reb Shmuel reassured Naftali and added, "Yoshiyahu, who was a great and righteous king, knew that the First Beis HaMikdash was destined to be destroyed. He was afraid that the Gentiles might get ahold of the *Aron*. Therefore, he went and hid it,[24] together with another four important objects: the original jar of *mahn*,[25] the bottle of anointing oil (*shemen ha-mishchah*),[26] the staff of Aharon with its blossoms and almonds,[27] and the box that the Philistines sent when they returned the Ark."[28]

Yechezkel joined the discussion and said that he had heard once that the prophet Yirmeyahu hid the *Aron* in Mount Nevo.[29]

"I also heard about it," Reb Shmuel said, "but we trust the opinion of our Sages who hold the view that the *Aron HaKodesh* is hidden here, in *Lishkas HaEitzim*.

"And now, let us move to the adjacent chamber, located in the northwestern corner.[30] It's called *Lishkas HaMetzora'im*(48)."[31]

---

23. Mishnah *Shekalim* 6:2; *Yoma* 54a.
24. *Yoma* 52b.
25. *Shemos* 16:33.
26. *Shemos* 30:22–33.
27. *Bemidbar* 17:25.
28. *I Shemuel* 6:8.
29. *Yosiphon*, chap. 3.
30. Mishnah *Middos* 2:5.
31. *Metzora'im* — people afflicted by *tzara'as*.

"Don't the *metzora'im* live outside the city?" Chananya interrupted Reb Shmuel's words.

"They do indeed," Reb Shmuel replied patiently, "but on the morning of the eighth day of their period of purification from the *tzara'as*, when they must bring their *korbanos*, they immerse themselves here in this chamber's *mikveh*."

"But how could they have entered the *Ezras Nashim* if they haven't yet immersed in a *mikveh*?" inquired Gamliel.

"An excellent question!" Reb Shmuel exclaimed with pride. "*Metzora'im* immerse on the seventh day of their purification.[32] Therefore, they are allowed to enter the *Ezras Nashim* on that day."

The children proceeded on their way, headed by their *rebbi*, until they reached *Lishkas HaShemanim*(49) [Oil Chamber], which was in the southwestern corner. There were many jugs full of oil for the lighting of the Menorah and for the *menachos* [meal-offerings], and wine for the *nesachim* [poured-offerings]. Sacks of fine-quality wheat flour [*soles*] were arranged there as well.

Their next site was *Lishkas HaNezirim*(46) [Nazarites Chamber], which was in the southeastern corner of the *Ezras Nashim*. There they watched the *nezirim* cook their *korbanos shelamim*. One of the *nezirim* was shaving the hair of his head, because it was the day of his purification. Another one, who had already shaved his hair off, was standing in the corner, throwing the hair into the fire that was underneath the pot cooking the *shelamim* that he had offered.[33] "That's exactly what the Torah says to do in *Bemidbar*," Naftali said excitedly.

---

32. *Vayikra* 14:9.

33. *Bemidbar* 6:18: "[After the service] at the entrance of the Tent of Meeting the *nazir* shall shave [the hair of] his head and put [it] on the fire that is underneath [the pot cooking] the *Shelamim*-offering."

After a brief pause, Reb Shmuel remarked: "There are actually two more chambers: those of the musical instruments[34] [*Lishkos Klei HaShir*](50). They are located on both sides of the Fifteen Steps(21) ascending from the *Ezras Nashim* to the *Ezras Yisrael*(4). The musical instruments of the Leviyim are kept in these rooms, and that's where the Leviyim are taught those heavenly, moving melodies that they sing on the *Duchan*(5) [Platform].

"And now we are going to end our visit with a story, as we always do according to the custom that we have established," Reb Shmuel said with a smile. "You see Nikanor Gate(30) on top of the Fifteen Steps there, right in front of us?"

The children nodded.

"Well, there is an exciting story attached to it.[35]

"Nikanor was the man who traveled to Alexandria in Egypt in order to bring copper doors for one of the gates of the Beis HaMikdash. He returned by sea, with the heavy doors on board the ship. All of a sudden a dreadful storm broke out at sea, and it threatened to sink the ship together with all the passengers.

"The passengers tried to save themselves by lightening the burden of the ship, so they took one of Nikanor's doors and threw it overboard into the sea. The sea, however, did not grow quiet and continued to rage. The travelers were about to throw the other door overboard as well, but Nikanor held the remaining door with both of his hands and said, 'If you want to throw out the door, throw me out as well, together with it!'

"The sea stopped raging instantly, and the ship continued on its route. The loss of the first door distressed Nikanor very much, but there was nothing he could do. How great was his surprise, then, when the ship entered the port of Acco! He suddenly saw

---

34. Mishnah *Middos* 2:6.

35. *Yoma* 38a.

the first door. Some say that it appeared from underneath the ship, glittering in the sun's bright rays. Others say that a sea monster swallowed the door and later spat it out onto dry land.

"In commemoration of that miracle, they installed those doors in front of the entrance to the Beis HaMikdash.[36] Of course, they could have put them up in any gate they wished, because all the gates that have doors[37] are the same size: ten *amos* wide and twenty *amos* high.

"During a later period, when the nation became wealthier,[38] they overlaid all the doors of the Temple with gold, except Nikanor's doors. Some say that they remained as they were in remembrance of the miracle. Others say they were not overlaid because the copper they were made from was of such fine quality that it looked exactly like gold.[39] Therefore, there was no need to overlay these doors with actual gold."

36. Mishnah *Yoma* 3:10, *Tiferes Yisrael* #64.

37. Mishnah *Middos* 2:3.

38. Ibid.

39. *Yoma* 38a.

Chapter Six

Eighty Million Sacrifices

We have already learned that the location of the *Mizbeach*(7) [Altar] is of a very high degree of holiness," Reb Shmuel told his pupils in class one day. "It is the spot where *Akeidas Yitzchak* [the binding of Yitzchak] took place,[1] when Avraham Avinu built the Altar upon which he was going to sacrifice his son, Yitzchak. This is where Noach built an Altar after he had left the Ark and this is where Adam offered sacrifices after he was created. How many *korbanos*, do you think, are sacrificed on the *Mizbeach* every year?"

"Let me see," Yechezkel began to calculate. "The regular *korban Tamid* is sacrificed daily, in the morning and in the evening, as the verse says: 'You shall carry out the service of one sheep in the morning and carry out the service of the second sheep in the afternoon,'[2] in which case about seven hundred and thirty *temidim* are sacrificed annually."

---

1. Rambam, *Hilchos Beis HaBechirah* 2:2: "It is a tradition, commonly known, that the place where David and Shlomo built the Altar on Aravna's threshing-floor was the place where Avraham built the Altar and bound Yitzchak on it..."

2. *Bemidbar* 28:4.

"There is a hint to the number in the verse even before that,"
Binyamin said cleverly. "It says,[3] '**Two perfect** [*temimim shnayim*]
sheep in their first year **per day** [*layom*] as a regular burnt-offering.' The first letters of 'two,' 'perfect,' and 'per day' are *tav, shin,*
and *lamed*, which equal 730 in *gematria*."[4]

The boys were greatly impressed.

"But you forgot the *musafim*!" Yonasan shouted. "Right, the
additional sacrifices pertaining to Shabbos, Rosh Chodesh and
the Festivals," Yehoshua supported him. "Once my father and
I calculated the number of the communal sacrifices besides the
regular *temidim*, and it came to 551 *musafim* and *korbenos tzibur*.

"And what about *korban Pesach*?" Naftali interjected. "This
year more than twelve million Jews have made *aliyah le-regel*.
I heard a Kohen say that more than one million *korbenos Pesach*
were brought this year!"

"A million *korbanos* in just one day? How did they manage to
bring so many *korbanos*?" Chananya wondered.

Binyamin made a rapid calculation. "There are about twelve
hours of daylight per day, and sixty minutes in each hour. That
makes 720 minutes of daylight. If we divide one million by 720,
we'll come up with about fourteen hundred *korbenos Pesach* a
minute."

"You made a mistake in the calculation," Reuven said.

"No I didn't," Binyamin insisted. "If we divide a million by
720, we come up with exactly 1388 *korbanos*."

"I meant to say, the calculation is correct, but you forgot that
the *korban Pesach* is sacrificed in the afternoon [*bein ha-arbayim*],[5]

---

3. *Bemidbar* 28:3.

4. 400(ת) + 300(ש) + 30(ל). Consult *Ba'al HaTurim*'s commentary to *Bemidbar* 28:3.

5. *Shemos* 12:6: "...and [then] all the assembled congregation of Yisrael
shall slaughter it in the afternoon."

only after the regular *korban Tamid* has been sacrificed.[6] There-fore, there are only about three hours to sacrifice all the *korbenos Pesach*—not twelve hours," Reuven explained himself.

"Okay, then. In that case, let's divide a million by 180 min-utes, which is three hours. That means that 5,555 *korbanos* were sacrificed every minute," Binyamin said.

Reb Shmuel sat in the corner, without interfering, his face glowing with joy and satisfaction.

"My father told me that more *korbanos* are sacrificed on the first day of Yom Tov than on the eve of Pesach," Naftali said.

"Quite logical," Reuven agreed. "Each *oleh regel* must bring an *olas re'iyah* (burnt-offering)[7] and a *chagigah* [Festival] *Shelamim*-offering.[8] Although it is possible to bring them on any day dur-ing the seven days of the Festival,[9] it is considered more proper to sacrifice them on the first day.[10] It's not considered appropriate to put it off until later."

"So if twelve million[11] people perform *aliyah le-regel*, and each male brings at least two *korbanos*, it turns out that ten million *korbanos* will be sacrificed," Bo'az reckoned.

"Why not twenty-four million?" Yonasan wondered. "If I am not mistaken, twelve times two equals twenty-four."

"Women, and boys under the age of thirteen [*ketanim*] are exempt from bringing these *korbanos*," Bo'az said, "so there are

---

6. *Pesachim* 58a.

7. *Chagigah* 2a, 7a. It is a burnt-offering offered by men upon appearing in the Beis HaMikdash on one of the three principal Festivals: "[The people shall] not [then] appear before Me emptyhanded" (*Shemos* 23:15).

8. *Chagigah* 9a.

9. Ibid.

10. Rambam, *Hilchos Chagigah* 1:5.

11. *Pesachim* 64b.

about five million men among the twelve million *olei ha-regel* obligated to bring these korbanos."

"Don't forget about the obligation to bring *simchah Shelamim*-offerings[12] besides these *korbanos*," Yehoshua added.

Alexander HaKohen from Tzippori remarked, "And there are always ordinary *korbanos* that a person vows [*nedarim* or *nedavos*] to offer during the current year. He must fulfill these obligations promptly on the first Festival after he makes the vow.[13] The verse says,[14] 'You shall come there,' and 'you shall bring there,' which means, when you make *aliyah le-regel*, bring along the *korbanos* that you are obligated to offer. Our family alone sacrificed fifteen *korbanos* during the recent Pesach Festival."

"Hey, we have entirely forgotten the thousands of *korbanos* that are known as *chagigas arba'ah asar* [a voluntary Festival-offering sacrificed on the *arba'ah asar* — the 14th of Nisan[15] together with the *korban Pesach*, on the eve of Pesach]," Chananya called out from the far end of the classroom.

Binyamin summed up. "So it is quite clear that about twenty million animals are sacrificed every year on the *Mizbeach* during the Festival of Pesach."

"Twenty million *korbanos* on one *Mizbeach* in just one week! Unbelievable!" Chananya exclaimed in amazement.

Finally, Reb Shmuel's quiet voice was heard in the classroom. "Also on other Festivals millions of *korbanos* are sacrificed. And if we add the sin- and guilt-offerings which Jews who have

---

12. *Pesachim* 109a; *Devarim* 27:7: "And you shall sacrifice *Shelamim*-offerings and eat [them] there, and rejoice before the Eternal, your God."

13. Rambam, *Hilchos Ma'asei HaKorbanos* 14:13.

14. *Devarim* 12:5,6: "You shall… come there. You shall bring there your burnt-offerings, [*Shelamim*]-offerings, tithe-offerings, hand-brought selected offerings, vow-fulfilling offerings and gift-offerings, etc."

15. *Pesachim* 69b-70a.

committed sins must bring, plus the *korbanos* of *nezirim* and *metzora'im*, the firstborn animals born annually in Eretz Yisrael, the *ma'aser beheimah*, which is the tenth of all the animals that are born during the year, and a variety of miscellaneous *olos* [burnt-offerings] and *shelamim* [peace-offerings] that Jews bring as voluntary sacrifices, we will come up with an approximate number of at least eighty million *korbanos* per year! And they are all sacrificed on an area of only twenty-four square *amos*."

"Twenty-four square *amos*?!" asked Yonasan in surprise. "I learned that the area of the *Mizbeach* is thirty-two square *amos*!"

"And my father told me that it occupies an area of twenty-eight square *amos*," Yehoshua said.

Naftali looked confused. "They can't all be correct, can they?" he wondered to himself. Reb Shmuel's next remark cleared up his confusion.

"Both Yehoshua and Yonasan are correct. And...you'll be surprised to hear that I am also correct. The Base of the Altar is thirty-two *amos* long and thirty-two *amos* wide. The total area of the roof of the *Mizbeach* is twenty-eight by twenty-eight *amos*. But

How the Mizbeach Was Built

Corners (Turrets)
1 amah

Roof of the Mizbeach
28 amos

Sovev (Circuit)
30 amos

Yesod (Base)
32 amos

the part of the roof taken up by the *ma'arachos* [the Pyres], where the *korbanos* are burnt, is only twenty-four by twenty-four *amos*.

"To give you a better idea of the shape of the *Mizbeach*, I will describe to you how it was constructed. They took four big boards, each thirty-two *amos* long[16] and one *amah* high, and joined them together in the shape of a square, whose sides were thirty-two *amos* wide and one *amah* high. They placed that square frame onto the floor of the *Azarah*, the holy site where Hashem commanded to build the *Mizbeach*.

"Afterwards, they took whole stones of various sizes. They had to be whole, because the *Mizbeach* must be built of stones unaltered by metal tools.[17] They put these stones into the square frame and poured lime, pitch and lead over the stones. When everything became dry and hard they removed the wooden frame, and a square-shaped stone block remained inside, whose length and width was thirty-two by thirty-two *amos* and whose height was one *amah*. This block is called the Base of the Altar(103)(104)(105) [*Yesod HaMizbeach*].

"After they had finished building the *Yesod*, the Base, they built another wooden frame of four boards, each one thirty *amos* long and five *amos* high. They placed this square frame in the center of the square *Yesod*, an *amah* away from each edge, and filled it with stones, lime, pitch and lead. After they had removed the frame, a perfect square was formed, rising above the lower square of the *Yesod*. The top of the square block is called the *Sovev*(96) [the Circuit]. We will see that there is a third square on top of this, so the *Sovev* will be just one *amah* wide on all sides. Now, who can figure out how high the *Sovev* rises above the floor of the *Azarah*?" Reb Shmuel asked.

---

16. *Zevachim* 54a.

17. *Shemos* 20:22. The stones were not to be touched by an iron tool (Mishnah *Middos* 3:4).

Building the Mizbeach

"The *Sovev* rises six *amos* above the floor of the *Azarah*," the children answered on the spot, "since the *Yesod* is one *amah* high and the *Sovev* is five *amos* above it."

Reb Shmuel continued his explanation. "The builders of the *Mizbeach* built a third square on top of the second one. This time it occupied an area of twenty-eight square *amos* and was three *amos* high. This square platform serves as the roof of the *Mizbeach*. Now you can understand how it is possible for all of us to be correct. The *Yesod* of the *Mizbeach*, which stands on the floor, occupies thirty-two square *amos*, whereas the size of the roof of the *Mizbeach* is only twenty-eight square *amos*. Yet the area of the *ma'arachos* is twenty-four by twenty-four *amos*."

"If that's the case, then the total height of the *Mizbeach* is nine *amos*," Yechezkel concluded.

"But I heard that the height of the *Mizbeach* is ten *amos*,"[18] Gamliel wondered, sounding confused.

"Don't worry, you heard correctly," Reb Shmuel reassured him, "except that you must have been told that its height is ten *amos* with the *kranos*(97)(98)(99)(100) [Corners or Turrets]. Each one of these four square cubes,[19] whose sides and height are one *amah*, is built onto a separate corner of the *Mizbeach*, in the same manner as the other parts of the *Mizbeach*. Thus, the *Mizbeach*, including the *kranos*, is ten *amos* high."

Bo'az posed a clever question. "If the roof of the *Mizbeach* occupies an area of twenty-eight square *amos*, why are the *korbanos* sacrificed on an area of only twenty-four square *amos*?"

"There is a need for unhampered walking space where the Kohanim are able to move about comfortably. A width of only one *amah* to walk between the *kranos* is not enough because the

---

18. Rambam, *Hilchos Beis HaBechirah* 2:5.
19. *Zevachim* 54a.

The Mizbeach

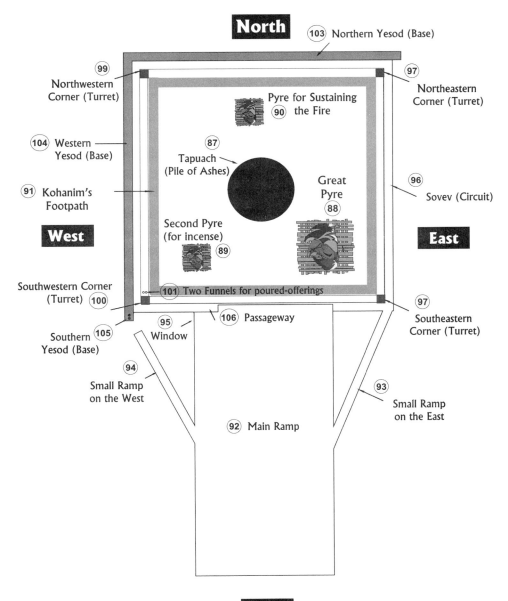

North

(103) Northern Yesod (Base)

(99) Northwestern Corner (Turret)

(97) Northeastern Corner (Turret)

(90) Pyre for Sustaining the Fire

(104) Western Yesod (Base)

(87) Tapuach (Pile of Ashes)

(96) Sovev (Circuit)

Great Pyre (88)

(91) Kohanim's Footpath

West

East

Second Pyre (for incense) (89)

(101) Two Funnels for poured-offerings

(100) Southwestern Corner (Turret)

(97) Southeastern Corner (Turret)

(106) Passageway

(95) Window

(105) Southern Yesod (Base)

(94) Small Ramp on the West

(93) Small Ramp on the East

(92) Main Ramp

South

kranos block the corners. Therefore, an additional *amah*'s width walking space is provided on the roof. This gives the Kohanim a width of two *amos* to walk around the *Mizbeach*. This path is called the Kohanim's Footpath(91) [*Mekom Hilluch HaKohanim*].[20] Therefore, if two *amos* on each edge of the roof are utilized in order to create the path, the area will be left with twenty-four square *amos* only."

"Is this entire area used for offering *korbanos*?" Chananya asked.

"No, the whole area is not entirely designated for offering *korbanos*. There are other things on the roof of the *Mizbeach* as well. The large Pile of Ashes right in the middle[21] is called the *Tapuach*(87). The Great Pyre(88) [*HaMa'arachah HaGedolah*] is fixed on the eastern side[22] of the *Mizbeach*. The smaller Second Pyre for incense(89) [*HaMa'arachah HaSheniyah shel ketores*] is located in the southwestern corner[23] of the roof. Live coals are taken from this pyre to burn the incense [*ketores*] on the Golden Altar(89) [*Mizbach HaZahav*] in the *Heichal*(11). The function of the Third Pyre(90)[24] is to ensure that there will always be fire on the *Mizbeach*, as the verse says in *Vayikra*, 'A fire must always burn on the Altar; it must not be extinguished.'[25]

"Now, the second square platform, which is built on top of the *Yesod*(103)(104)(105), leaves over a jutting base, one *amah* wide, along the entire length of the northern(103) and western(104) sides. This

---

20. Mishnah *Middos* 3:1.

21. Mishnah *Tamid* 2:2.

22. Mishnah *Tamid* 2:4.

23. Mishnah *Tamid* 2:5.

24. *Yoma* 45a: "Rabbi Yosei says, 'Every day there were three pyres... the Great Pyre, the Second Pyre for incense, and one for the preservation of the fire.'"

25. *Vayikra* 6:5.

base juts out one extra *amah* on both sides. This leaves only a one square *amah* piece on the eastern and southern sides.[26] It is upon either the long western base [*Yesod Ma'aravi*] or the one square *amah* base on the southern side of the *Mizbeach* [*Yesod Dromi*], that the Kohen pours the leftover blood of the *korbanos*.[27]

"If we ascend five *amos* higher we shall reach the *Sovev*(96), which is also one *amah* wide. The Kohanim walk along it when they sacrifice the sin-offering [*chatas*]. We shall add more details during our forthcoming lessons."

"I have a question," Reuven said, and everybody listened carefully, knowing that he always asked good questions.

"You said that the *Yesod*(103) extends along the entire length of the Altar only on its northern and western sides, and there is no real *Yesod* on the southern and eastern sides other than a one square *amah* piece. So the *Yesod* really isn't thirty-two square *amos*. Why, then, did they make a square frame, thirty-two *amos* by thirty-two *amos*, to serve as a mold for the *Yesod*, as you told us?"

"An excellent question, Reuven!" Reb Shmuel exclaimed enthusiastically. "I'm so happy that you noticed this important detail which I forgot to explain. After they built the first mold, just before filling it up with stones, lime, etc., they took two beams, each thirty-one *amos* long, one *amah* wide, and one *amah* thick.[28] They put one of them on the eastern side of the *Mizbeach* and one on the southern side. This blocked the stones and other material from entering so that there was no long *Yesod* on either of those sides. They did this because the Tribe of Binyamin was promised that the *Mizbeach* would be built on their property. However, the area bordering on the southern and eastern sides of the *Mizbeach*

---

26. Mishnah *Middos* 3:1.

27. *Zevachim* 47b, 53a.

28. Mishnah *Middos* 3:1, Bartenura; *Zevachim* 54b.

Measurements of the Mizbeach's Height
(Western View)

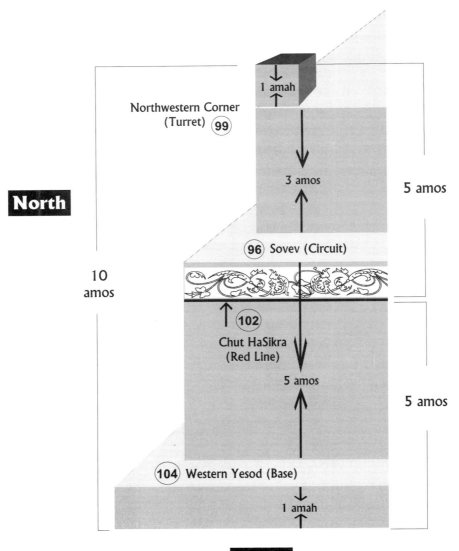

1 amah

Northwestern Corner
(Turret) 99

North

3 amos

5 amos

10
amos

96 Sovev (Circuit)

102

Chut HaSikra
(Red Line)

5 amos

5 amos

104 Western Yesod (Base)

1 amah

West

Measurements of the Mizbeach's Height
(Eastern View)

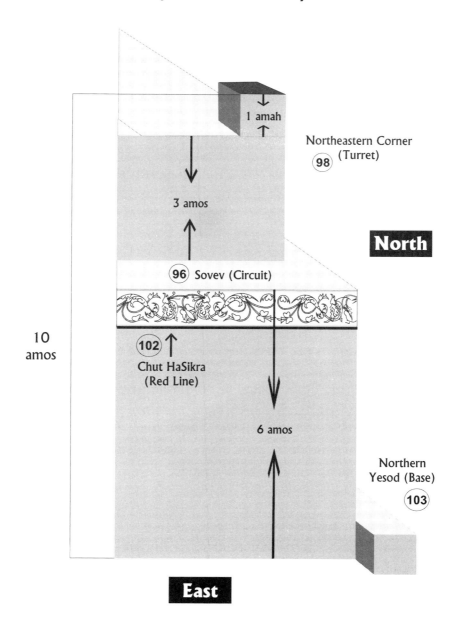

1 amah

Northeastern Corner
(98) (Turret)

3 amos

North

(96) Sovev (Circuit)

10 amos

(102) Chut HaSikra
(Red Line)

6 amos

Northern
Yesod (Base)

(103)

East

is in the domain of the Tribe of Yehudah. Therefore, no *Yesod* was built on those sides, so that the Altar would be entirely in the portion of Binyamin."[29]

Reuven nodded his head in understanding, whereupon Reb Shmuel continued.

"The Main Ramp(92) [*HaKevesh HaGadol*] was built on the southern side of the *Mizbeach*.[30] Kohanim use it to ascend to the *Mizbeach*. Its length is thirty-two *amos* and its width is sixteen *amos*. Kohanim use it to reach the roof of the *Mizbeach*, whose total height is, as we said, nine *amos*. Two Small Ramps(93)(94) extend from the middle of both sides of the Main Ramp, the eastern one leading to the *Sovev*(96) and the western one leading to the Southern Base(105).[31] When we watch the actual service of the

The Mizbeach and Its Ramps

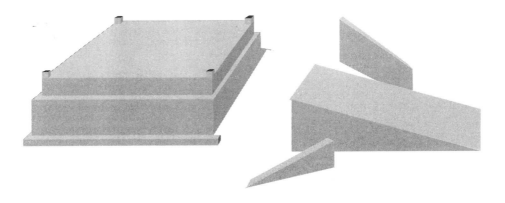

---

29. *Zevachim* 53b.

30. Mishnah *Middos* 3:3.

31. *Zevachim* 62b. The Kohanim were not permitted to use steps, because the Torah says, "Nor may you go up onto My Altar with steps, so that your nakedness not be exposed on it" (*Shemos* 20:23).

korbanos, you'll be able to see it."

"I noticed a red line encircling the middle of the *Mizbeach*. What is it for?" Bo'az asked.

"The *Chut HaSikra*(102) [Red Line] marks the exact middle of the height of the *Mizbeach*, which is five *amos* from the floor of the *Azarah*, and it shows the Kohanim where the blood has to be placed.[32] The blood of some offerings is splashed onto the *Mizbeach* below the *Chut HaSikra*, and the blood of other offerings is applied to the *Mizbeach* above it. The *Sovev* enables the Kohanim to climb up and apply the blood above the *Chut HaSikra*, when required.

"And now listen to this miracle that has become a daily occurrence on the *Mizbeach*," Reb Shmuel finished his lesson enthusiastically. "Every year, about eighty million *korbanos* are burnt on the *Mizbeach*. A continual fire blazes upon it. And yet, it remains intact and never cracks or falls apart. Even an Altar made of one huge whole stone would crack and the stone would melt because of the enormous heat—not to mention one made of small stones held together by lime, pitch and lead. And the *Mizbeach* of the Beis HaMikdash withstands enormous daily heat for years on end! It's an open miracle!"[33]

---

32. Mishnah *Middos* 3:1: "A red line went around it in the middle to separate between the upper blood and the lower blood."

33. *Tiferes Yisrael*, Introduction to Mishnah *Middos*, chap. 3.

Chapter Seven

An Interesting Evening

The children sat in a circle in the courtyard of the house, as the sweet-smelling Yerushalmi breeze stroked their faces and ruffled their sidelocks. They eagerly waited for their *rebbi*'s fascinating story, which he was accustomed to tell them in the evenings.

All of a sudden, Bo'az from Macedonia turned to Alexander and said, "You certainly have an interesting name. Isn't it a gentile name, though? Why did they give you such a name? Everyone in Macedonia is familiar with Alexander of Macedonia [Alexander the Great], although he died three hundred years ago. He was a powerful ruler and captured almost the whole world. However, there is not a single Jew in Macedonia who bears such a name."

"I was named after my righteous grandfather whose name was Alexander. He was named after his own grandfather, the famous *tzaddik*," Alexander replied somewhat defensively.

"Jews have a very reliable tradition to give their children the name Alexander," Reb Shmuel remarked suddenly. "The name Alexander has a very interesting story attached to it."

The boys became very excited, knowing that this was an introduction to a gripping story. They waited in suspense for Reb Shmuel to begin. And this is what he related:

"In the beginning of the period of the Second Beis HaMik-dash [*Bayis Sheini*] — that is, about three hundred years ago — a young Emperor ascended to the throne in Macedonia, which some people call Greece. Soon afterward, the new Emperor launched a large-scale military campaign with the purpose of capturing as many countries as possible. It was quite obvious that Hashem Yisbarach crowned his campaign with great success. During Alexander's reign, Greece became an enormous empire that controlled almost the entire world.

"Daniel, who was endowed with *ru'ach ha-kodesh*, predicted Alexander's rise to power, and this is what he wrote in his book: 'And as I was contemplating, behold, a he-goat came from the west across the face of the whole earth and not touching the ground.'[1] The 'he-goat' is an allusion to the Greek Empire, led by its young Emperor, Alexander the Great.[2]

"Alexander even succeeded in conquering Persia, which was a formidably powerful empire in those days. Daniel alludes to this, saying, '…And he came to the ram that had two horns… and ran at him in the fury of his power… and smote the ram and broke his two horns.'[3] The ram represents the Persian Kingdom that was subjugated by Greece.

"On his way[4] to wage war against Persia, Alexander of Macedonia passed by Eretz Yisrael. The members of the Kusim sect,[5] who lived on Mount Gerizim and had always hoped to destroy the Beis HaMikdash, viewed Alexander's coming as a wonderful

---

1. *Daniel* 8:5.

2. Ibid., Ibn Ezra.

3. *Daniel* 8:6,7.

4. *Yosiphon*, chap. 5.

5. Kusim — A heretic sect, hostile to Torah Judaism (see *II Melachim* 17:24–41); *Yoma* 69a.

opportunity to realize their desire. They therefore hastened to visit the Emperor with a false claim that the Jews intended to rebel against him.

"'You will be able to bring them to their knees only if you destroy their Temple,' the Kusim said.

"The Emperor became convinced, and led his army to capture Yerushalayim in order to destroy the Beis HaMikdash. Fast messengers rushed to inform Shimon HaTzaddik—who served as the *Kohen Gadol* after Ezra the Scribe had passed away[6]—that Alexander was approaching Yerushalayim with the purpose of destroying the dwelling place of the *Shechinah*. Shimon Ha-Tzaddik donned the special garments worn by the High Priest, and gathered the most venerable and esteemed Jews of Yerushalayim. Together, this honorable delegation went out to meet the Emperor.

"The two parties met in the middle of the road, and all of a sudden, something quite incredible happened. The great and awesome king, Alexander of Macedonia, dismounted from his horse, bowed down, and prostated himself before Shimon Ha-Tzaddik! Alexander's knights and noblemen were shocked and amazed, and cried out, 'Your Majesty! It is not befitting your royal status to prostrate yourself before a Jew!'

"'Leave me alone!' the great Emperor scolded them. 'I saw his venerable image, defeating my enemies in all my wars. How can I not bow down before him?

"'Why did you come to meet me?' the king continued, turning to Shimon HaTzaddik. The *Kohen Gadol* replied respectfully, 'I beg Your Majesty to forgive me, but how was it possible for those pagan heretics to dupe Your Majesty into wishing to destroy the Temple? It is there that we pray to God for your well-being and success!'

---

6. Mishnah *Avos* 1:2, Bartenura.

*The great and awesome Alexander of Macedonia
prostrated himself before Shimon HaTzaddik*

"Upon hearing such words, Alexander immediately annulled the evil decree, and even permitted the Jews to destroy the Kusim's house of worship on Mount Gerizim."

"What a great story!" Chananya exclaimed in delight. "But what does it mean that Alexander saw Shimon HaTzaddik's image defeating his enemies?"

"I'm not sure this information is accurate, but once I heard that on the night before their meeting, Alexander dreamed of an angel dressed in the garments of the *Kohen Gadol*, brandishing a sword in his hand.[7]

"'Why do you want to kill me?!' asked the frightened Emperor, to which the angel answered:

"'In all your wars, God sent me to conquer every single one of your foes. All of them were great kings, yet I subdued them before you. But now, you will surely die because of your desire to go up to Yerushalayim to destroy God's own Dwelling!'

"'O, please forgive me!' Alexander entreated. 'Give me a chance to repent!'

"The angel seemed to be pacified, and said to him, 'All right then; go up to Yerushalayim, and when you see a man dressed in the same clothes as mine, bow down and protrate yourself before him, and do whatever he commands you.'

"When Alexander saw Shimon HaTzaddik the next day, he said that it was this image who had defeated all his enemies before him in all his conquests.

"After the two leaders had made peace, Shimon HaTzaddik arranged for Alexander to visit the Beis HaMikdash. The great king was beside himself with amazement over its beauty and splendor. He then expressed a desire to donate a large amount of gold in order to cast a statue of himself to be exhibited in the Beis HaMikdash.

---

7. *Yosiphon*, chap. 5.

"The *Kohen Gadol* was at a loss as to what should be done. On the one hand, he could not agree to put up a molten image in the *Heichal*. On the other hand, he feared that if he refused to fulfill the Emperor's request, who knew what could happen if he flew into a rage. So Shimon HaTzaddik thought of a clever answer: 'Perhaps Your Majesty could contribute the promised gold for the sake of poor priests, and I will perpetuate Your Majesty's memory for generations! All the male children that will be born this year to the priests of Judea and Yerushalayim will be named after Your Majesty—Alexander of Macedonia!'

"Needless to say, the king was thrilled to hear Shimon Ha-Tzaddik's idea.

"Most likely our Alexander HaKohen, who studies in our group, bears the name of his forefathers who were named after Alexander the Great." Reb Shmuel smiled at Alexander, who smiled in return.

"You see, my dear boys," Reb Shmuel continued, "when the people of Yisrael do the will of Hashem, they do not need a large army to fight against their enemies, because HaKadosh Baruch Hu brings down great and mighty kings before them. And that reminds me of another story…

"Many years after Alexander the Great, King Seleucus ruled in Macedonia. His attitude toward the Jews was tolerant and favorable. He did not oppress or enslave them.

"One day some wicked men came to see King Seleucus and told him about the vast treasures of gold and silver hidden in the Beis HaMikdash.

"'It is befitting a great Emperor like Seleucus to own such precious treasures, not some lowly Jews,' they poured sweet poison into his ears.

"The temptation was great, and the king could not resist it. He sent his general Heliodorus to plunder the Beis HaMikdash treasury and to transfer its contents to Macedonia. The general led his army to Yerushalayim, and upon arrival asked to speak to the High Priest. The general arrogantly announced to the *Ko-hen Gadol* why he was there, and all the holy man's entreaties to reach a compromise fell on deaf ears.

"The wicked general Heliodorus put up guards around the Beis HaMikdash so that the Jews would not be able to prevent him from fulfilling his sinister mission.

"It was a night of doleful moaning and lamenting for the Jews. The tearful, heartrending weeping of the adults mingled with the wailing of the children. All the residents of Yerushalayim, young and old, spent a mournful night in heartfelt prayer and supplication before the Master of the world, that He prevent the villain from realizing his wicked intentions, and that Hashem's holy Name not be desecrated publicly.

At dawn the next day, Heliodorus led his army into the Beis HaMikdash. All of a sudden a terrible noise was heard in the *Heichal*, and all the general's regiments fled the holy site in panic. Only Heliodorus remained standing alone in the courtyard of the House of God. And then the general beheld an awesome sight: a giant man dressed in golden apparel, girded with a golden sword and riding a mighty stallion, was coming toward him steadily. With one kick of the stallion's powerful leg, Heliodorus was knocked to the ground.

"While Heliodorus was on the floor, the giant man ordered his two companions to whip the general mercilessly, which they did very thoroughly — until he was sorely beaten and bleeding profusely, mute with fright. He was barely alive when the Ko-hanim picked him up and delivered him into the care of his subordinates. They put him on a bed in his tent, where he lay in the throes of death, having no strength to utter a word.

"The soldiers of Heliodorus's army who had followed him to Yerushalayim went to see the *Kohen Gadol* and begged him to pray for the welfare of their general. The *Kohen Gadol* prayed for his recovery, and Heliodorus miraculously recovered soon after.

"Shamefaced, he went to the *Kohen Gadol* and bowed down

before him in deep gratitude, promising to contribute a vast amount of gold to the treasury of the Beis HaMikdash.

"After Heliodorus returned to Macedonia, he told King Seleucus, 'If Your Majesty has enemies whom he wishes to kill, don't bother fighting against them: just send them to Yerushalayim to torment the Jews, and they will certainly perish there all by themselves.'

"The Emperor was shocked to hear what had happened to Heliodorus, and from then on he sent a lavish gift to the Beis Ha-Mikdash once a year."

When Reb Shmuel finished his story, the boys rubbed their eyes, as if waking up from a dream. Then they suddenly noticed Reb Avraham, the elderly man from Tiveriah who had organized their class, sitting quietly in the corner. At the sight of their surprised looks, Reb Avraham smiled and said, "I came into the room a few minutes ago, but you were so engrossed in the story that you didn't notice me.

"I have come all the way back from Tiveriah to bring a *korban*," Reb Avraham said. "I've been on the road for the last two days. Tomorrow I intend to bring a guilt-offering [*asham*], which I am obligated to bring. Afterwards I shall return to Tiveriah, *b'ezras Hashem*.

"I became obligated to bring an *asham taluy*[8] as a result of a very upsetting incident. Two types of fatty meat lay in front of

---

8. *Vayikra* 5:17,18,19: "And if a person sins by doing one of any of the Eternal's commandments that may not be done, but he is uncertain [whether he actually transgressed] he will nevertheless incur guilt and bear the consequences of his transgression. He shall bring to the priest a perfect ram from flocks of the prescribed value of a guilt-offering and the priest shall make an atonement for him for the inadvertent sin he may have committed but is uncertain thereof, and he will be forgiven. It is a guilt-offering, he has surely incurred guilt before the Eternal."

me. They were absolutely identical, but one of them — as I found out later — contained none other than *chelev* [forbidden fat of an animal], and the other one contained *shuman* [permitted fat of an animal]. I ate one of them,[9] and after I found out that one of them had *chelev*, I wasn't sure which one I had eaten. I might have mistakenly eaten the forbidden one!

"Now, if I had known for sure that I had inadvertently eaten a piece of *chelev*, I would have been obligated to bring a sin-offering [*chatas*]. This is because a person who, *chas ve-shalom*, eats *chelev* deliberately, is liable for the *kares* penalty.[10] If he eats *chelev* by mistake, he has to bring a *korban Chatas*. But I am in doubt as to which piece I ate. Therefore, I have to bring an *asham taluy*," Reb Avraham concluded.

The silence that ensued in the room was broken by Naftali.

"Excuse me, Reb Avraham, may I ask a question?"

"Certainly," Reb Avraham encouraged him.

"Was it really so necessary for you to undertake such a long and difficult journey from Tiveriah — especially considering your age — just in order to offer a *korban* for a *safeik issur*?" Naftali asked hesitantly.

"It certainly *was* absolutely necessary," Reb Avraham began emphatically. "Being in doubt as to whether one inadvertently transgressed at all [*safeik issur*], is much more serious than knowing for sure that he inadvertently transgressed [*issur vaday*].[11] A person who is obligated to bring a *chatas* to atone for an inadvertent *issur vaday* may bring a sheep worth one *me'ah*[12] or even

---

9. *Vayikra* 5:17, Rashi (ד"ה ולא ידע).

10. Excision, death penalty executed by Heaven.

11. Rabbeinu Yonah, beginning of his commentary on *Berachos* 1b.

12. *Me'ah, sela*: silver coins. Twenty-four *me'ah* make one *sela*.

less.[13] However, to atone for an inadvertent *safeik issur*, one must bring a ram as a *korban Asham*, worth two *sela'im*[14] — which are worth forty-eight times more than a *me'ah*. How could this be?

"A person who is aware of having transgressed an *issur*, regrets it sincerely and wholeheartedly and repents completely. On the other hand, a person who is in doubt as to whether he has definitely sinned or not, has a guilty conscience, but he consoles himself, saying, 'Maybe I haven't sinned at all.' This is the reason why the Torah obligates a person whose sin is in doubt to bring a more expensive *korban* — as if to remind him that he must regret it and repent completely on account of the sin that he might have committed."

"And what is the halachah if you find out later that you definitely ate *chelev* and not *shuman*?" Naftali persisted.

"If that happens then I will be obligated to sacrifice a *korban Chatas*[15] in order to atone for the inadvertent transgression of a sin [*aveirah be-shogeg*]," Reb Avraham replied patiently.

"So, dear pupils, if you would like to know how a *korban Asham* is offered, you can join me on my way to the Beis HaMikdash tomorrow to see it being done in actual practice."

---

13. *Zevachim* 48a, Rashi.

14. *Vayikra* 5:15, Rashi; *Kerisos* 26b, Rashi.

15. *Vayikra* 5:18, Rashi.

Chapter Eight

Reb Avraham Brings an Asham

After all the children had assembled the next morning, Reb Shmuel announced, "Because we want to watch Reb Avraham sacrifice his *korban Asham* today, I am going to give a short description of the *Ezras Yisrael* and the *Ezras Kohanim*. I will then explain a few *halachos* pertaining to the offering of the *korban Asham*, whereupon we'll hurry to the Beis HaMikdash."

The boys took their seats, and Reb Shmuel started the lesson.

"Yesterday we visited the *Ezras Nashim*(3) and reached Nikanor Gate(30), which is actually the border between the *Ezras Nashim* and the *Ezras Yisrael*(4).

"The *Ezras Yisrael* is an area designated for Jews who want to either bring *korbanos* to the Beis HaMikdash or watch the holy service of the Kohanim. This *Azarah* [courtyard] is eleven *amos*[1] wide and 135 *amos* long. From the *Ezras Yisrael* one arrives at the next *Azarah*, called the *Ezras Kohanim*(6), which is also eleven *amos* wide and 135 *amos* long.

"The entire area from Nikanor Gate until the back wall of the Beis HaMikdash is simply called the *Azarah*. The *Azarah* is 135 *amos* wide and 187 *amos* long, and includes the *Ezras Yisrael* and *Ezras Kohanim*.

---

1. Mishnah *Middos* 2:6.

Ezras Yisrael and Ezras Kohanim

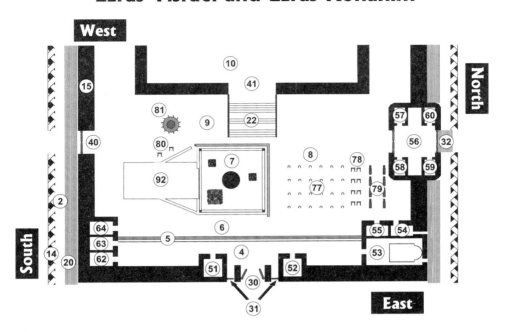

2. *Cheil*
4. *Ezras Yisrael* (Israelites' Courtyard)
5. Platform (consisting of 4 steps)
6. *Ezras Kohanim* (Kohanim's Courtyard)
7. *Mizbeach* (Altar)
8. *Beis HaMitbechayim* (Abattoir)
9. Between the *Ulam* and the *Mizbeach*
10. *Ulam* (Antechamber)
14. *Soreg* (lattice fence)
15. Wall of *Azarah*
20. 12 Steps ascending from *Cheil* to *Azarah*
22. 12 Steps ascending to *Ulam*
30. Nikanor Gate (entrance to *Ezras Yisrael*)
31. Two Side Doors on either side of Nikanor Gate
32. Pyre Hall Gate (Music Gate)
40. Water Gate
41. Entrance to *Ulam*
51. Chamber for the Preparation of the *Kohen Gadol*'s Flour-offering
52. Chamber of Pinchas, Keeper of the Priestly Garments

53. Chamber of Hewn Stone (seat of the Sanhedrin)
54. Parhedrin Chamber (where the *Kohen Gadol* was sequestered for seven days before Yom Kippur)
55. Chamber of the Diaspora
56. The Pyre Hall
57. Chamber of Sacrificial Lambs
58. Chamber for preparation of Showbread
59. Chamber of the Receipts
60. Small Pyre Chamber
62. Salt Chamber
63. *Parvah* Chamber
64. Rinsing Chamber
77. Rings to secure the animals for slaughter
78. Tables used for rinsing the flayed animals
79. Low Pillars for flaying the slaughtered animals
80. Two Tables near Altar
81. *Kiyor* (Washing Basin)
92. Main Ramp

"In the *Azarah*, immediately after the eleven *amos* of the *Ezras Kohanim*, are the *Mizbeach*(7) and the *Beis HaMitbechayim*(8) [*Slaughtering Area*].[2] The *Mizbeach* is situated in the southern and central *Azarah*, and the *Beis HaMitbechayim* is located north of the *Mizbeach*. Does anyone know where the guilt-offering [*asham*] is slaughtered?"

"In the *Azarah*," Yechezkel replied. "A person who slaughters a *korban* outside of the *Azarah* is liable for the *kares* punishment, isn't he?"[3]

"Do you think it can be slaughtered in the *Ezras Nashim*?"

"I guess it's okay, since it's also a type of *Azarah*," Yechezkel replied again.

Bo'az disagreed with him. "I was told that it is permissible to slaughter only in the *Azarah* you described before, past Nikanor Gate," he said.

"Bo'az is correct," confirmed Reb Shmuel. "Sacrifices are slaughtered within Nikanor Gate only. However, the *Azarah* has four sides. So on which of the four sides is the *asham* slaughtered?"

"How could I possibly forget?" Yonasan shouted out. "The verse in *Vayikra* says, 'In the [same] place where they shall slaughter the burnt-offering (*olah*) they shall slaughter the guilt-offering (*asham*).'[4] Burnt-offerings are slaughtered to the north of the *Mizbeach*, as it says, 'He shall slaughter it by the northern side of the Altar before the Eternal.'[5] This indicates where the *asham* is to be slaughtered — by the northern side of the *Mizbeach*."[6]

---

2. Mishnah *Middos* 5:1.

3. *Vayikra* 17:4.

4. *Vayikra* 7:2.

5. *Vayikra* 1:11.

6. *Zevachim* 54b.

"And where is the blood to be splashed?" Reb Shmuel prodded.

"And [the priest] shall splash its blood against the Altar, all around,"[7] the boys quoted in chorus.

"And how is the blood splashed against the *Mizbeach* all around?"

Yehoshua spoke up. "The Kohen makes only two splashes, described in the Mishnah as 'Two splashes that constitute four.'[8] He makes one splash against the Northeastern Corner of the *Mizbeach*(98), so that part of the blood reaches the northern wall, and another part the eastern wall. Then he proceeds toward the Southwestern Corner of the *Mizbeach*(100) and performs another splash in the same manner, so that the blood may reach both the western and the southern walls of the *Mizbeach*. The Kohen performs only two splashes, but the blood touches on all four walls of the *Mizbeach*: 'Two splashes that constitute four.'"

Reb Shmuel's face radiated sheer contentment.

"And what do they do with the blood that is left in the vessel [*shyarei ha-dam*]?"

"Perhaps the leftover blood is poured onto the Southern Base(105), just like the leftover blood of the *olah*[9] [burnt-offering]," Naftali replied.

"Beautiful!" Reb Shmuel commended him. "Now, what they do with the meat of the *korban Asham*?"

"The *emurim* are burned on the Altar, and the meat is eaten by the priests in the *Azarah*," Yehoshua was well-versed enough to answer.[10]

---

7. *Vayikra* 7:2.

8. *Zevachim* 53b, Rashi (ד"ה שתי מתנות).

9. *Zevachim* 51a, Rashi (ד"ה אל יסוד).

10. *Vayikra* 7:5,6.

The group headed for the Beis HaMikdash. On their way, Reb Shmuel suddenly changed direction and headed for the *mikveh* [ritual immersion pool].

"The Sages are divided over the issue of whether one is always obligated to immerse himself in the *mikveh* before entering the *Azarah*.[11] I suggest we follow the stringent view and purify ourselves properly before we enter," Reb Shmuel told the pupils.

When they came to the Beis HaMikdash, they quickly passed through the *Ezras Nashim*(3). At the entrance to Nikanor Gate(30), Reb Shmuel stopped them and said: "Now we are about to enter the *Ezras Yisrael*(4) [Israelites' Courtyard]. Its sanctity is of a higher degree than that of the *Ezras Nashim*. Even a *mechusar kippurim*[12] may not enter the *Ezras Yisrael*, although his *tum'ah* is considered to be a minor one."

"What is a *mechusar kippurim*?" Yonasan asked.

"It is someone who has already immersed in a *mikveh* but has not sacrificed his obligatory *korban* to atone for his *tum'ah* completely," answered the *rebbi*.

Naftali looked sympathetically at the people who stood at the gate. "They must be *mechusarei kippurim*," he thought.

Reb Shmuel's warning interrupted his thoughts: "Whoever enters the *Azarah* should walk at a slow pace and imagine that he is standing before Hashem,[13] as the verse says about His presence in the Beis HaMikdash, 'My eyes and My heart shall be [present] there for eternity.'[14] One must walk there with dread, fear and trepidation, as King David said, 'In the House of God we shall walk with trepidation.'"[15]

---

11. *Yoma* 30a, Rashi (ד"ה לעבודה); Rambam, *Hilchos Bi'as HaMikdash* 5:4.

12. Mishnah *Keilim* 1:8.

13. Rambam, *Hilchos Beis HaBechirah* 7:5.

14. *I Melachim* 9:3.

15. Literal meaning of the verse in *Tehillim* 55:15.

The pupils passed through Nikanor Gate(30) in perfect order, whereupon they found themselves in the *Ezras Yisrael*. The service of sacrificing the morning *korban Tamid* [*Tamid shel shachar*] had finished not so long before, and now the Kohanim started to sacrifice individual *korbanos*. At that time there were hundreds of Jews with their sheep and bullocks in the *Ezras Yisrael*. Here and there turtledoves and pigeons were heard cooing.

The boys spotted Reb Avraham in one of the corners of the *Azarah* after a few minutes of searching. He was pouring his heart out in an emotional recitation of *Tehillim*, reading from an ancient scroll. They stood there silently for some time until Reb Avraham took notice of them. He signaled to Reb Shmuel to take the ram from him, so that it should not disturb his recitation.

While they waited for Reb Avraham to finish his preparations, Reb Shmuel taught them a few *halachos*.

"Look there," he pointed with his finger. "That's the northern side of the *Mizbeach*, and that's where the *kodshei kodashim* [sacrifices of the most holy order] are slaughtered. This entire area — from the northern wall of the *Azarah* up to the wall of the *Mizbeach*[16] that faces it, and from the wall of the *Ulam*(16) up to the eastern wall of the *Azarah* that faces it — is appropriate for the slaughter of *kodshei kodashim*.

"On the northern side of the *Mizbeach*, the *Beis HaMitbechayim*(8) is seen. There are twenty-four *Taba'os*(77) [Rings], which are used to secure the animals for slaughter. The *Taba'os* are made in the shape of semicircles. Besides the Rings, there are eight *Nanasin*(79), which are low pillars used for flaying the slaughtered animals, and eight *Shulchanos*(78) — tables used for rinsing the flayed animals — in the *Beis HaMitbechayim*.

"There were no *Taba'os* in the First Beis HaMikdash, and

---

16. Rambam, *Hilchos Beis HaBechirah* 5:15,16.

The boys watched Reb Avraham pouring out his heart
in an emotional recitation of Tehillim

there were no *Taba'os* at the beginning of the Second Beis Ha-Mikdash either. Yochanan the *Kohen Gadol* installed twenty-four *Taba'os* on the northern side of the Altar.[17] He had those Rings made to assist with the *shechitah* [slaughter]: before the *korban* is slaughtered, the animal's head is placed into a Ring which prevents it from squirming during the slaughter and receiving of the blood.

"The *Taba'os* themselves are used in a very curious way: they are partially attached to the floor of the *Azarah*, so that before the heads of the animals are placed into them, they are turned upwards and "unlocked." After the animals' heads are lowered onto the floor, the *Taba'os* are turned back, locking the heads inside them. Then they are attached back to the floor of the *Azarah* again."

"What a clever device!" the boys expressed their admiration.

A Kohen approached the waiting group and asked, pointing at the ram, "Would you like to offer a *korban*?"

"It's not our *korban*," Reb Shmuel answered, and the Kohen turned around and went away.

Reb Shmuel continued. "The *Nanasin* are eight low stone Pillars, with a square block of cedar wood on top of each. Three hooks, each one higher than the other, are fixed into the blocks of cedar wood. They are used to hang three kinds of animals on them: a small animal is hung on the lowest hook, a medium-sized one is hung on the middle hook, and a large animal is hung on the top hook.[18]

---

17. *Sotah* 48a.

18. Mishnah *Middos* 3:5: "The *Beis HaMitbechayim* was on the north of the Altar, and there stood eight low pillars, with square blocks of cedar wood on them. Iron hooks were fixed on them. There were three rows of [iron hooks] on each of them."

Slaughter Area for
Kodshei Kodashim

(area shaded in gray)

West

South

North

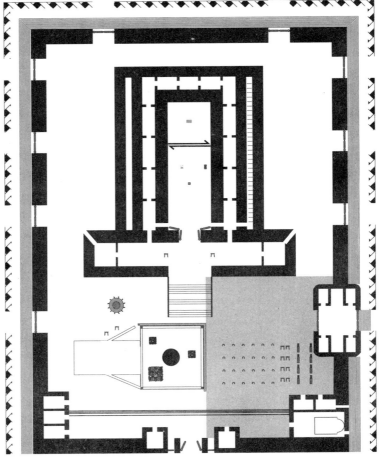

East

"After the animals are hung on the hook, they are flayed and cut into sections. Then the *emurim*[19] are rinsed on one of the eight *Shulchanos*.[20] The meat of the *korbanos* is also rinsed, so that it can later be cooked for the Kohanim to eat."[21]

In the meantime Reb Avraham had finished reciting the entire *Sefer Tehillim*. Then he took his ram[22] [a one-year-old sheep[23]] and signaled to the children to join him. The group turned to the *Duchan*, the Platform of four steps(5) that led to the *Ezras Kohanim*(6).[24] A Kohen quickly approached them.

"What kind of *korban* would you like to sacrifice?" he asked Reb Avraham respectfully.

"A *korban Asham*," Reb Avraham replied.

The Kohen and Reb Avraham pulled the ram up the *Duchan* steps on their way to the *Ezras Kohanim*. Reb Avraham led the ram to the north of the *Mizbeach*, toward the area of the *Beis HaMitbechayim*(8).

The pupils found it difficult to see the Kohen in action, because the *Ezras Kohanim*(6) at the top of the stairs was two and a half *amos* higher than the *Ezras Yisrael*(4). They could not climb up either, because the stairs themselves were part of the *Ezras Kohanim*, which no Israelite could enter without a special need.[25]

---

19. *Emurim*: Sacrificial portion; the innards of the offering that are burnt on the Altar. See *Vayikra* 3:9–11.

20. Mishnah *Tamid* 4:2.

21. Rambam, *Hilchos Beis HaBechirah* 5:14.

22. *Vayikra* 5:18: "He shall bring to the priest a perfect ram from flocks… and the priest shall make an atonement for him…"

23. Mishnah *Parah* 1:3.

24. Mishnah *Middos* 2:6, *Tiferes Yisrael* #65.

25. Mishnah *Keilim* 1:8: "The *Ezras Kohanim* is holier than [*Ezras Yisrael*], and Israelites are not to enter it, except when they have a need to: [i.e.] for *semichah*…"

Therefore, they had to content themselves with watching from the *Ezras Yisrael*(4). But they knew they wouldn't miss anything important thanks to their friend, Alexander HaKohen… He smiled at them from upstairs.

They were sincerely happy for him because, as a Kohen, he could watch the scene from above.

One of the boys wanted to know why Reb Avraham couldn't perform *semichah*[26] in the *Ezras Yisrael*, so they could see it too. Reb Shmuel explained that *semichah* needed to be done next to the *Taba'os*(77) where the ram would be slaughtered, because *shechitah* had to be done immediately after *semichah*.

"I can see Reb Avraham[27] placing his two hands on the ram's head[28] and leaning on the ram with all his strength,[29] confessing his sin,[30] crying bitterly…" Alexander was commenting from above. "What a heartrending sight he is! Just think, if Reb Avraham's sorrow and regret about *possibly* having transgressed *be-shogeg* [by mistake] are so great, how careful must we be not to *actually* transgress *be-shogeg* —not to mention deliberately, God forbid!" Alexander said to himself quietly, but his friends heard him.

Reb Shmuel, who was obviously taller than his pupils, could see and report what was happening.

"Right now the Kohen is slaughtering the ram, and his fellow Kohen is receiving the blood, gathering it into a bowl [*mizrak*]. This Kohen is on his way to the *Mizbeach*(7) now, holding the *mizrak* in

---

26. *Semichah*: Placing one's hands and leaning with full weight on the head of his offering; *Menachos* 93a.

27. *Menachos* 92a.

28. *Menachos* 93a.

29. *Zevachim* 33a.

30. *Yoma* 36a.

The Order of the Asham Offering

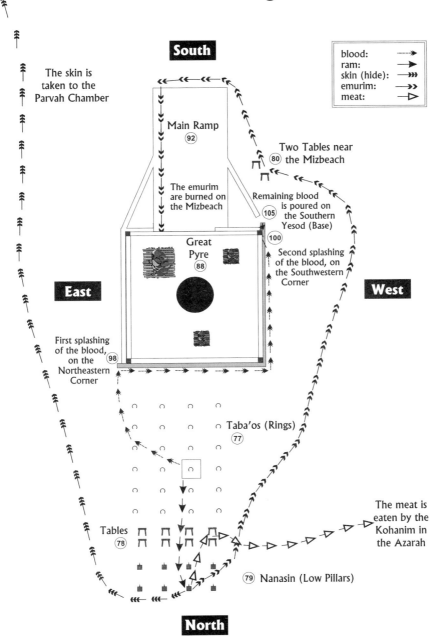

South

The skin is taken to the Parvah Chamber

Main Ramp (92)

The emurim are burned on the Mizbeach

Two Tables near (80) the Mizbeach

Remaining blood (105) is poured on the Southern Yesod (Base)

Great Pyre (88)

Second splashing (100) of the blood, on the Southwestern Corner

East

First splashing of the blood, on the Northeastern Corner (98)

West

Taba'os (Rings) (77)

The meat is eaten by the Kohanim in the Azarah

Tables (78)

(79) Nanasin (Low Pillars)

North

blood:	- - -▸
ram:	⟶
skin (hide):	⟶⟩⟩⟩
emurim:	⟶⟩⟩
meat:	⟶▷

his hand... He has reached the *Mizbeach* and is now splashing some of the blood onto the Northeastern Corner(98), below the *Chut HaSikra*(102) [red line]. Now he is turning westwards and going around the *Mizbeach*. I can't see him, but he is surely splashing another quantity of blood onto the Southwestern Corner(100), and pouring the leftover blood onto the Southern Base(105)."

One of the Kohanim took the slaughtered ram to the *Nanasin*(79), and hung it on the middle hook of one pillar. He flayed the ram and gave the skin to the Kohen.

"Where is this Kohen taking the skin of the ram?" Alexander asked of his fellow Kohanim.

"He is taking it to *Lishkas Beis HaParvah*(63) [*Parvah* Chamber],[31] where it will be salted and distributed among Kohanim,"[32] the Kohen explained. "The distribution of the skins among all the Kohanim of the *mishmar*[33] takes place at the end of the week."[34]

The boys, who were standing on their toes, managed to see how the *emurim* were removed from the animals. One of the Kohanim took the innards with him to the South of the *Azarah*, and entered one of the chambers there.

Reb Shmuel pointed at the chamber and explained: "This chamber is called *Lishkas HaMadichin*(64) [Rinsing Chamber]. In this chamber, two parts of the ram's stomach — the *keres* and the *keivah* — are carefully rinsed. Also, the intestines are rinsed there for the first time, after which they are placed on the tables of the *Beis HaMitbechayim* to complete their rinsing."[35]

---

31. Mishnah *Middos* 5:3. *Parvah* means animal hide or skin (*Tosfos Yom Tov*). Bartenura and Rambam give other explanations for this chamber's name.

32. *Zevachim* 103a.

33. *Mishmar*: A division of Kohanim. All the Kohanim were divided into twenty-four *mishmeros*, which served in weekly rotation.

34. *Pesachim* 57a.

35. Mishnah *Middos* 5:3, *Tosfos Yom Tov*.

Reb Shmuel pointed at the two doors that adjoined *Lishkas HaMadichin* and said, "The first one is the entrance door to the *Lishkas Beis HaParvah*(63), where the skins of the *kodashim* are salted. The second one is the entrance door to *Lishkas HaMelach*(62) [Salt Chamber], from where the salt for the salting of the sacrifices is taken, as the verse commands [*Vayikra* 2:13], '...on every offering of yours you shall bring salt.'"

The children peeked inside and saw a Kohen arranging vessels, filled with salt, in their proper places.

The meat of the ram was placed on one of the *Shulchanos*(78)[36] that were next to the *Nanasin*(79). It was rinsed there, and then taken to the place where the distribution of the *kodshei kodashim* to the Kohanim was carried out. In the meantime, the *emurim* had been taken and placed on the marble table(80) that was on the western side of the Main Ramp(92) [*HaKovesh HaGadol*] .[37]

Another Kohen appeared on the premises and removed the *emurim* from the marble table(80). He ascended the Main Ramp(92) carrying them in his hands. On his way up the Ramp he salted them, went up to the *Mizbeach*, and threw the salted *emurim* into the large fire of *HaMa'arachah HaGedolah*(88) [the Great Pyre] that was burning on it.[38]

"Well, have you learned all the *halachos*?" the children were surprised to hear Reb Avraham's voice. He had actually been standing next to them, but they were so enraptured that they did not notice that he had descended the *Duchan*(5) and joined them again. His face shone with great inspiration and joy, as his

---

36. Rambam, *Hilchos Beis HaBechirah* 5:14.

37. Mishnah *Tamid* 7:3.

38. *Vayikra* 6:5: "The fire on the Altar shall be lit on [the Altar] itself [and] must not be extinguished, and each morning the priest shall burn wood upon [the wood-pyre]. He shall arrange the [daily] burnt-offering upon it, and then burn up on it the fats of the peace-offerings."

worries about the transgression that he might have committed had been relieved.

"As we leave the *Azarah*, we must remember not to turn our backs to this holy place,[39] but to walk slowly backwards with our faces toward the *Heichal*(11) until we actually exit from the *Azarah*," Reb Shmuel reminded the group.

Reb Avraham continued, "There are two small side doors on either side of Nikanor Gate(30), called *Pishpeshim*(31).[40] They do not exactly face the entrance of the *Heichal*; therefore, it is preferable to leave through them."

They turned in the direction of the *Pishpeshim*, left the *Azarah*, and walked home.

---

39. Rambam, *Hilchos Beis HaBechirah* 7:4.

40. Mishnah *Middos* 2:6, *Tiferes Yisrael* #83: "Two small doors, one drawn toward the south and the other drawn toward the north, so that those who exit through them should not have to actually turn their backs to the *Heichal*, as Nikanor Gate faced the *Heichal*."

Chapter Nine

"This Is the Law of a Sin-Offering"

T he next day, after the morning prayer, the children parted warmly from Reb Avraham. He had a long two-day journey ahead of him — to Tiveriah, in the Lower Galilee, in the north of Eretz Yisrael.

Reb Avraham was not young, and he climbed into his wagon cart with some difficulty. The wagon pulled off, and they waved good-bye to him until he disappeared from their sight.

The children learned Torah diligently, with great *hasmadah*, the entire day. The night before, Reb Avraham had told them stories about the devotion and self-sacrifice with which the Chashmonaim learned Torah and kept Hashem's commandments. The stories had inspired them anew to learn with intensity.

In the evening a pleasant surprise awaited them. Yehoshua, who was standing at the window watching the sunset at that moment, suddenly exclaimed, "I can't believe it's him!"

"What can't you believe, and who is 'him'?" Naftali asked, smiling.

"It's him, Reb Avraham! He's parked his wagon in the courtyard! Now he is coming to us!" Yehoshua shouted. "Reb Shmuel, Reb Avraham has arrived!"

After the initial excitement had abated and Reb Avraham had refreshed himself with a cold drink, he told his anxious listeners the following story.

"I was on my way up north and had almost reached Shechem.

Suddenly, I saw two men on horseback who were making their way toward me. I identified them as my own servants.

"Reb Avraham! Our master!" they hurried to break the news to me, "you definitely ate *chelev*, by mistake of course! It wasn't *shuman* that you ate, because we had removed the plate with the *shuman* from the table previously!"

"I was heartbroken to realize I had sinned accidentally [*be-shogeg*]. But once I had calmed down, I thanked Hashem that my servants had caught me when they did! If I had met them later, I might have had to return to Yerushalayim all the way from Tiveriah again!

"I am now obligated to sacrifice a sin-offering [*korban Chatas*].[1] According to halachah, I can postpone offering the *korban* until the next Festival,[2] which is Shavous. However, I'd like to do it as soon as possible, because I am not getting any younger — and one never knows when his last day will be. If a person selects an animal and designates it for a *korban Chatas* and then dies, it is impossible for his heirs or anyone else to sacrifice it for him.[3]

"I will therefore offer the *korban Chatas* tomorrow, *im yirtzeh Hashem*, and I'll stay here for Shabbos. My business interests in Tiveriah will have to be put off until later. I don't always have the opportunity to breathe in so much *yiras Shamayim*. It's in the very air of Yerushalayim, so close to the *Beis HaBechirah*, the Chosen House of God. And needless to say, I'll enjoy my stay here even more in your gracious company!" he gave them a broad smile, and the flattered children nodded their heads vigorously, as if to say, "It's mutual!"

---

1. *Kerisos* 2a.
2. *Rosh Hashanah* 4b.
3. *Horios* 6b.

When the boys woke up the next morning, they did not find Reb Avraham, because he had gotten up at dawn in order to be able to witness the sacrificing of the *Tamid shel shachar*, the regular morning sacrifice. Later, after the boys had immersed themselves in the *mikveh*, they went to the Beis HaMikdash.

Reb Avraham had been waiting impatiently for them with a sheep. He could hardly wait to atone for his unintentional sin by offering the *korban Chatas*.

As soon as Reb Avraham saw the children, he climbed the *Duchan's*(5) stairs, entering the *Ezras Kohanim*(6) with his sheep. This was not so easy for the elderly man.

There he performed *semichah* with all his might[4] and burst out crying. He sobbed bitterly, confessing his sin with sincere regret.[5]

Alexander HaKohen was again able to report on the procedure from where he stood in the *Ezras Kohanim*. His friends listened with rapt attention:

"Now the Kohen has placed the sheep's head[6] onto the floor of the *Azarah* underneath an open Ring(77) and closed it on the sheep's neck. The animal's neck and head are tightly locked in the Ring, without it being able to squirm. The Kohen is now slaughtering the sheep[7] with a steady hand, and a fellow Kohen is collecting the blood into the *mizrak* [sprinkling bowl].[8] The *mizrak* is now filled with the blood of the slaughtered sin-offering, and the Kohen who has received it is taking it to the *Mizbeach*(7)."

---

4. *Vayikra* 4:29: "He shall rest his hand on the head of the sin-offering, and [then] slaughter the sin-offering in the same place as the burnt-offering."

5. *Yoma* 36a.

6. Mishnah *Middos* 3:5.

7. *Vayikra* 4:29.

8. *Zevachim* 52b.

Applying the Blood to the Corners of the Mizbeach for the Sin-Offering (Chatas)

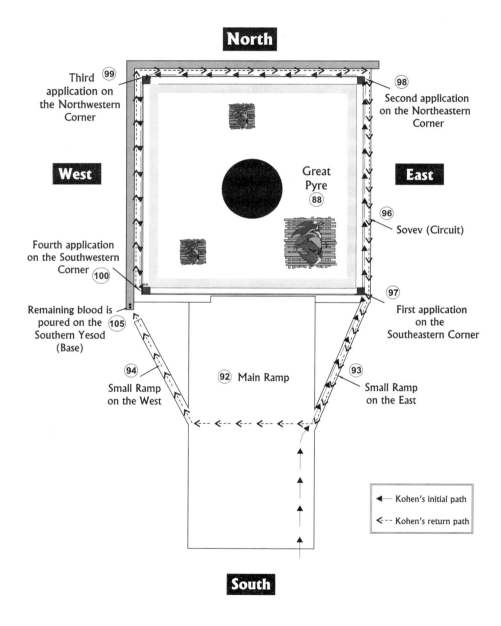

North

Third ⑲ application on the Northwestern Corner

⑱ Second application on the Northeastern Corner

West

East

Great Pyre ⑧⑧

⑯ Sovev (Circuit)

Fourth application on the Southwestern Corner ⑩⑩

⑰ First application on the Southeastern Corner

Remaining blood is poured on the ⑩⑤ Southern Yesod (Base)

⑭ Small Ramp on the West

⑨② Main Ramp

⑨③ Small Ramp on the East

◄— Kohen's initial path

◄-- Kohen's return path

South

After the Kohen had ascended the Main Ramp(92), Alexander's commentary became unnecessary; his non-Kohen friends could vividly see the Kohen ascending the Ramp(92), which was to the south of the *Mizbeach*(7).[9] In the middle of his ascent, the Kohen turned to the Small Ramp [*HaKevesh HaKatan*] to the East(93) of the Main Ramp. From there the Kohen could get to the *Sovev*(96). As the children already knew, the *Sovev* surrounded the entire *Mizbeach*(7), and was six cubits high.[10]

The Kohen reached the *Sovev* and stopped next to the Southeastern Corner(97) [*keren*]. He dipped the index finger[11] of his right hand into the blood that was in the bowl, and put the blood on the corner [*keren*] of the *Mizbeach*.[12]

Then the Kohen proceeded on his way along the *Sovev* northwards, stopped at the Northeastern *keren*, dipped his finger into the blood again, and applied it to that corner. He then went to the other two *kranos* and applied blood to them.

After the Kohen had finished applying blood to all four corners of the *Mizbeach*, he turned around and walked back along the *Sovev* until he returned to the Main Ramp again. He crossed it[13] widthwise, and then descended to the Southern *Yesod* [Base](105) via the Small Ramp on the West(94). He poured out the leftover blood there.[14]

Another Kohen took the slaughtered sheep to the *Nanasin*(79),

---

9. *Zevachim* 53a.

10. Mishnah *Middos* 3:1.

11. *Zevachim* 53a.

12. *Vayikra* 4:30: "The priest shall then take [some] of its blood with his finger and put it on the corners of the Altar, and all the rest of its blood he shall pour onto the base of the Altar."

13. *Zevachim* 62b, Rashi (ד"ה שני כבשים); *Zevachim* 64a, Rashi (ד"ה צבר את).

14. *Zevachim* 53a.

Western View of the Mizbeach

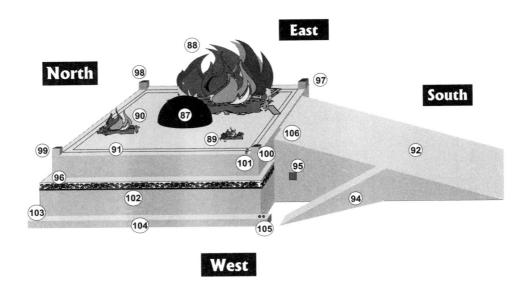

87. *Tapuach* (Pile of Ashes)

88. Great Pyre

89. Second Pyre (for incense)

90. Pyre for Sustaining the Fire

91. Kohanim's footpath

92. Main Ramp

94. Small Ramp on the West

95. Window, on the west side of Main Ramp, where disqualified burnt-offerings of birds were placed

96. *Sovev* (Circuit)

97. Southeastern Corner (Turret)

98. Northeastern Corner (Turret)

99. Northwestern Corner (Turret)

100. Southwestern Corner (Turret)

101. Two Funnels for *nesachim* (poured-offerings)

102. *Chut HaSikra* (Red Line)

103. Northern Base (Yesod)

104. Western Base (Yesod)

105. Southern Base (Yesod)

106. Passageway between Main Ramp and Altar leading under the Altar

where it was flayed and its *emurim* were removed.[15] The *emurim* were burnt up on the *Mizbeach*(7), and the meat was distributed to Kohanim. They were to eat it in a state of ritual purity [*taharah*], following all the laws of *kodshei kodashim* sacrifices.[16] The laws required the meat to be eaten within the *Azarah*, only by the male Kohanim, and finished on the same day and the evening right after it—preferably before midnight.

After Reb Avraham left the *Azarah* relieved and in a good mood, Alexander HaKohen told his friends, "While the animal was being slaughtered, I heard Reb Avraham say to himself:[17] 'Due to Hashem Yisbarach's great mercy, this animal is being slaughtered now instead of me! It is I who actually should have been slaughtered for having transgressed the will of the living God, even if I did it unintentionally! I should have died now, instead of the sheep!' And then he wept bitterly. Then, when the Kohen placed the blood on the Corners of the *Mizbeach*, I heard Reb Avraham burst out crying all over again and moan, 'My own blood should have actually been spilled now!' Thus he stood and cried all through the offering of the *korban Chatas*. Also, when the *emurim* were burning he kept saying to himself: 'I was liable for the death penalty, and it is I who should have been burned, but Hashem Yisbarach in His great compassion, let this sheep be brought instead of me! The sheep's *emurim* are burning up on the *Mizbeach* instead of me!'"

Reb Shmuel had been listening to Alexander's recount and commented, "Reb Avraham's behavior while offering the *korban*

---

15. *Vayikra* 4:31: "And he shall remove all its fat in the same way as the fat was removed from the peace-sacrifice, and the priest shall burn [it] up on the Altar to be a pleasing aroma [before] the Eternal, and [thus] the priest will make an atonement for him, and he will be forgiven."

16. *Zevachim* 53a.

17. *Vayikra* 1:9, Ramban.

Chatas seems to be extraordinary to you. But in reality, every single Jew who is obligated to offer a *korban Chatas* must behave in the same way. Let me explain.

"When a person does an *aveirah*, he sins intellectually when he thinks about the forbidden act or object, he sins verbally when he speaks about it, and he sins practically when he actually commits the *aveirah*! Therefore, Hashem commanded three things for the sinner to do: *semichah* with his hands on the *korban* to atone for the actual act of sinning, verbal confession to atone for speaking about the sin and, finally, to atone for his sinful thoughts, the sinner must think in his mind that all that is done to the sacrificial animal — the slaughtering, the placing of blood on the *kranos*, and the burning of the *emurim* on the *Mizbeach* — should really be done to him. Only then will the atonement for his sin be complete."

"Now I'm beginning to understand Reb Avraham's behavior," Alexander said. "Your explanation is scary, but very convincing! By the way, there's something else that I remember Reb Avraham saying when his *chatas* was being offered: '*Sekillah*! [execution by stoning]; *Sreifah*! [execution by burning], *Hereg*! [execution by a sword]; *Chenek*! [execution by strangulation],' Reb Avraham whispered to himself. What did he mean by all those frightening words?"

"It sounds like he meant that instead of meting out the four capital punishments[18] to him, the Kohen gives them to the animal," Bo'az conjectured. "When it is laid onto the floor before *shechitah*, that is like *sekillah*, because someone getting *sekillah* is pushed down[19] from a height onto the ground.

"The *shechitah* is like *hereg*, because *hereg* is death by sword.

---

18. *Vayikra* 1:9, Rabbeinu Bachya.
19. *Sanhedrin* 45a.

In the end, the animal is burnt up on the *Mizbeach*, which is identical to *sreifah*."

"But what about *chenek*?" Reuven inquired.

"I noticed once that right before slaughtering the animal, the *shochet* pressed on its throat. I guess that's a kind of strangulation — *chenek*," Yehoshua proposed.

"It may also be that the Ring(77) into which the animal's head is put chokes it slightly," Naftali suggested.

Gamliel added another thought. "I once heard that the dead body of an idol-worshiper who is punished by *sekillah*[20] is hung on a tree, as the verse says, 'And if a man committed a sin that carries the death sentence and is put to death, you shall hang him on a gallows.'[21] This sounds similar to what must be done with the animal after it is slaughtered; it is hung on a hook of one of the *Nanasin*!"

Reb Shmuel could not hide his joy. "I am so happy to be your *rebbi*! You are making the right assumptions! Because you are all so interested in what is going on here, why don't we stay in the Beis HaMikdash a bit longer and learn some more *halachos*!

"There are two chambers on the eastern side of the *Ezras Yisrael*, one on each side of Nikanor Gate. One of them is called *Lishkas Pinchas HaMalbish*(52) [Chamber of Pinchas, keeper of the priestly garments]. All the priestly garments are kept in this chamber: the shirts [*kutanos*], the trousers [*michnasayim*], the belts [*avnetim*] and the head-coverings [*migba'os*]. Twenty-four *mishmeros kehunah*[22] [divisions of Kohanim] perform the service in the Beis HaMikdash in weekly shifts. Each *mishmar* uses its own garments. Because each *mishmar* needs four cells to keep its

---

20. *Sanhedrin* 45b.

21. *Devarim* 21:22.

22. *Ta'anis* 27a.

four priestly garments in, there are ninety-six compartments in this chamber.[23]

"Interestingly, the number of the *Taba'os*(77) [Rings] into which the animals' necks are placed before *shechitah* is also twenty-four,[24] corresponding to the twenty-four *mishmeros kehunah*. Alexander, did you notice an interesting detail of the slaughter of the *korbanos*?" Reb Shmuel asked the young Kohen from the Galilee.

Alexander tried to recall the sights of the past few days in his memory.

"The *rebbi* must be referring to the fact that the Kohanim used the same *Taba'as* (Ring) all the time," Alexander ventured to reply, "but I am not sure..."

"Yes, yes, you are absolutely right, that's exactly what I meant. Congratulations on your being so observant!" Reb Shmuel exclaimed delightedly. "Each *mishmar* has its own *Taba'as* that it uses for slaughtering during its weekly shift. However, there are two exceptions. The first one concerns the *shechitah* of the regular daily sacrifice [*korban Tamid*]. The *Tamid* must be slaughtered in broad daylight. Therefore, the morning *Tamid* is slaughtered in the second *Taba'as* from the Northwestern Corner(99) of the *Mizbeach*, in order to expose it to the rays of the sun rising in the east in the morning. This *Taba'as* is far from the ten-cubit-high *Mizbeach*(7), and therefore the *Mizbeach*'s gigantic shadow does not block the sunlight. It is also far from the shadow of the high eastern wall of the *Azarah*.[25]

"The second *Taba'as* from the Northeastern Corner(98) of the *Mizbeach* is used for the slaughter of the evening *Tamid* for the

---

23. Mishnah *Tamid* 5:3, *Tiferes Yisrael*.
24. Mishnah *Middos* 3:5.
25. Mishnah *Tamid* 4:1, Bartenura and *Tiferes Yisrael*.

same reason: it is far from the *Mizbeach* and the *Heichal*, so that their shadows cannot block off the light of the sun that shines on it from the west toward evening. *B'ezras Hashem*, I intend to take all of you to the Beis HaMikdash this week in order to witness the slaughtering of the *korban Tamid shel shachar*.

"The second exception is the Ring that was once used by the *mishmar* of the Bilgah priestly family. This Ring is locked on purpose: it is fixed to the floor of the *Azarah* so strongly that no one can open it and use it for the *shechitah* of sacrificial animals."

"Who is Bilgah?" someone asked.

"Why is the *Taba'as* of their *mishmar* locked?" inquired another.

"How do they slaughter *korbanos* without a *Taba'as*?" a third person wanted to know.

"Just a minute," Reb Shmuel said with a smile on his face, "I will answer all your questions in due course!

"Bilgah is one of the twenty-four *mishmeros kehunah*. The Kohanim of this *mishmar* are compelled to use the *Taba'as* of a different *mishmar*. They incurred this humiliating punishment after the daughter of one of their families married a heathen Greek official. Consequently, during the period of the Chashmonaim, when the Greeks broke into the *Heichal* to desecrate it, that wicked woman entered with them. She kicked the *Mizbeach* and hurled shockingly insulting words at it and at Hashem Yisbarach Himself.

"The Jews, faithful to Hashem and His holy Torah, could not tolerate such criminal behavior. The Torah Sages of that generation proclaimed: 'The priestly family from whom this woman came must be punished, because it seems that something is wrong with the upbringing which they give their children.' Therefore, the *Chachamim* imposed this penalty on the Bilgah family."[26]

---

26. *Sukkah* 56b.

"And why is the Chamber of Priestly Garments called after Pinchas? Which Pinchas does this name allude to?" Yechezkel wanted to know.

"The man appointed as the keeper of the priestly garments is called Pinchas," Reb Shmuel replied.

"*Called* Pinchas? So it sounds like the name of this particular chamber changes according to the name of its keeper," Yechezkel concluded. He smiled as a sudden idea flashed through his mind: "In that case, it's very possible that, if our dear friend Alexander gets appointed to serve as the keeper of this chamber one day, it'll be called '*Lishkas Alexander HaMalbish!*'"

Everybody smiled, but...

Reb Shmuel gave him a surprise. "As a matter of fact," he said seriously, "the name of the current keeper of the chamber is not Pinchas either.[27] 'Pinchas' is just a nickname given to everyone who is in charge of the chamber. It comes from the very first official, whose name really *was* Pinchas. Pinchas was the first '*malbish*' of the Second Beis HaMikdash."

"And what is the name of the other chamber, the one immediately south of Nikanor Gate?" Chananya asked.

"This chamber is called *Lishkas Osei Chavitin*[28] (51) [Chamber for the preparation of the *Kohen Gadol*'s flour-offering]. The *Kohen Gadol* brings a flour-offering every day, and this is where it is prepared."[29]

Something caught the boys' attention at Nikanor Gate(30) .

Two distinguished-looking men passed through the gate, taking measured steps toward the Beis HaMikdash. They looked like people who were aware of their importance — and were proud of

---

27. Mishnah *Shekalim* 5:1.
28. Mishnah *Middos* 1:4.
29. *Vayikra* 7:12–16.

it. One of them was dragging a thin sheep; it was obvious that its owner had chosen it as a sin-offering, to atone for some sin he had committed. The man looked extremely wealthy, and he appeared to be annoyed.

"I'm so aggravated about having to part with this little sheep of mine, you know," the boys heard the wealthy man complain to his companion, "but what can I do? I don't have a choice. I desecrated Shabbos — unintentionally of course — and am obligated to bring a *korban Chatas* to atone for my *chilul Shabbos be-shogeg*. I spent a whole hour looking for the skinniest and cheapest sheep in my flock, and I finally found this one. Just imagine! What did I do, really? I never intended to desecrate Shabbos; I did it by sheer mistake. I'm sure such a trifling sin can be atoned for with this kind of sheep as well."

The boys were astonished to see such a striking contrast between this *korban Chatas* and the one that they had seen only an hour before. The sight of the distraught Reb Avraham, crying bitterly over his inadvertent sin and begging Hashem to forgive him was still fresh in their memories. And now they saw this arrogant man, who didn't seem too bothered about his transgression. All he was sorry about was his wretched little sheep! Is that how one comes to the Beis HaMikdash?!

A Kohen approached the wealthy sinner and asked him what he wanted.

"I have to bring a sin-offering," he muttered with contempt. As soon as the Kohen heard the reply, he gave a sign to the Leviyim[30] who were standing on the *Duchan*(5), and they started singing verses from *Tehillim* that inspired people to repent and rectify their sins — and to regret their past attitudes.

The wealthy man stood and waited. As he was listening to

---

30. *Ma'or VaShemesh, Parashas Shemini.*

One of the distinguished-looking men was dragging a thin sheep

the special music that began to fill the air, his eyes began to water. Finally, the man burst into bitter tears, which he could not suppress.

"Woe unto me! Woe to my soul!" the man began to moan. "I sinned, I committed a terrible transgression—I desecrated Shabbos! I could have prevented it if I had been more careful! What have I done?! I have caused my Creator great anguish. I received a pure, holy soul from Hashem, and I stained it with this terrible sin!" He bemoaned his fate and could not stop crying. "And if that wasn't bad enough," he continued, "I added more sin to my iniquity by treating the *korban Chatas*, which I was obligated to bring, with contempt."

He turned to his companion and said, "I have not yet consecrated this sheep for a *korban Chatas*. Could you perhaps, then, do me a big favor? If you please, run to my flocks, select the healthiest, fattest, and most expensive sheep you can find, and bring it to me!"

The children were very moved by the dramatic change in the man's attitude, and they stood watching the scene without uttering a word.

When they were about to leave the place, Yonasan asked Reb Shmuel, "Why didn't the Leviyim sing when Reb Avraham sacrificed his *korban*?"

"By the time Reb Avraham actually sacrificed his *korban Chatas* he had already done perfect *teshuvah*, and there was no need to encourage him to repent by means of song," his *rebbi* explained.

The group turned toward the north of the *Azarah* and reached *Lishkas HaGazis*(53) [Chamber of Hewn Stone], the seat of the Great Sanhedrin.

The children entered the chamber and stood on the side by the door, in great awe and reverence and in absolute silence. They saw the seventy-one sages of the Sanhedrin, in all their glory. Today they were busy investigating the priestly lineage of certain Kohanim.[31] At the end of the session the sages announced their ruling.

"You were found to be kosher Kohanim of undisputed priestly lineage," one of the *Chachamim* said in a deep, mellow voice.

The Kohanim were overjoyed, having been proven to be authentic priests. Right then and there, they put on the white garments of the Kohanim in order to do the service in the Beis HaMikdash.[32]

"These Kohanim will celebrate this day — the day that their ancestral lineage that connects them to the decendants of Aharon has been proven," Reb Shmuel commented.[33]

"There are two chambers adjoining *Lishkas HaGazis*(53)," Reb Shmuel added after they had left the Chamber of Hewn Stone. "They are in the *Ezras Kohanim*(6)[34] so we won't be able to go there. One of them is called *Lishkas HaGolah*(55).[35] Inside it is a well, from which fresh water is drawn for the needs of the *Azarah*. We are not sure today whether the term *golah* means 'Diaspora,' and this chamber is named for the Jews of the Diaspora who dug the well, or whether the actual term is '*gullah*,' which denotes the round bowl that is permanently attached to the wall of the well, serving as a vessel with which the water is drawn.

"The other chamber is called *Lishkas Parhedrin*(54), in which the *Kohen Gadol* is sequestered for seven days before Yom Kip-

---

31. Mishnah *Middos* 5:4.

32. Ibid. The Mishnah continues to say that if they were found to be non-kosher *kohanim*, they would put on black garments as a sign of mourning.

33. Ibid., *Tosfos Yom Tov*.

34. Mishnah *Middos* 5:3, *Tiferes Yisrael*, Bo'az #2.

35. Mishnah *Middos* 5:4.

pur, separated from his family, so that he may reach a high level of spiritual holiness prior to the holiest day of the year."

"My father once told me that the *Kohen Gadol's* chamber is called *Lishkas Balvuti*,"[36] Reuven said, wondering what it meant.

"And *my* father told me that this chamber is called *Lishkas HaEitzim* [Tree Chamber]."[37]

"You are both correct," Reb Shmuel said with a smile. "During the First Temple and at the beginning of the Second Temple, it was indeed called '*Balvuti*,' which means *sarim* — ministers, high officials.[38] This was to show that High Priests are as important and highly esteemed as great *sarim*.

"Later, after the Kohanim began the corrupt custom of bribing the king in order to be appointed High Priest, this chamber became known as *Lishkas Parhedrin* — the Chamber of the King's Officers [*pekidim*]. The new name intimated that the priests were similar to the king's *pekidim* who only served for one year, after which new ones replaced them. Because the priests of that period wanted to be appointed as High Priest for the honor and glory of the position and not in order to serve Hashem, they died the very first time they officiated in the *Kodesh HaKodashim*."

"I once heard a beautiful thought that relates to this," Binyamin said. The children turned to him, anticipating an interesting *gematria*.

"The verse in *Vayikra* says:[39] '*Bezos* — with this procedure Aharon may enter the inner Sanctuary...' The word *bezos* has the numerical value of 410, corresponding to the number of years the First Temple stood. The question is: what does this number have

---

36. *Yoma* 8b.

37. Mishnah *Middos* 5:4.

38. *Yoma* 8b.

39. *Vayikra* 16:3.

to do with Aharon? He surely did not serve in the Beis HaMikdash for 410 years. The answer is as follows: The High Priests who served in the First Beis HaMikdash were *tzaddikim*, like Aharon was. Therefore, when they served in the inner Sanctuary, it was as if Aharon himself was doing the *avodah* all those 410 years."[40]

"I had the privilege of seeing the *Kohen Gadol*, Rabbi Yishmael ben Piyachi,"[41] Gamliel said. "His face glows and he looks like a big *tzaddik*. I was also told that he is a great Torah scholar. Is it possible that he will die this year, *chas ve-shalom*?" Gamliel found it hard to believe.

"Look, our generation has a special *zechus*, which the previous generations did not have," Reb Shmuel reassured him.[42] "In our times, Rabbi Yishmael, who is a great and righteous *Kohen Gadol*, has been serving in the Beis HaMikdash for the last eight years. I once witnessed an amazing, awe-inspiring occurrence: I stood in the *Azarah* when Rabbi Yishmael was serving there, when all at once a Heavenly voice was heard[43] from the walls of the *Azarah* — 'Lift up your heads, O gates! Let Yishmael ben Piyachi, the disciple of Pinchas, enter and serve as High Priest.'"

While Reb Shmuel was telling them the story, the boys could still see on his face what a deep, unforgettable impression that occurrence had made on him.

Naftali was still waiting for an answer and repeated his question: "Why is the chamber also called *Lishkas HaEitzim*?"

"For many reasons," Reb Shmuel replied patiently, "but I'll give you one now. *Lishkas HaEitzim* is actually a symbol.[44] This

---

40. *Midrash Vayikra* ad loc.
41. *Sotah* 49a.
42. *Yoma* 9a.
43. Pesachim 57a.
44. Mishnah *Middos* 5:4, *Tiferes Yisrael* #26.

particular name is supposed to remind the *Kohen Gadol* that if he perverts his deeds he will be likened to a dying tree whose inside is rotten. On the other hand, if he perfects his deeds, he will flourish like a fruit-bearing tree deeply rooted alongside brooks of water, as the verse in *Tehillim* says, 'The righteous will flourish like a palm tree...'"[45]

---

45. *Tehillim* 92:13.

Chapter Ten

A Sudden Change of Plans

The boys spent an inspiring Shabbos in the company of Reb Avraham, and enjoyed every minute of it. And Reb Avraham had a lot of *nachas* from testing the children and seeing their wonderful erudition.

After the Shabbos morning meal the children sat in a circle, with Reb Avraham in the center. He immediately began his favorite pastime, to sharpen the children's memory by testing their knowledge.

"Tell me, please, which *halachos* do the *korban Chatas* and *korban Asham* have in common?" The stream of answers started to flow:

"Both are slaughtered in the north of the *Azarah*,"[1] Gamliel said first.

"Both require *semichah*[2] and *viduy*,"[3] Yehoshua replied immediately afterwards.

"The *emurim* of both are burnt upon the *Mizbeach*,[4] and the

---

1. *Vayikra* 6:18, 7:2.
2. *Vayikra* 4:29, *Zevachim* 11a.
3. *Yoma* 36a.
4. *Vayikra* 4:31, 7:3–5.

meat of both is eaten by the Kohanim,"[5] Bo'az added.

"The meat of the *chatas* and the *asham* is eaten only by male Kohanim and only in the *Azarah*,"[6] Alexander HaKohen replied.

Last but not least, Chananya offered his answer. "Both are eaten only on the day of the offering and during the following night."[7]

"Beautiful!" Reb Avraham exclaimed, full of emotion and pride. "But—do you know the differences between the *korban Chatas* and the *korban Asham* as well as you know their similarities?"

The stream continued to flow.

"The *korban Asham-taluy* must be a male ram,[8] whereas for a *chatas* one brings a female sheep[9] or a female goat."[10]

"The price of a *chatas* animal can be even a very small amount,[11] whereas the *asham* animal must be worth at least two silver *shekels* of the type mentioned in the Torah, which equals two *sela'im*."[12]

"The blood of a *korban Asham* is splashed from a bowl,[13] whereas the blood of a *chatas* is placed with the Kohen's finger on the *kranos* of the *Mizbeach*."[14]

"The blood of a *korban Asham* is splashed twice,[15] in such a

---

5. *Vayikra* 6:19, 7:6.
6. Ibid.
7. *Zevachim* 53a, 54b.
8. *Vayikra* 5:18.
9. *Vayikra* 4:32.
10. *Vayikra* 4:28.
11. *Zevachim* 48a.
12. *Kerisos* 26b.
13. *Vayikra* 7:2.
14. *Vayikra* 4:30.
15. *Zevachim* 54b.

way that it reaches all four sides of the *Mizbeach*, whereas the blood of a *korban Chatas* is applied four times."[16]

"The blood of the *korban Asham* is applied below the *Chut HaSikra*(102),[17] whereas the blood of a *Chatas*-offering is applied to the *kranos*,[18] which are above the *Chut HaSikra*."[19]

Their pleasant discussion lasted a very long time, and was enjoyed both by the examiner and the examinees.

On Sunday afternoon, Reb Avraham left for his home in Tiveriah. When the boys went to bed on Sunday night, their minds were full of the images they had seen during the previous days. They couldn't wait for the coming week — Reb Shmuel was taking them to the Beis HaMikdash to watch the offering of the *Tamid shel shachar*. They were counting the hours, so eagerly were they looking forward to this highly spiritual experience.

But, as King Shlomo said, "There are many thoughts in a man's heart [as he makes plans], but it is Hashem's plan that will actually stand."[20] Something very sad had happened during the night which disrupted all their plans.

Reb Shmuel burst into their room before sunrise and woke up Alexander HaKohen.

"Alexander, you must get up this minute," he urged him.

"What's the matter?" Alexander muttered sleepily.

"Just get dressed immediately and leave the house! Don't ask questions!"

Alexander obeyed his *rebbi*; he dressed quickly and ran out the door. Through the open window, Reb Shmuel called out and

---

16. *Zevachim* 53a.
17. *Sifra* 7:1.
18. *Vayikra* 4:30.
19. Mishnah *Kinim* 1:1.
20. *Mishlei* 19:21.

explained himself. "I'm sorry, Alexander, but you are a Kohen."

"I had to leave because I am a Kohen?" Alexander wondered in amazement. "What does the *rebbi* mean?"

"I'm so sad to have to tell you this, but our elderly neighbor in the next room, Reb Yissachar, passed away during the night. *Baruch Dayan HaEmes!*" Reb Shmuel said with feeling. "Alexander, you are a Kohen; you're not allowed to be in the same house with a *meis*, a dead person. I didn't tell you right away because if I had, you wouldn't have been allowed to get dressed first."[21]

Even a Kohen who has already become *temei meis* (impure through contact with a corpse) must distance himself from further *tum'ah* (impurity),[22] and cannot remain in the place where the *meis* is. It is likewise forbidden to cause a Kohen *katan* (i.e. less than 13 years old), like Alexander, to become *tamei*.[23] Actually, Alexander was sleeping already and nobody was physically bringing him into the house in order to make him *tamei*. Therefore, because he was not yet bar mitzvah, there would have been no transgression in letting him sleep.[24] Nevertheless, Reb Shmuel woke him for the sake of the boy's education and upbringing, so he would get used to the mitzvah of guarding himself against *tum'as meis*.

The other children had also awoken and were sitting up in their beds, rubbing their eyes. It was a sad way to start the day. They remembered the sweet, elderly Reb Yissachar, who had been quite sick, but never complained.

"*Oy*," Naftali thought to himself, "and we have all become *teme'ei meisim* now! We won't be able to visit the Beis HaMikdash

---

21. *Shulchan Aruch, Yoreh De'ah* 372:1.

22. Rambam, *Hilchos Avel* 3:4.

23. *Vayikra* 21:1, Rashi; Yevamos 114a.

24. *Shulchan Aruch, Yoreh De'ah* 373:1, *Orach Chayim* 343:1.

this week!" Instantly he was ashamed for his thoughts. They seemed trivial compared to the tragedy of the man's passing. Still, he couldn't hide his disappointment, together with the others. They had been so much looking forward to watching the sacrifice of the *Tamid shel shachar*, and now it had to be postponed for a whole week!

"Come on, boys," Reb Shmuel said mildly, seeing their faces, "have you forgotten that *kol de'ovad Rachamana — le-tav avid*?[25] It is obviously part of Hashem's plan that we should become *teme'ei meis*! As far as our visit to the Beis HaMikdash is concerned, we'll visit it some other week, as soon as we are able — *b'ezras Hashem*. Don't forget, we are going to spend at least another five weeks in Yerushalayim."

"Is it possible that we haven't become *tamei* at all, since the *meis* did not die in *our* apartment?" offered Chananya.

As if Reb Shmuel had been waiting for that question, he answered on the spot: "No, the Torah says, 'This is the law: if a man dies in an *ohel* [tent], whoever enters the *ohel*, and whatever is in the *ohel*, will become impure for seven days.'[26] There was a window open between the two rooms; therefore, we all became *tamei* because we were under the same roof as the *meis*.

"But it is such a small window! Does it have the prescribed *shiur*[27] fit for conveying *tum'ah*?" Chananya tried again.

"A window bigger than a *tefach* by a *tefach*[28] is big enough to impart *tum'as meis* through it. This window is much wider than a *tefach* by a *tefach*," Reb Shmuel concluded.

---

25. *Berachos* 60b: "All that the Merciful [God] does, He does for an [ultimately] good purpose."

26. *Bemidbar* 19:14.

27. *Shiur* — Minimum measurement, or size, prescribed by the Torah.

28. *Tefach* — handbreadth. See Mishnah *Ohalos* 13:1.

Alexander was still standing outside, under the open window, listening to Reb Shmuel's explanations.

"Let's go outside so that your friend Alexander can also participate in the lesson," Reb Shmuel suggested.

The boys got dressed and went outside with their *rebbi*, who began his discourse on the subject of ritual impurity of a *meis*. "A *meis* is defined as *avi avos ha-tum'ah*[29] — the highest level of *tum'ah*. Whoever touches a *meis* or turns out to be in the same house with one also becomes *tamei*, but to a lesser degree, and is defined as *av ha-tum'ah*.[30] Someone who is an *av ha-tum'ah* can render people, utensils and food *tamei*.[31] Because we are *teme'ei meisim* now, all the people, utensils and food that we touch during the next seven days will become *tamei*."

"If that's the case," Gamliel expressed his apprehension, "how will we be able to walk in the street? We may cause all the passers-by to become *tamei*!"

"Yes, indeed," Reb Shmuel replied seriously, "we'll have to be very careful. A person or a non-metal utensil that touches us will become *rishon le-tum'ah* [first degree of *tum'ah*,[32] of lesser gravity than *av ha-tum'ah*]. When a *rishon le-tum'ah* wishes to purify himself, he must immerse himself in a *mikveh* before sunset[33] and then wait until the evening to become completely *tahor*. The same holds true for utensils."[34]

"And before he immerses, is he liable to render other people *tamei*?" Naftali wondered.

---

29. *Bava Kamma* 2b, Rashi (ד"ה וטמא מת); *Bemidbar* 19:22, Rashi.
30. Mishnah *Keilim* 1:1.
31. *Bava Kamma* 2b.
32. *Pesachim* 14a.
33. *Vayikra* 22:4–7.
34. *Bemidbar* 19:22.

"Not people, or even vessels," replied Reb Shmuel. "A *rishon le-tum'ah* can only render food *tamei*,[35] and thus turn it into *sheini le-tum'ah* [second degree of *tum'ah*, of lesser gravity than *rishon le-tum'ah*].

Gamliel was still apprehensive. "We can always try to avoid bumping into people who will pass us, or avoid touching them when we pass by them, but there will always be some people who might touch us unwillingly, not being aware that we are *tamei*. Maybe it's better for us to stay at home during the coming week."

"There is no need to overdo it," Reb Shmuel calmed him. "Before we go outside we'll put on the special emblems that people who are *tamei* wear on their clothes,[36] so that passers-by are able to keep away from us."

"Can I have two emblems?" Gamliel asked. "I want to make sure I don't make anyone *tamei*!"

Reb Shmuel, who already knew the boy well enough, willingly agreed, suppressing a little smile that stubbornly kept trying to appear on his face.

"As we have already learned, a person who is *temei meis* is forbidden to enter the *Azarah*,[37] and any such person who enters is liable for the *kares* punishment,"[38] Reb Shmuel continued. "However, our Sages issued a decree forbidding his entrance even to the *Cheil*(2).[39] He is also forbidden by the Torah to eat

---

35. *Bava Kamma* 2b.

36. *Sefer HaChinuch*, mitzvah 171.

37. *Bemidbar* 5:2.

38. *Bemidbar* 19:13: "Whoever touches the corpse [of] a human being who dies, and does not purify himself [with the ashes], has defiled the Dwelling of the Eternal [if he enters there]; that person will be cut off from Yisrael." See *Kerisos* 2a.

39. Mishnah *Keilim* 1:8.

kodashim,[40] and one who eats *kodashim* in a state of impurity is also punished by *kares*.[41]

"Because of all these strict laws, we will not enter the Beis HaMikdash so soon. We also can't eat *kodashim kalim*, meat that comes from sacrifices of lesser holiness — like *shelamim* — which normally would be permissible for us to eat."

"When we first met Reb Avraham from Tiveriah, he told us that it is prohibited to eat *ma'aser sheini* food that became *tamei*,"[42] Yonasan recalled.

"That is correct. It is absolutely forbidden to eat such *ma'aser sheini*."

Gamliel was worried. "Will we have to burn all the *ma'aser sheini* food we have in the house, because it has become *tamei* through a *meis* being under the same roof with it?"

"Sure, we'll have to burn it all. We are not allowed to eat it," Reuven interjected.

"We are not allowed to eat it in its present state of *tum'ah*," confirmed Reb Shmuel, "but there is a way to make it 'edible' for us. We can redeem the impure *ma'aser sheini*[43] food onto money, and then the food will become *chullin* [non-holy]. We are allowed to eat *chullin* in our present state of *tum'as meis*. After we purify ourselves, we'll buy other food with the money. This new food will then have the same level of *kedushah*, holiness, as *ma'aser sheini*."

"And how is a *temei meis* purified?" Binyamin asked.

"On the third and seventh day of his state of impurity, a *temei meis* is sprinkled with *mei chatas*, which is special water mixed

---

40. *Vayikra* 22:4.

41. *Vayikra* 22:3; see also *Kerisos* 2b.

42. *Yevamos* 73b.

43. *Makkos* 19b.

with the ashes of the *Parah Adumah*.[44] Therefore, on Wednesday and next Sunday we will have to be sprinkled with *mei chatas*. Are all of you familiar with the purification procedure?"

"Of course," Bo'az answered. "We were all purified before Pesach so that we'd be able to eat the *korban Pesach*. We all know that a person must purify himself in honor of the Festival."[45]

"And you probably went to '*Taharah* Street,'[46] where a man known as the 'purifier' sprinkles water on every passer-by." The children nodded their heads in reply.

"This time, when we go through the process of *taharah*, we'll be able to learn all the details of the *haza'ah* [sprinkling]. You are a Kohen, Alexander, and I am sure you experienced it many times, when you wanted to eat *terumah* food. A non-Kohen, however, sees it less. Now that we are impure, we all have the opportunity to study it together..."

The children smiled. They liked their *rebbi's* wonderful ability to see the best in everything.

"And what about the utensils and the dishes in the house?" Reuven asked.

"Well, the dishes will have to go through the same process of purification[47] — except those made of clay, which cannot be purified.[48] They'll have to be broken into pieces and thrown in the garbage."

---

44. *Bemidbar* 19:12.

45. *Rosh Hashanah* 16b.

46. Mishnah *Parah* 12:4.

47. *Bemidbar* 19:18: "A pure man shall then take [a bunch of] hyssop, immerse [it] in the water, and [with it], sprinkle [the water] on the tent, the vessels and the people who were [in the tent], or on him who touched the bone, the slain person, the one who died or the grave."

48. *Eiruvin* 104b.

"And will we also have to break that huge earthenware jar full of wine?" Yechezkel asked hesitantly. "We only bought it yesterday. Wouldn't it be *bal tashchis* if we broke it?"[49]

"First of all, if the Torah itself commands us to throw something out, it cannot possibly have anything to do with *bal tashchis*," Reb Shmuel replied. "But in this case, the wine never became *tamei*. Nor will the jar have to be destroyed. An earthenware vessel does not become *tamei* unless it is unsealed at the time when it was exposed to *tum'ah*. Our jar, however, has a tight seal[50] over it; therefore, neither the jar nor the wine became impure."

Yechezkel heaved a sigh of relief.

Before they went to the funeral, Reb Shmuel handed out emblems to his young disciples, and they pinned them onto their robes in a visible spot. Gamliel wore two emblems, one on his front and one on his back.

---

49. *Bal tashchis* — lit., "You shall not destroy." The transgression of destroying things of material value for no purpose.
50. *Bemidbar* 19:15.

Chapter Eleven

"Enter His Gates with Thanksgiving"*

O n Tuesday Reb Shmuel took the boys for an interesting tour around the *Azarah*, with the purpose of getting acquainted with its thirteen gates.[1] Even though they were *teme'ei meis*, they were nevertheless allowed on *Har HaBayis*, but not past the *Soreg*. Needless to say, before they left, they were strictly warned not to come near other people, neither on their way to nor in the *Har HaBayis*(1) area. At the eastern Chuldah Gate(25), Reb Shmuel and his pupils took their shoes off. They passed through the gate and turned right, in the direction of the Eastern Gate(29) of the Beis HaMikdash. Gamliel followed Reb Shmuel closely, glancing to his right and left, fleeing from the slightest likelihood of bumping into a *tahor* person.

"We have passed by the Eastern Gate of the Beis HaMikdash," Reb Shmuel announced. It is actually the entrance to the *Ezras Nashim*(3), which leads to the *Ezras Yisrael*(4) and the *Ezras Kohanim*(6) as well."

"Is this the only gate leading to the *Azarah*?" Yechezkel asked.

---

* *Tehillim* 100:4

1. Mishnah *Middos* 2:6.

"No, it's not the only gate. As we proceed further on we will see other gates through which one can enter directly into the *Ezras Yisrael* and the *Ezras Kohanim*," Reb Shmuel answered.

They continued to walk northwards. When they reached the edge of the *Soreg*(14) they turned westwards and continued to walk.

"Where do these two gates lead to?" Yehoshua asked suddenly. He pointed at the northern wall of the Beis HaMikdash.

"I wouldn't call these little doors 'gates,'" Reb Shmuel said. "There are four gates in this northern wall of the *Azarah*, and these doors are not part of them. Instead, one is the entrance door to *Lishkas HaGazis*(53)[2] and the other is the entrance to *Lishkas Parhedrin*(54)."[3]

"If so, both *Lishkas HaGazis* and *Lishkas Parhedrin* have two entrances," Yonasan remarked.

"That's correct," Reb Shmuel smiled, "they have one entrance from the *Cheil* and one from the *Azarah*."

The group proceeded on their way cautiously, taking extreme care not to come near the *Soreg*(14) and accidentally pass through it. They stopped opposite a big building adorned with a dome.[4] The building was built into the *Azarah* wall, and it protruded toward the *Cheil*(2). Reb Shmuel prostrated himself fully before the building's gate,[5] extending his hands and feet on the ground, and the students imitated their *rebbi*.

"Does one have to prostrate oneself before each gate of the *Azarah*?" Yonasan wondered out loud.

"Each time one passes by a gate through which the Beis

---

2. *Yoma* 25a.

3. Mishnah *Middos* 5:4, *Tiferes Yisrael* #27.

4. Mishnah *Tamid* 1:1.

5. Mishnah *Shekalim* 6:1, *Tiferes Yisrael* #2.

HaMikdash is seen, he prostrates himself. It's an expression of gratitude[6] to HaKadosh Baruch Hu for the beauty of the Beis HaMikdash," Reb Shmuel replied. "This building is called the Pyre Hall(56) [*Beis HaMoked*],[7] and the gate(32) is called *Sha'ar Beis HaMoked* or *Sha'ar HaShir* [Music Gate]."[8]

"So, is this *Sha'ar Beis HaMoked* or *Sha'ar HaShir*?" Chananya failed to understand.

"This gate has two names,"[9] Reb Shmuel explained patiently. "It is called *Sha'ar HaShir*, because the musical instruments of the Leviyim are brought in through it.[10] It is also called *Sha'ar Beis HaMoked* because of the building to which it leads. *Beis HaMoked* is a big building, as you can see. It contains five rooms.[11] One of them is the central room, through which one passes to the other four rooms located in its four corners.

"A big fire is burning in that large room,[12] and the whole building is called after this fire [*Moked* — Pyre], which the Kohanim use to warm themselves up after serving in the *Azarah*.[13] Right now it's spring and the weather is pleasantly warm, but you must not forget that the Kohanim who serve in the Beis Ha-Mikdash walk around barefoot on the marble floor even in winter, wearing only the four priestly garments — which do not keep them particularly warm. Three of them — the *kutones*, the *migba'as* and the *michnasayim* — are made of linen only, and it is only the

---

6. Mishnah *Shekalim* 6:3, *Tosfos Yom Tov*; *Middos* 2:6, *Tiferes Yisrael* #68.

7. *Yoma* 19a.

8. Mishnah *Shekalim* 6:3, Mishnah *Middos* 2:6.

9. Mishnah *Middos* 2:6, *Tiferes Yisrael* #78.

10. Mishnah *Shekalim*, 6:3, Bartenura.

11. Mishnah *Middos* 1:6.

12. *Shabbos* 19b.

13. Mishnah *Tamid* 1:1, *Tiferes Yisrael* #3.

The Pyre Hall (Beis HaMoked)

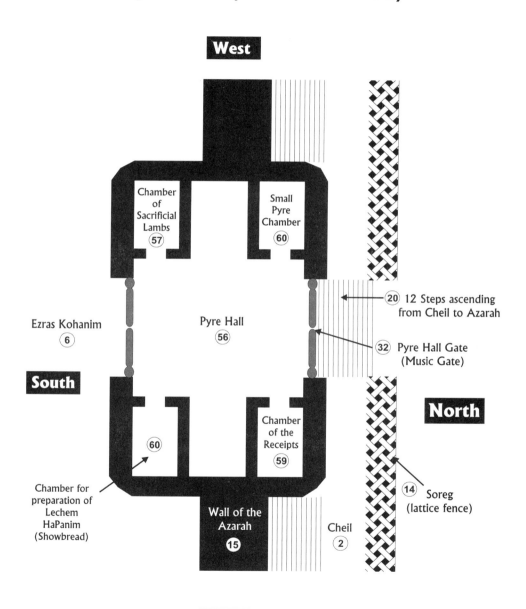

West

Chamber of Sacrificial Lambs
(57)

Small Pyre Chamber
(60)

(20) 12 Steps ascending from Cheil to Azarah

Ezras Kohanim
(6)

Pyre Hall
(56)

(32) Pyre Hall Gate (Music Gate)

South

North

(60)

Chamber of the Receipts
(59)

Chamber for preparation of Lechem HaPanim (Showbread)

Wall of the Azarah
(15)

Cheil
(2)

(14) Soreg (lattice fence)

East

avnet that contains wool as well.[14] So the Kohanim tend to suffer from cold.

"On the days when the cold penetrates their bones, they come here to warm up near the fire. And at night they sleep here."[15]

"Can't they walk barefoot on a wooden surface or on rugs, so that they don't get so cold?" Yehoshua asked sympathetically.

"*Chalilah!*" Reb Shmuel exclaimed emphatically. "Kohanim are not allowed to stand on any surface while they perform the service.[16] They must walk on the floor of the *Azarah*, with nothing intervening between their bare feet and the floor. By the way, did you know that there is a special person appointed to heal the Kohanim? His name is Ben Achiya.[17] He heals the Kohanim who suffer from intestinal diseases caused by the severe cold and by the consumption of the meat of *kodshei kodashim* that has to be eaten in great quantities right away. Remember — this meat cannot remain over until the next day."

"And what purpose do the smaller rooms serve?" Reuven inquired.

"Each room has its own special purpose.[18] The room located in the southwestern corner is called *Lishkas Tela'ei Korban*(57) [Chamber of Sacrificial Lambs], in which six perfect, unblemished lambs are always kept for the offering of the *korban Tamid*."[19]

"Why specifically six lambs, and not more or less?" Yechezkel asked.

"Because two lambs are needed for the two regular daily sac-

---

14. Rambam, *Hilchos Klei HaMikdash* 8:1.

15. Mishnah *Tamid* 1:1.

16. *Zevachim* 24a.

17. Mishnah *Shekalim* 5:1.

18. Mishnah *Middos* 1:6.

19. *Arachin* 13a.

rifices, and the lambs have to be checked[20] for bodily blemishes four days before they are offered," answered Reb Shmuel.

"The chamber located in the southeastern corner is called *Lishkas Osei Lechem HaPanim*(58) [Chamber for the Preparation of the Showbread].[21] That's where the *lechem ha-panim* is baked."

"Aren't the Garmu family the bakers of the *lechem ha-panim?*" Binyamin remembered.

"Yes, they are indeed called Garmu. The *Chachamim* always mention them disparagingly,[22] because the Garmu family refused to teach them how to prepare the *lechem ha-panim*," Reb Shmuel explained.

"The room located in the northeastern[23] corner is called *Lishkas HaChosamos*(59) [Chamber of the Receipts]. In this room the Kohanim sell special receipts to people who need *nesachim* for their sacrifices.[24] Later on, these people get flour and oil for their meal-offerings and wine for their poured-offerings in *Lishkas HaShemanim*(49) [Oil Chamber] in exchange for their receipts. The Oil Chamber is located in the *Ezras Nashim*(3). *Lishkas HaChosamos* is also the place where the stones of the *Mizbeach*, desecrated by the *tamei* Greeks during the rule of the wicked king Antiochus, were later entombed.[25]

"The last room is called *Beis HaMoked HaKatan*(60) [Small Pyre Chamber].[26] In this room, a special tunnel was dug in the ground through which Kohanim go down to immerse themselves

---

20. *Arachin* 13b.

21. Mishnah *Middos* 1:6.

22. *Yoma* 38a.

23. Mishnah *Tamid* 3:3.

24. Mishnah *Shekalim* 5:4.

25. Mishnah *Middos* 1:6, *Tiferes Yisrael* #49.

26. Mishnah *Middos* 1:6.

The Thirteen Gates of the Azarah

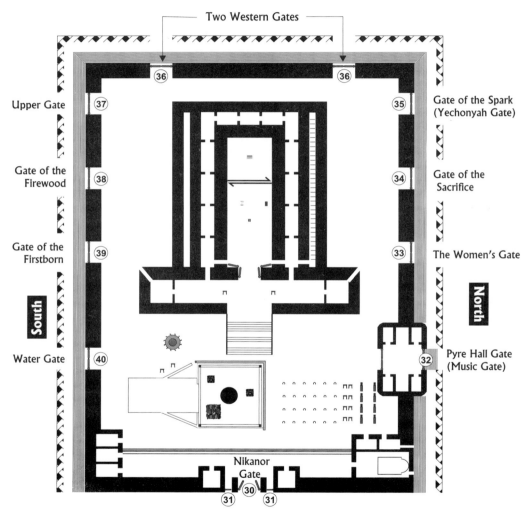

West

Two Western Gates

36   36

Upper Gate 37   35 Gate of the Spark
                                       (Yechonyah Gate)

Gate of the 38   34 Gate of the
Firewood   Sacrifice

Gate of the 39   33 The Women's Gate
Firstborn

South   **North**

Water Gate 40   32 Pyre Hall Gate
                                       (Music Gate)

Nikanor
Gate
31   30   31

Two Side Doors on either
side of Nikanor Gate

East

in a *mikveh*. There is another bonfire burning underground, close to the *mikveh*, so that the Kohanim can warm themselves up after they emerge from the *mikveh*."[27]

"That's really interesting!" Naftali exclaimed.

The group continued walking together, and as soon as they approached *Sha'ar HaNashim*, the Women's Gate (33),[28] they prostrated themselves before it.

"This gate is for the use of women who want to watch the slaughtering of their *korbanos*. They can get straight to the *Beis HaMitbechayim*(8) via this gate, without having to pass through the *Ezras Yisrael*(4)," Reb Shmuel explained. "We will soon reach the third gate — *Sha'ar HaKorban*(34) [Gate of the Sacrifice].[29] *Kodshei kodashim* that must be slaughtered in the north of the *Azarah* are transferred through this gate.

"The fourth gate(35) — the last one on the northern side — has two names:[30] *Sha'ar Yechonyah* [Yechonyah Gate] and *Sha'ar HaNitzotz* [Gate of the Spark].[31] It is called *Sha'ar HaNitzotz* because of the fire that is burning there constantly.[32] This fire is used for the needs of the *Azarah*. It is called *Sha'ar Yechonyah* after the Judean king Yechonyah[33] who passed through this gate when he left Yerushalayim for Babylonia, when he was exiled by King Nevuchadnetzar. Yechonyah was exiled eleven years before the destruction of the First Temple.[34] The artisans and the gatekeepers

---

27. Mishnah *Tamid* 1:1.

28. Mishnah *Shekalim* 6:3.

29. Ibid.

30. Mishnah *Middos* 2:6, *Tiferes Yisrael* #80.

31. Mishnah *Middos* 1:5.

32. *Tiferes Yisrael* #40, commentary on his map of the Beis HaMikdash.

33. Mishnah *Middos* 2:6.

34. *Megillah* 11a.

were also exiled with him, as the verse says, '...as well as the artisans and the gatekeepers, one thousand mighty men and makers of war, and the king of Babylonia brought them into exile to Bavel.'[35] And by the way, our Sages explain that the terms 'mighty men' and 'makers of war' refer to Torah scholars who fight 'the battle' of the Torah.[36]

"After Yechonyah had been exiled to Babylonia, Tzidkiyahu became king of Judea.[37] Eleven years later the rest of the Jewish People were exiled to Babylonia, following the destruction of the Beis HaMikdash. They were fortunate that those Torah scholars had settled in Babylonia before them.[38] Those *talmidei chachamim* provided their exiled brothers with the type of spiritual support needed to insure that the Torah would not be forgotten among Yisrael."

"I once visited Yechonyah's synagogue," Chananya HaLevi said.

"Really? Wow!" his friends got excited.

"Where is it?" Reb Shmuel wondered.

"I joined my family on a trip to the city of Nehardea a few years ago, and there we saw Yechonyah's synagogue. It was built by Yechonyah and his group from stones and earth that they had brought along from Yerushalayim.[39] They wanted to fulfill the verse, 'For Your servants have desired her [Yerushalayim's] stones and favor her earth.'"[40]

The boys reached the northwestern corner of the Beis HaMik-

---

35. *II Melachim* 24:16.

36. Gittin 88a.

37. *II Melachim* 24:17,18.

38. Gittin 88a.

39. *Megillah* 29a, Rashi (ד"ה דשף).

40. *Tehillim* 102:15.

dash, where they changed direction and started walking southward. On their way they encountered two gates[41](36), and they certainly did not forget to prostrate themselves, as they were supposed to.

"These gates do not have special names," Reb Shmuel said.

At the end of the western wall of the Beis HaMikdash they turned east. Shortly after they had started to walk along the southern wall, they encountered the first gate, called the Upper Gate(37) [*Sha'ar HaElyon*].[42]

"The Temple Mount is on a slope.[43] It rises from east to west. This gate, situated on the western end of the southern wall, is in the highest place; hence, its name — Upper Gate," Reb Shmuel explained.

"The second gate is called *Sha'ar HaDelek*(38) [Gate of the Firewood], through which[44] wood for the fire on the *Mizbeach* is brought in. The third one is called *Sha'ar HaBechoros*(39) [Gate of the Firstborn], through which firstborn animals and other *kodashim kalim*[45] are brought into the Beis HaMikdash.

"*Kodshei kodashim* are slaughtered only in the north, and they are brought in through the northern *Sha'ar HaKorban*(34), as we said before," Reb Shmuel continued. "However, firstborn animals, tithed animals [*ma'aser beheimah*], *Shelamim*-offerings and thanksgiving offerings — all of which are *kodashim kalim* — can also be slaughtered in the south, which is why they are brought in through the south."

"And why does this gate bear the name of this specific *korban*

41. Mishnah *Middos* 2:6.

42. Mishnah *Shekalim* 6:3.

43. Mishnah *Shekalim* 6:3, Bartenura.

44. Mishnah *Middos* 1:4, Bartenura.

45. *Tiferes Yisrael* #35, commentary on his map.

Where Kodashim Kalim
Can Be Slaughtered

(area shaded in gray)

West

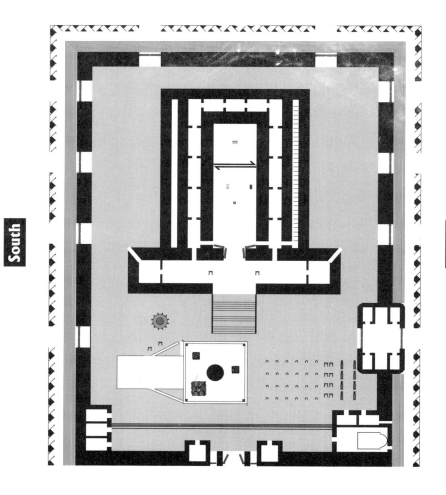

South

North

East

and not any of the other *kodashim kalim* you mentioned?" Bo'az asked.

"It was given the name *Sha'ar HaBechoros* in order to prevent mistakes,"[46] Reb Shmuel replied. "Firstborn animals are similar to *kodshei kodashim* in that both are consumed by Kohanim only. Therefore, it is possible to make a mistake and assume that the prescribed slaughtering site of firstborn animals is also in the north only, like that of the *kodshei kodashim*. It is specifically for this reason that the southern gate was named *Sha'ar HaBechoros*(39), so that everyone may know that, as *kodashim kalim*, they may be slaughtered in the south as well.

"The last southern gate is called *Sha'ar HaMayim*(40) [Water Gate].[47] This gate is close to the *Mizbeach*. Water that has been drawn from the Spring of Shilo'ach [*Ma'ayan HaShilo'ach*] is brought in through this gate. It is used specifically for the water libation [*nisuch ha-mayim*] offered on the *Mizbeach* during on the Festival of Sukkos."

Gamliel's eyes sparkled with excitement when he reminisced, "I remember spending Sukkos with my parents in Yerushalayim. The *nisuch ha-mayim* ceremony was absolutely fantastic, so special! The joy was tremendous, everyone became enveloped in such a holy fervor…"

One could still see the inspiration light up Gamliel's face when he related the story.

"Yes, the *nisuch ha-mayim* offering is a very special event and a spectacular sight!" Reb Shmuel commented.

"Now, boys, there is another reason that this gate is called *Sha'ar HaMayim*. When Mashiach comes, a tiny trickle of water will originate from the *Kodesh HaKodashim*. It will gain strength,

---

46. Mishnah *Middos* 1:4, *Tiferes Yisrael* #33.

47. Mishnah *Middos* 2:6.

emerging from under the threshold of the *Heichal* as a stream as wide as the opening of a jug. It will flow through *Sha'ar HaMayim*, until it will reach the House of David, where it will become a rushing spring, in which *tamei* people will immerse themselves in order to become *tahor*."[48]

Reb Shmuel pointed at *Sha'ar HaMayim* again and added, "There is another chamber just above *Sha'ar HaMayim*(40).[49] It is called *Lishkas Beis Avtinas*(65) [Avtinas Family Chamber]. The incense is prepared there, and there is also a *mikveh*(67) where the *Kohen Gadol* immerses himself for the first time on Yom Kippur."[50]

"What does the *rebbi* mean by 'the first time?'" Yechezkel wanted to know. "Doesn't he perform all his *tevillos* (immersions) in this particular *mikveh*?"

"No," Reb Shmuel replied. "You see those windows along the wall? These are the windows of *Lishkas HaMelach*(62) [Salt Chamber], *Lishkas Beis HaParvah*(63) and *Lishkas HaMadichin*(64) [Rinsing Chamber]. There is another *mikveh*(66) above *Lishkas Beis HaParvah*.[51] That's where the *Kohen Gadol* performs his other immersions on Yom Kippur."

Naftali totaled the number of the *mikvaos*. "We learned about four *mikvaos* in the Beis HaMikdash: one in *Lishkas HaMetzora'im*(48),[52] which is used for the immersion of *metzora'im* [people afflicted with *tzara'as*], one in *Beis HaMoked HaKatan*(60),[53] which is used for the immersion of Kohanim, and another two for the immersion of the *Kohen Gadol*."

---

48. *Zechariah* 13:1; Mishnah *Middos* 2:6; *Yoma* 77b–78a.

49. Mishnah *Middos* 1:1, *Tiferes Yisrael* #2.

50. *Yoma* 31a.

51. Mishnah *Middos* 5:3.

52. Mishnah *Middos* 2:5, Bartenura.

53. Mishnah *Middos* 1:6.

"Excellent!" complimented Reb Shmuel.

"Aren't there supposed to be thirteen gates?" queried Ye-hoshua. "I counted and came up with only ten: four on the northern side, two in the west, and four in the south. What happened to the other three?"

"We have already seen and discussed these three gates," Reb Shmuel replied. "In fact, the other day we entered the *Ezras Yisrael*(4) from the *Ezras Nashim*(3) through them. These are Nikanor Gate(30)[54] and the two *Pishpeshim*(31) on either side of it. So we have thirteen altogether."

---

54. Mishnah *Middos* 2:6.

Chapter Twelve

A Fascinating Shiur on the Mount of Olives

O n Wednesday, in the late morning hours, the boys heard a knock on the door. Chananya, who was standing not too far from the door, went to open it. A stranger stood in the entrance, holding a covered bowl of water in one hand and some *eizov* (hyssop) branches in the other. Chananya stared at him with questioning eyes. The man smiled at him and remained silent. Finally, Chananya understood: he had come to sprinkle upon them the water that would make them *tahor*!

"He has come! He is here!" Chananya shouted excitedly to his friends.

Purification of *tum'as meis* is carried out with the ashes of the *Parah Adumah*.[1] The *Parah Adumah* is burned and some of its ashes are put into a bowl of *mayim chayim* — spring water. This

---

1. *Bemidbar* 19:17,18: "They shall take for the impure person [some] of the ashes [from] the burning of the purifying [cow], and [someone] shall put spring water on [them], in a vessel. A pure man shall then take [a bunch of] hyssop, immerse [it] in the water, and [with it], sprinkle [the water] on the tent, the vessels and the people who were [in the tent], or on him who touched the bone, the slain person, the one who died or the grave."

mixture of water and ashes is sprinkled onto a person who is *te-mei meis*, on the third and the seventh day of his *tum'ah*.

The man walked into the room, saying, "Hello, my name is Yerachmiel. I'm sure you have all guessed why I am here. Please be careful not to touch me, so that I do not become *tamei* like you. If that happens, I won't be able to purify you,[2] as the Torah says, 'The pure person shall sprinkle on the impure person.'[3] The one who sprinkles must be *tahor*."

The boys distanced themselves from Yerachmiel, but watched everything he did with interest. He put down the bowl and tied three branches of *eizov* into a bundle.[4] Then he lifted the lid off the bowl; inside was a mixture of water and ashes.

"This mixture of spring water and ashes is called '*mei niddah*,'[5] because it is water (*mei*, from the word *mayim*) that is 'thrown' (i.e. 'sprinkled') onto the impure person," Yerachmiel explained to the boys. "The term '*niddah*' is derived from the word '*va-yaddu*' in the verse, '*Va-yaddu ehven bi* — And they threw stones at me.'[6] It is also called '*mei chatas*' — *chatas* from the word *chitui*, which means to purify."

As Yerachmiel was explaining the details of the purification procedure, he dipped the bunch of *eizov* in the *mei niddah*[7] and sprinkled the boys with it.

"There is no prescribed quantity [*shiur*] of *mei niddah* that has to touch a person's body.[8] Even a small amount purifies an impure person."

---

2. Rambam, *Hilchos Parah Adumah* 11:1.

3. *Bemidbar* 19:19.

4. Mishnah *Parah* 11:9.

5. *Bemidbar* 19:9.

6. *Eichah* 3:53.

7. *Bemidbar* 19:18.

8. *Zevachim* 93a; Rambam, *Hilchos Parah Adumah* 12:1.

"The pure person shall sprinkle on the impure person"

After Yerachmiel had finished sprinkling all those present, he turned to Reb Shmuel and asked, "Do the dishes and other utensils in the house have to be sprinkled as well?"

"Certainly," Reb Shmuel replied. "Our neighbor died in the adjacent apartment, so all our utensils became *tamei*."

"Fine, I'll sprinkle them as well," Yerachmiel said, and proceeded to move about the house, sprinkling all the wooden and metal utensils, as well as the furniture: the beds, the tables, and the chairs.[9]

When Yerachmiel left the room for a minute, Naftali whispered to Reb Shmuel, "Shouldn't we pay him for his work?"

"It is forbidden to charge for preparing or sprinkling the *mei chatas*,"[10] Reb Shmuel whispered back.

When Yerachmiel was about to leave the house, Naftali asked him, "Will our friend, Alexander HaKohen, also be able to sprinkle *mei chatas* when he grows up?"

"Well, the one who sprinkles *mei chatas* does not haveto be a Kohen.[11] Even an intelligent young boy [*bar da'as*] can do it," he replied with a smile, and bade them good-bye.

Reb Shmuel hurried to warn his pupils, "Don't forget, boys: although we have already been sprinkled once, we are still considered *teme'im* just as we were before the sprinkling. Only after we have been sprinkled for the second time and after we have immersed in the *mikveh*, we will become *tahor*!"[12]

*   *   *

---

9. *Bemidbar* 19:18.

10. Bechoros 29a.

11. Mishnah *Parah* 12:10.

12. *Bemidbar* 19:12: "He shall purify himself with [the cow's ashes] on the third day, and on the seventh day will become pure, but if he does not purify himself on the third day and on the seventh day, he will not become pure."

In the afternoon, a pleasant surprise awaited the children when they heard their *rebbi* announce, "Get ready, we're going out! We are going to tour *Har HaMishchah* [*Har HaZeisim* — the Mount of Olives]. We will visit the site where the *Parah Adumah* is burned. There are two very good reasons I'm taking you there now. First of all, we were just purified with the ashes of the *Parah Adumah* this morning! Second, I heard that a *Parah Adumah* is going to be burned soon, and I'd like you to become familiar with the burning site."

The boys were excited, and marched along the streets of Yerushalayim with great joy. They left the city through its eastern gate, the one that was opposite the Mount of Olives. Then they crossed the valley and made a fifteen-minute climb up to the site.

They found a shallow pit[13] (*gummah*) in the ground, like for a wine-press. The boys sat down on the rocky earth, just above the pit, and Reb Shmuel started his lecture.

"The *Parah Adumah* must be slaughtered and its blood sprinkled toward the *Heichal* precisely here, where we are. There is no other place in the world where these activities, along with the burning of the *Parah Adumah*, can be done."

"Do you mean specifically at this particular spot or anywhere on *Har HaZeisim*?" Yechezkel wanted to have the precise information.

"On this particular mountain[14] and at this particular spot," Reb Shmuel clarified. "Only at this particular spot on the mountain can one see a bit of the Entrance to the *Heichal*(42). The Torah says,[15] 'Elazar the priest shall then take some of its blood with his forefinger and sprinkle some of its blood seven times directly to-

---

13. Mishnah *Parah* 3:10, Bartenura.

14. Mishnah *Parah* 3:6.

15. *Bemidbar* 19:4.

ward the front of the Tent of Meeting.' In other words, the priest must be able to see the Entrance to the *Heichal* from where he stands on the mountain.[16] Therefore, he must stand at a spot located exactly opposite the entrances of the walls that surround the *Heichal*(11); otherwise, these walls will block the view of the Entrance to the *Heichal*."

Reb Shmuel got up and shook some dust off his clothes.

"Let's climb a little higher up the mountain," he said. "Can you see the Entrance to the *Heichal* from here?"

He didn't expect to get an affirmative answer, because it was so obvious that the walls hid it completely.

"Now let's go down a little and cross the *gummah*."

"We can't see the entrance from here either," one of the boys said.

"Okay, let's go back to where we were and stand next to the *gummah*. What do you see now?"

The boys stood around the hole in the ground and looked toward the Beis HaMikdash. They turned their eyes to the top of the eastern wall of the Temple Mount. The wall was low, so that it would not hide the Entrance to the *Heichal* from the eyes of the Kohen.[17] They looked through the Eastern Gate(29) and through Nikanor Gate(30) — which started seven and a half cubits higher than the Eastern Gate[18] because there were Fifteen Steps(21) between the *Ezras Nashim*(3) and the *Ezras Yisrael*(4),[19] each step half a cubit high.[20]

"I can see the fire that is burning on the *Mizbeach*(7)!" Naftali shouted.

---

16. Mishnah *Middos* 2:4.
17. Ibid.
18. *Yoma* 16a.
19. Mishnah *Middos* 2:5.
20. Mishnah *Middos* 2:3.

Reb Shmuel smiled at his excitement. "Yes indeed, you see the edge of the Great Pyre(88) [*HaMa'arachah HaGedolah*]. Now take a look at the right side of the fire. Can you see something there that looks like a little hole?" The children nodded their heads. "This hole is part of the Entrance to the *Heichal*(42). It is only possible to see it from exactly this spot, where we are standing now, and from nowhere else.

"The Entrance to the *Heichal* is actually twenty *amos* high, like the Eastern Gate and Nikanor Gate. We can only see one *amah* of the Entrance because the roof of the *Mizbeach* is nineteen cubits higher than the bottom of the Eastern Gate. This is how we come up with this figure: the Fifteen Steps are seven and a half cubits high. The *Ezras Kohanim*(6) is two and a half cubits higher than the *Ezras Yisrael*,[21] and the height of the roof of the *Mizbeach* is nine cubits.[22] This makes nineteen cubits altogether.

"I heard that in two more days, the red cow from Ovadiah's herd in the Valley of Sharon will 'celebrate' its second birthday," Reb Shmuel confided after they had sat down on the stones again.

"How can a cow celebrate its birthday?" Yonasan asked innocently.

"Let's buy her a birthday present," Yechezkel joked. "We Romans buy birthday presents, you know."

The boys burst out laughing.

Reb Shmuel waited until the laughter subsided, then continued. "Only a cow in its third year[23] is considered kosher for this mitzvah, because prior to that it is not yet considered a *parah*, a cow. It's still a calf. And one does not wait until the cow is

---

21. Mishnah *Middos* 2:6.

22. Mishnah *Middos* 3:1.

23. Mishnah *Parah* 1:1; Rambam, *Hilchos Parah Adumah* 1:1.

older than that, because it is extremely rare to find a red cow. It cannot have even two non-red hairs,[24] it must be unblemished and it must never have carried anything—otherwise it is *pasul* [invalid].[25] Therefore, as soon as the cow reaches the age of two, we don't give it a chance to develop a blemish or otherwise become *pasul*, and it is slaughtered and burned right away. Do you have an idea of how much a *Parah Adumah* is worth?"

"Ten thousand golden *dinars*?" Gamliel tried to guess.

"It couldn't be worth *so* much! Perhaps five thousand," Naftali asserted.

Reb Shmuel smiled. "Listen to this! Once, the *Chachamim* bought a *Parah Adumah* for *six hundred thousand* golden *dinars!*"[26]

"Wow!" the boys cried.

"You see," Reb Shmuel said, "red cows are so rare that they are very, very valuable."

"Why is Ovadiah's cow still in his possession? Hasn't it already been bought by the Beis HaMikdash?" Yehoshua wondered.

"The red cow stays in her master's herd until she is two, because the verse says,[27] 'They shall take on your behalf a completely red *cow*.' Our Sages interpret this to mean that the heifer is not 'taken,' or bought, until it is a cow—that is to say, more than two years old."[28]

"Who pays for such an expensive cow?" a bewildered Alexander asked.

"The money for the purchase of the *Parah Adumah* is taken

---

24. Mishnah *Parah* 2:5.
25. *Bemidbar* 19:2.
26. *Kiddushin* 31a.
27. *Bemidbar* 19:2.
28. Rambam, *Hilchos Parah Adumah* 1:1.

from the *Terumas HaLishkah*,[29] from the half-*shekels* that every adult Jewish male contributes each year. This money can be used for buying a *Parah Adumah* because the Torah calls it a '*chatas*.'[30] This gives it a status similar to a sin-offering."

"And who gets the privilege of burning the cow? The *Kohen Gadol*? Or his deputy? Or perhaps a regular Kohen?" Yonasan asked.

"The very first *Parah Adumah* was burned by Elazar,[31] the son of Aharon HaKohen, who was his father's deputy," Reb Shmuel answered. "Since then, any *Kohen Gadol* or *kohen hedyot* can do it.[32] From the time we received the Torah at Mount Sinai, eight Red Cows have been burned.[33] The first one was in the time of Moshe Rabbeinu, as we said. Then, many hundreds of years later, in the period of Ezra the Scribe during the time of the Second Beis HaMikdash, the second one was burned. It's quite amazing that the ashes of Moshe's *Parah Adumah* lasted and served the Jews for such a long time. How many years do you think the first cow's ashes were used?"

"Almost a thousand years," Binyamin answered immediately. "In the book of *Melachim* it says that 480 years elapsed from the time of the Exodus from Mitzrayim until the building of the First Beis HaMikdash.[34] The First Beis HaMikdash stood for 410 years[35] — that's 890 years altogether. And if we add the seventy

---

29. Mishnah *Shekalim* 4:2.

30. *Bemidbar* 19:9.

31. *Bemidbar*19:3: "You shall give it to Elazar the priest and he shall take it outside the camp, and [someone]   shall slaughter it in his presence."

32. Rambam, *Hilchos Parah Adumah* 1:11.

33. Mishnah *Parah* 3:5; Rambam, *Hilchos Parah Adumah* 3:4.

34. *I Melachim* 6:1.

35. *Yoma* 9a.

years of the Babylonian exile,[36] we get 960 years."

"Very good, Binyamin! A precise calculation!" Reb Shmuel commended him.

"Now, Shimon HaTzaddik[37] burned two cows, and Yochanan *Kohen Gadol* also burned two. Eliyahu Eyni ben HaKof burned one, and Chananel HaMitzri also burned one. That makes eight Red Cows altogether. Soon the ninth one will be burned, *b'ezras Hashem*," Reb Shmuel finished. Then he sighed. "May it not become *pasul* like the last one."

"When did that happen?" the children wanted to know.

"About half a year ago[38] the *Parah Adumah* was declared *pasul* after it had been slaughtered."

"But why, what happened?" Yechezkel asked.

"The cow was slaughtered by the righteous *Kohen Gadol*, Rabbi Yishmael ben Piyachi, and was absolutely kosher. However, the *Chachamim* rendered it *pasul* nevertheless, due to an argument with the heretical Tzedokim."

Silence descended upon the small group on the mountain. Only the chirping of the birds and the wind in the trees were heard in the background. The children waited expectantly to hear their teacher tell them the story of this *Parah Adumah*.

---

36. *Yirmeyahu* 29:10.
37. Mishnah *Parah* 3:5.
38. Mishnah *Parah* 3:5, *Tiferes Yisrael* #45.

Chapter Thirteen

The Heretic Tzedokim and Baytosim

efore I start telling you the story," Reb Shmuel began, "I'd like to tell you how the Tzedokim appeared on the scene of history, and about the background of their false outlook. About two hundred and fifty years ago, there lived a great Sage named Antignos Ish Socho, a prominent man in Socho."

"Wasn't he the student of Shimon HaTzaddik, who was one of the last of the *Anshei Knesses HaGedolah*?"[1] Yechezkel asked.

"Yes, that is correct. Antignos Ish Socho was one of the most important students of Shimon HaTzaddik. He achieved high levels in *avodas Hashem*, the service of Hashem, until he reached such a height that he served the Creator out of pure love for Him, and not just out of fear of punishment—or for the sake of reward for fulfilling the *mitzvos*. One day he taught his students what he practiced in life: 'Do not be like servants who serve their master for the sake of receiving a reward, but rather be like servants who serve their master without the intent of receiving a reward.'[2]

---

1. Mishnah *Avos* 1:2,3.
2. Mishnah *Avos* 1:3.

"Two disciples sat among those who drank in their mentor's words thirstily: Tzadok and Baytos,[3] who were quite different from all the others. Those two were not particularly firm in their faith, and, as they made their exit from the class, one of them said to his friend, 'Did you hear our *rebbi*'s words? The *rebbi* stated quite clearly that there are no consequences for a man's deeds. So if there is no reward or punishment and no hope for a world to come, what's the purpose of our toil in fulfilling the *mitzvos*?'

"They certainly misunderstood the implication of their *rebbi*'s words. Their *rebbi* only intended to say that one should be motivated to serve Hashem out of love, and not for the sake of receiving reward, or out of fear of punishment.

"Those two *talmidim* caused the people of Yisrael tremendous damage for many generations. They decided to renounce their belief in the God of Yisrael and to reject the entire Torah.[4] However, Tzadok and Baytos knew that if they were to come to the people of Yisrael and tell them, 'Forsake the Torah and do not observe the commandments,' the people of Yisrael might rise against them and kill them, and no one would be enticed to follow them. Therefore, they claimed that they believed in the Written Torah, and they only disputed the oral tradition of our Sages — that is to say, the Oral Torah. In such a way they disguised their true intentions.

"We Jews, faithful to Hashem and His Torah, know and believe that Moshe Rabbeinu received the Oral Torah on Mount Sinai,"[5] Reb Shmuel proclaimed. "The Oral Torah interprets and explains the Written Torah. There are even cases where the Oral Torah explains certain verses differently from their literal meaning.

---

3. Mishnah *Avos* 1:11, Bartenura.
4. Mishnah *Avos* 1:3, Rambam.
5. Rambam, Introduction to *Mishneh Torah*.

"For instance, the Torah says, 'An eye for an eye.'[6] According to the literal meaning of the words, it appears that a person who pokes his fellow Jew's eye out is punished by getting his eye poked out. However, we interpret this verse according to our Sages' tradition, which rules that a person who causes damage to his fellow must compensate him with money or property.[7] There is proof for this in the Torah, but even without proof we would be ready to act according to the tradition that we received from our *Avos*.

"Besides these, there are *halachos* that are called "*halachah le-Moshe mi-Sinai*." This means that the Oral Torah contains *halachos* to which there is no reference in the Written Torah,[8] such as the black color of the tefillin straps [*retzuos*].[9]

"The *Chachamim* of all the generations made a fence[10] [*siyag*] around the Torah. They issued various decrees, and made enactments and 'fences,' in order to prevent Jews from actual sin. The observance of all these *siyagim* is obligatory,[11] for Hashem commanded us in His Torah,[12] 'You must not deviate from what they [the *Chachamim*] tell you, even if what seems to be right they say is left, or what seems to be left they say is right.'

"Tzadok and Baytos conveyed their heretical views to their students. They said there was no obligation to observe our Sages' decrees and regulations, and the entire Torah was to be interpreted literally, without an Oral Law. There was something uniquely strange about those two wicked men," Reb Shmuel

---

6. *Shemos* 21:24.

7. *Bava Kamma* 83b.

8. Rambam, Introduction to the Talmudic order *Zerayim*.

9. *Shabbos* 28b.

10. Mishnah *Avos* 1:1.

11. *Shabbos* 23a.

12. *Devarim* 17:11.

smiled bitterly. "Usually the rabbi is more pious and righteous than his disciples. In this case, however, the 'rabbis' were much more sinful than their disciples. Tzadok and Baytos rejected the entire Torah, whereas their disciples learned from them to reject only the Oral Torah and the decrees of the Sages.

"Now, tell me, my dear *talmidim*, if you know any verses that were deliberately misinterpreted by the Tzedokim and Baytosim."

Naftali raised his hand and answered fervently, "They distorted the meaning of the verse that describes the date to bring the *Omer*-offering.[13] The verse literally says, 'From the day after *ha-shabbos*…you shall count for yourselves.'[14] Its correct meaning is, 'From the day after the rest day (i.e. Yom Tov) of Pesach.' They wrongly claim that the *Omer*-offering is to be brought from the day after Shabbos—always on a Sunday. And because the Festival of Shavuos occurs fifty days after the bringing of the *Omer*, their date for that Festival also becomes wrong."

Bo'az added, "I learned in the Mishnah[15] that before Yom Kippur the *Kohen Gadol* was made to swear that he would not deviate from all the halachic requirements that he had studied. This was done because when the Tzedokim burned the incense, they put it on top of the coals in the *Heichal*(11) and not in the *Kodesh HaKodashim*(12). They did this because, according to their heretical opinion, the verse '*Ki be'anan eira'eh al ha-kapores*'[16] means that the Kohen must enter the *Kodesh HaKodashim* within the incense cloud. Its correct meaning is, 'For I reveal Myself in the cloud that is over the Ark's cover.'"

---

13. *Menachos* 65a.

14. *Vayikra* 23:15.

15. *Yoma* 53a.

16. *Vayikra* 16:2.

"Once upon a time a *tzedoki* served as the *Kohen Gadol*," Reb Shmuel informed the group. "He offered the incense in the *Heichal* and got his punishment on the spot. A loud noise was suddenly heard in the *Azarah*. An angel came down from Heaven and knocked him to the ground. When the Kohanim came inside to carry him out, they saw an imprint in the shape of a calf's footprint between his shoulders.[17] They understood that he must have been punished by an angel, for the sole of an angel's foot looks similar to that of a calf."[18]

"The Tzedokim also distort the meaning of the verse that deals with the *korban Tamid*,"[19] Yehoshua said. "They claim that it may be brought by any individual Jew who feels like contributing an offering out of the goodness of his heart, because the command to bring the *korban Tamid* is expressed in the singular form.[20] Of course, the verse really means that the *Tamid* is a public sacrifice, which is paid for out of public funds and brought by the community as a whole. The community is one entity, and that's why the singular form is used."

Reuven added his own piece of knowledge: "We learned in class that whoever places his tefillin on either his forehead or the palm of his hand betrays himself as a heretic.[21] This is because he acts like the heretical Tzedokim, who understand the Torah literally, so that the passage[22] '*al yadecha*' is translated 'on your hand,' and '*bein einecha*' becomes 'between your eyes,'— meaning, 'on your forehead!'"

---

17. *Yoma* 19b.
18. *Yechezkel* 1:7.
19. *Menachos* 65a.
20. See *Bemidbar* 28:4.
21. *Megillah* 24b.
22. *Shemos* 13:9.

Naftali guffawed.

"Yes, it sounds hilarious, but if people stick to these lies, it becomes terrible," Reb Shmuel responded. "And what do you say to situations where the Tzedokim are quite stringent? They do this in order to demonstrate that they do not falsify the entire Torah by striving to be lenient. But of course it's very obvious that they are stringent only about things that do not prevent them from living an easygoing, godless existence. For instance, when it comes to the *Parah Adumah*, the Tzedokim claim that a *tevul yom* is not fit for burning it."[23]

The children were familiar with the concept of "*tevul yom*," which is a *tamei* person who has immersed during the day in order to purify himself,[24] but is not yet entirely *tahor* until the evening.

Reb Shmuel continued. "The Tzedokim claim that the Kohen who slaughters and burns the red cow must wait until evening to become entirely *tahor* from his *tum'ah*, because they misinterpret the verse '*Ve-asaf ish tahor*'[25] — 'a pure man shall then gather the cow's ashes.' The *Chachamim* disagree,[26] saying that the word *tahor* in the verse refers to a *tevul yom*. He is pure in that he can eat *ma'aser sheini*, although he is not totally pure for he must wait until the evening to eat *terumah*."

"But why don't the *Chachamim* agree to a *chumrah* anyhow?" Gamliel asked. "It's always good to be more stringent, isn't it? A bit of a *chumrah* here and there won't hurt, will it?"

Reb Shmuel gave an insightful answer. "Well, the *Chachamim* didn't want to accept a heretic *chumrah* either, so that people

---

23. Mishnah *Parah* 3:7.

24. Mishnah *Zevachim* 12:1, Bartenura.

25. *Bemidbar* 19:9.

26. *Yoma* 43b.

should not be mistaken and imitate the Tzedokim's leniencies as well. The Tzedokim's customs are not based on any Torah source at all. The *Chachamim* want to show that the Tzedokim's interpretations are totally incorrect, so they go out of their way to reject them: the Kohen who is to burn the cow is deliberately made *tamei*,[27] whereupon he immerses himself in the *mikveh*, and while he is a *tevul yom*, slaughters the cow, sprinkles its blood and burns it."

"What happened half a year ago, when the *Parah Adumah* became *pasul*?" Yonasan remembered to ask.

"On that occasion the *Parah Adumah* was actually prepared in accordance with halachah, but after they had slaughtered it, they suddenly realized that they had not caused[28] the Kohen to become *tamei* first. Therefore, they made it *pasul*. This was in order to remove any possible claim that all the previous cows had not been burned properly, because they had been slaughtered and burned by a *tevul yom*. *B'ezras Hashem*, in two weeks' time a new red cow will be burned."

"Reb Shmuel, we also want to see the burning of the cow," Reuven pleaded.

"Certainly! God-willing, I'll take you with me at the appointed time. It will be a great privilege for you to witness such an important type of Divine service, which is performed so rarely!"

"Reb Shmuel, what kind of bridge is over there, in the distance? It almost reaches the *gummah*," the observant Yehoshua asked suddenly. "I noticed it before, but I didn't want to interrupt you."

---

27. Mishnah *Parah* 3:7.
28. Mishnah *Parah* 3:5, *Tiferes Yisrael* #45.

"I must say, you asked the question at the right moment," Reb Shmuel smiled. "Because the *Chachamim* allow a *tevul yom* to slaughter and burn the *Parah Adumah*, they were afraid that people would think they were negligent of the laws concerning the *Parah Adumah*. In order to prevent such a mistake, the *Chachamim* issued many stringent decrees and restrictions (*chumros*) concerning other laws connected with the *Parah Adumah*.[29] This bridge, leading from *Sha'ar Shushan*(26)[30] on the eastern[31] side of the Temple Mount to the place of the burning of the red cow, is actually one of the many *chumros*."

"Why do you call the bridge a *chumrah*?" Gamliel wondered.

"I'll explain," Reb Shmuel answered. "Do you see a number of workers on the bridge? The workers are fixing it now for the appointed day of the burning. A distinguished procession, including the Kohen who will burn the cow, the cow itself, and the people who will help the Kohen burn it, will pass along the bridge. The bridge is built in a very special way that prevents those who pass on it from becoming *tamei*. This is to protect against the very unlikely possibility of a dead person, unknown to anyone, being buried below. Even in such an eventuality, the bridge blocks the *tum'ah* from spreading upwards, thereby preventing those who pass on it from becoming impure. At some other opportunity I will explain to you how this is made possible.

"Another *chumrah* that was introduced by the *Chachamim* has to do with children being raised on a ro..."

Reb Shmuel suddenly interrupted his explanation. A strange

---

29. Rambam, *Hilchos Parah Adumah* 2:5.

30. Mishnah *Middos* 1:3.

31. Mishnah *Parah* 3:6.

figure was approaching the group. He wore torn clothes, and a large *tallis* over his head and face reached down to his mouth. A long, unkempt beard straggled out below. As he approached them, they heard him shout: "*Tamei, tamei!* Watch out for *tum'ah*, don't become *tamei*! *Tamei, tamei!* Be careful! Don't become *tamei*!"[32]

"What's *that*?!" Gamliel cried out in alarm. The boys started to back away in fright.

"Come closer boys, don't be afraid!" Reb Shmuel called his pupils. "There's nothing to fear. He is just a man shouting to us to be careful not to become *tamei* from him."

The man began to speak to them in a thick voice. "I apologize for having frightened you. My name is Yitzchak, and, to my deepest regret, I am afflicted by *tzara'as*, as you can see." The *metzora* rolled up his sleeve. The children were shocked at the sight of the *tzara'as* mark, which was exhibited before their eyes in all its "glory." A patch of skin was snow-white, and there were two long, white hairs in the middle of the mark.[33]

"Because I am a *metzora*, it is forbidden for me to live in the city," he told them, "and I cannot mix with people. I live here in the mountains, alone, as the Torah says, 'He shall live alone, his dwelling place being outside the camp.'[34] I devote all my time to repentance and praying to Hashem, that He may forgive my sins and cure me of my *tzara'as*. I come to this particular spot every day, to stand opposite the Beis HaMikdash and to ask HaKadosh Baruch Hu to have mercy on me and accept my *teshuvah*."

---

32. *Vayikra* 13:45: "And the *tzara'as*-affected person, who has the [impure] mark on him — his clothes shall be torn and his hair shall grow wild, and he shall cover [his head] up to [his] moustache and call out: Impure, Impure!"

33. See *Vayikra* 13:2,3.

34. *Vayikra* 13:46.

The children were shocked at the sight of the tzara'as mark

Reb Yitzchak began to recite *Tehillim*.[35] The words seemed to come straight from his heart:

> A hymn by David, to proclaim.
> O Eternal, rebuke me not in Your anger,
> nor afflict me in Your wrath.
> For Your arrows have sunk into me,
> and Your hand has come down upon me.

Then Reb Yitzchak stretched out his afflicted arm and exclaimed:

> There is no wholeness in my flesh,
> because of Your rage;
> there is no peace in my bones
> because of my sin.

He broke out in heart-wrenching weeping:

> For my transgressions
> have overwhelmed me;
> like a heavy burden,
> they are too heavy for me.

Tears filled the boys' eyes. Reb Shmuel guided them away gently, so that they would not disturb the *metzora*'s prayers to Hashem Yisbarach.

---

35. *Tehillim* 38:1–5.

Chapter Fourteen

The Metzora's Story

The next morning at the end of the class, Reb Shmuel suggested, "How would you like to go and visit the *metzora* now? I visited him yesterday and asked his permission to bring you to hear more details about *tzara'as* from him."

The children showed great interest and were ready to go right away.

Reb Yitzchak, the *metzora*, welcomed them with a friendly smile. Just like the day before, the boys seated themselves in a semicircle on the rocky ground, and Reb Yitzchak commenced his story.

"I am standing before you now like a vessel filled with shame and disgrace. Whoever looks at me can see how dismal my situation is. I live all alone here, outside the city, away from society and ostracized. My clothes are torn, my hair has grown wild, and my head is wrapped up — I am like a mourner![1] Because of my foolishness, I caused this terrible calamity to befall me.

"My situation was quite different until recently. I am a wealthy man, and I used to be a distinguished citizen of Beis Lechem. I own a vast number of cattle and sheep, and cultivated fields that stretch over wide areas. I also possess great treasures

---

1. *Vayikra* 13:45. See also *Targum Onkelos*.

of gold and silver in my cellars.

"But instead of thanking Hashem Yisbarach for all the good that He bestowed on me and giving *tzedakah* to poor people, I let my heart swell with false pride. I said to myself, 'Who can compare to me in accomplishments and success?' I sincerely believed that all of my possessions had been obtained by me thanks to my blessed talents. My pride caused me to treat simple people with contempt. I spoke to them arrogantly and looked down my nose at them. In addition to all of my 'accomplishments,' I excelled in stinginess, was tightfisted, and gave *tzedakah* grudgingly. I thought, 'Why should I give my money away? Did I toil with the sweat of my brow in order to give it away to a good-for-nothing pauper? Let him go and work like I did, and he'll be able to earn some money!' Due to my haughtiness, I regularly spoke ill of others [*lashon ha-ra*] and caused hatred between them [*rechilus*].

"One day about half a year ago, I returned home after a day's work in high spirits. Lo and behold, a very unpleasant surprise awaited me. An enormous, ugly, deep red[2] mark appeared in the corner of my luxurious living room, which had been renovated and painted only two weeks before. I called in my neighbor and he carefully examined the mark. An expression of great alarm appeared on his face, and he said to me, 'Hurry, call a Kohen immediately. I think it's a *tzara'as* mark.'

"The Kohen, who arrived very soon, ordered me to take all my belongings out of the house.[3]

---

2. *Vayikra* 14:37–38: "He shall look at the mark, and [if he sees that] the mark on the walls of the house is a sunken-looking deep green or deep red [that] appears recessed from [the rest of] the wall, the priest shall go out of the house [and stand] at the entrance of the house and quarantine the house for seven days."

3. *Vayikra* 14:36: "The priest shall then order [that] they empty out the house before the priest comes to look at the mark, [so that] whatever is in-

"I was completely humiliated. I wished I could find a place to hide because of my tremendous embarrassment. All the neighbors, who stood outside watching the scene with great curiosity, suddenly saw several objects being carried out of my house. Some were things that they had requested to borrow and I had refused to lend, claiming I didn't have them. Now my falsehood and stinginess became revealed to all.[4]

"After the whole house had been emptied out, the Kohen entered the living room. After a thorough examination of the mark, he decided that it was a case of house *tzara'as*. He left the house, and locked it for seven days of quarantine.[5]

"During the time my house was locked, I stayed at the home of one of my friends together with my family. It never occurred to me that I had to repent if I wanted the mark to disappear. In fact, when the Kohen tried to tell me why my house became afflicted, I shut him up. 'Who is he to reprimand me?' I thought in my pride.

"Meanwhile, I suddenly recalled a Midrash, in which the *Chachamim* say that house *tzara'as* is a sign of good tidings for the people of Yisrael:[6] The Emori nation who used to live in Kena'an before the Children of Yisrael had captured the land, hid treasures of gold, silver and diamonds inside the walls of their houses. If *tzara'as* marks appeared on the walls and the houses

---

side the house does not become impure, and after that the priest shall come to look at the house." See also Rambam, *Hilchos Tum'as Tzara'as* 14:4.

4. *Yoma* 11b, *Arachin* 16a: "Whoever uses his house utensils only for his own purposes and does not lend them to others, claiming he does not have any utensils, HaKadosh Baruch Hu publicizes the fact that he does own utensils when they empty out all that is inside the house because of the *tzara'as* that has afflicted it."

5. *Vayikra* 14:38.

6. *Midrash Rabbah, Vayikra* 80.

would have to be demolished, Jews would find the hidden treasures. I knew that my house was an ancient structure — thirteen hundred years old — so I was sure I'd find some hidden treasures in its walls. I sat and waited impatiently, looking forward to the great wealth that would soon fall to my lot.

"The Kohen returned on the seventh day, but when he saw that the mark [*nega*] had spread, he called some workers.[7] They extracted the affected stones and discarded them outside the city limits, whereupon the wall was repaired with new stones which replaced the afflicted ones that were removed. Then they replastered the whole house, painted it, and locked it up for another seven days. I was full of hope that the *tzara'as* would reappear, and I would have the *zechus* to collect the gold that must surely have been hidden inside the walls.

"After seven days had elapsed, the *nega* reappeared. My prayer had been answered! I thought. But woe to me and woe to such a prayer! The Kohen came and gave an order to demolish the whole house.[8]

"Strong-muscled, broad-shouldered workers came the next day and began to demolish the walls using heavy hammers. I specially ordered reliable workers who would not steal the gold, and I stood watching them the whole day. I tried to chase away curious on-lookers, so that the whole 'treasure business' would not become public.

"The house was smashed to pieces, but not even a small piece of gold was found. The stones, the wood and the dirt were discarded outside the city, to an impure place, and I was left with neither a home nor a treasure.

---

7. *Vayikra* 14:39–42. See also Rambam, *Hilchos Tum'as Tzara'as* 15:2.

8. *Vayikra* 14:45: "He shall [have] the house demolished — its stones, its wood and all the house's plaster — and have [them] taken outside the city to an impure place."

"I stood watching the workers the whole day"

"That's when I started soul-searching — making a *cheshbon ha-nefesh* — wondering what had caused such a misfortune to befall me. I arrived at the conclusion that it must have happened because of my excessive stinginess. So I accepted upon myself an obligation, from then on, to open my heart to the plight of poor people, and also to those neighbors who came to borrow things from me.

"Straight after this incident we moved to Yerushalayim. Don't imagine that I had suddenly become a big *tzaddik* and wanted to live closer to the *Shechinah* in order to attain more *yiras Shamayim*. No, that wasn't the case. I had just learned a halachah that says that the houses of Yerushalayim are not susceptible to *tum'as ha-nega'im*,[9] and I really wanted to be spared the disgrace in case it happened to me again.

"So I purchased a big house in Yerushalayim and we settled in the new place. I was very careful to lend out utensils to neighbors whenever they asked, according to the commitment I had made. I also gave *tzedakah* with an open hand. Things ran smoothly until I was afflicted with the following misfortune."

Reb Yitzchak stopped talking and heaved a deep, mournful sigh that came straight from his broken heart. Then he continued in a low voice.

"One day I was invited to a friend's wedding. When I went to get dressed in honor of the occasion, I took my best piece of clothing out of the closet: a beautiful linen garment that I had bought from a foreign merchant. All of a sudden I noticed a deep green mark on it.[10] I called the Kohen urgently. He gave it a penetrating look and ruled: '*Tzara'as begadim*! [*Tzara'as* of clothing].'

"The garment was quarantined for seven days. The inspec-

---

9. *Bava Kamma* 82b.
10. *Vayikra* 13:47–49.

tion afterwards showed that the *tzara'as* had spread, so the garment had to be burned.[11] I was glad nobody found out about it; at least I was spared the embarrassment. Again I began to soul-search. Because I had heard once that *tzara'as* is a punishment for *shevuas shav* (an oath taken in vain),[12] I decided that this was the reason why my garment had been affected with *tzara'as*. So I accepted an obligation upon myself from then on to avoid swearing in vain.

"O, how stupid I was! If I had listened to the first Kohen, or if I had consulted the Torah Sages, they would have told me that *nega'im* occur mainly on account of *lashon ha-ra*. Miriam the *nevi'ah* was afflicted by *tzara'as* because she spoke *lashon ha-ra*.[13] Moshe Rabbeinu's arm turned snow-white with *tzara'as* after he had spoken *lashon ha-ra* about Yisrael.[14] But I hadn't consulted the *Chachamim*, because I'd relied on my own wisdom and ability to solve problems.

"I then removed all the garments made of wool, linen and leather from my wardrobe, because I knew that only such garments are susceptible to *tum'as ha-nega'im*."[15]

Reb Yitzchak glanced at the faces of his young audience and pleaded with them:

"Please learn a lesson from my story. Learn from my mistakes, and do not repeat them!"

After a short pause he continued.

"HaKadosh Baruch Hu is a merciful and compassionate King. First He brings a *nega* upon a man's house. If the man fails

---

11. *Vayikra* 13:50–52.
12. *Arachin* 16a.
13. *Bemidbar*, chap. 12.
14. *Shemos* 4:6, Rashi.
15. Mishnah *Nega'im* 11:2, *Kilayim* 9:1.

to repent, He afflicts his clothes with *tzara'as*. If he fails to rectify his ways even then, his very body is stricken with it.[16]

"One morning, I woke up and went to wash my hands. I was terrified to see on my arm a snow-white patch of skin. I tried to soak it in water, to wash it with soap, but nothing helped. I had no other choice than to call a Kohen. His pronouncement had the effect of a bolt of lightning on me: 'This mark is white enough to be considered *tzara'as*. You must be quarantined for a seven-day period.'[17]

"But HaKadosh Baruch Hu's mercy is boundless. At that particular moment, the two typical signs of absolute *tzara'as* had not been detected on the mark of my arm. I had not yet been classified as an absolute *metzora*, although I had to be quarantined for seven days. I was sent away outside the city,[18] and locked in a house[19] until my condition was clarified."

"May I interrupt?" Reb Shmuel asked Reb Yitzchak. "I'd like to explain this issue to the children in detail." Reb Yitzchak nodded his assent, and Reb Shmuel began. "There are two ways that a person can become an absolute *metzora* right away, the first time he is seen by a Kohen. One way is if there are at least two white hairs in the middle of the white *tzara'as* mark.[20] The second is if there is healthy skin with a normal color within the white patch.[21] In either of these two cases, the man is immediately and absolutely declared a *metzora* [*metzora muchlat*].

---

16. Rambam, *Hilchos Tum'as Tzara'as* 16:10.

17. *Vayikra* 13:4: "And if the spot is white on his skin but does not appear deeper than the skin, and the hairs have not turned white, the priest shall quarantine [the person with] the mark for a seven-day period."

18. *Megillah* 8b.

19. *Vayikra* 13:4, Rashi.

20. *Vayikra* 13:3.

21. *Vayikra* 13:10–11.

"Reb Yitzchak had only a white mark, without another sign, so he fell into the category of a *metzora musgar*, a *metzora* who has to be quarantined. After seven days the Kohen returns, and if the white patch has spread further or if either of the other two signs that we just mentioned appear, then the man is declared a *metzora muchlat*."

Reb Yitzchak then continued. "At that point I understood I had to carefully investigate what was happening to me. 'Why have I been afflicted with such a great misfortune?' I finally humbled myself to ask the Kohen, and he told me that *nega'im* come because of *lashon ha-ra*.[22] I immediately accepted upon myself an obligation to stop speaking *lashon ha-ra*, although it was a major effort for me.

"Nevertheless, I did not fulfill my obligation perfectly. Because our Sages explain that the word *metzora* is formed from the words *motzi shem ra*[23] [someone who speaks false *lashon ha-ra*], I understood that it is specifically such a person who is stricken by *tzara'as*. So I stopped slandering people. However, I continued speaking *lashon ha-ra* that was true — but I'm sure you all know that this is also absolutely prohibited.

"On the seventh day, the Kohen detected these two[24] white hairs." Reb Yitzchak showed the white hairs to the children.

"'I certainly sympathize with you,' the Kohen told me, 'but you have failed to do proper *teshuvah*, so you are now declared a *metzora muchlat*.'

"I was compelled to leave my house and was banished from the city for an indefinite period of time. I have been here all alone for several months, far from my family, my friends, my beautiful

---

22. *Arachin* 16a.

23. *Arachin* 15b.

24. *Vayikra* 13:3.

house and my business. Reb Yitzchak started sobbing. "I am sitting here, awaiting Hashem's forgiveness, and I do not know when my *tzara'as* will go away.

"Regretfully, I defamed others, claiming that they had many 'impure marks' (i.e. flaws). But I ended up having the impure mark *on me*, as our Sages put it: '*Kol ha-posel, be-mumo posel*'[25]—whoever finds fault with others, is really revealing his own faults.

"The hair on my head (*rosh*) must grow wild to atone for my arrogance, because I wanted to be the '*rosh*' and lord over everybody. My clothes must be torn in order to atone for my stinginess, and I must cover my head up to my mouth in order to atone for what I sinned with my lips. I am *tamei*, and must call out, '*Tamei! Tamei!*—Impure! Impure!' I said about others that they were *tamei*, and now I am compelled to say it about myself![26]

"What more can I tell you, dear children—be extra careful and go out of your way to avoid speaking *lashon ha-ra*, even if what you're saying is true. Remember: 'Whoever guards his mouth and tongue, guards himself from calamity.'[27] You see what great misfortune fell to me because of my foolish tongue? I was punished very severely. Nevertheless, I am thankful, for now I know that I have to improve my ways! From now on, *bli neder*, I won't speak badly about any Jew!

"The Kohen told me that *tzara'as* of the body is considered a very light punishment, ten times lighter than the *tzara'as* of the soul.[28] 'Remember,' he said, 'whoever guards his mouth and tongue from *tzaros* (misfortune), guards his soul from *tzara'as*...'"

---

25. *Kiddushin* 70a.

26. *Vayikra* 13:45, *Keli Yakar*.

27. *Mishlei* 21:23.

28. *Yalkut Shimoni, Parashas Metzora.*

At the end of his speech, Reb Yitzchak got up and departed from the place, and the children watched him until he disappeared from sight. They were strongly affected by his words. Each of the boys made a silent decision: "I am not going to speak any more *lashon ha-ra* and *rechilus*!"

Chapter Fifteen

The Plot

Reb Shmuel," Naftali and Chananya asked, "both of us want to go and visit the *metzora* again!"

It was early afternoon of the same day, and the two children — who had some free time — wanted to go to Reb Yitzchak's temporary dwelling. They saw him as their new friend.

"We would like to thank him for his sobering words, which we found most helpful and enlightening. Perhaps, by doing that, we'll be able to boost his low morale," Naftali explained. Reb Shmuel willingly agreed, but warned them to be back in time for class.

Reb Yitzchak, the *metzora*, welcomed the two boys warmly.

"I am so happy to hear that my story had a good influence on you," he told the children. "And now may I ask you to do me a favor?"

"Of course," the boys answered.

"I have a very difficult question in halachah. I'd like you to carry a message to the *Beis Din* on *Har HaBayis* and bring me back their ruling," Reb Yitzchak said, signing the letter and handing it to Chananya. The children proceeded on their way after waving good-bye.

"We'll try to return as soon as possible," they called back.

They took a shortcut along the special bridge that was built for the procession of the *Parah Adumah*. While they were crossing the bridge, they were scolded by the workers who were toiling away at its renovation. After they had reached the eastern gate of the Temple Mount [*Sha'ar Shushan*(62)], which was opposite the Mount of Olives,[1] the children removed their shoes, shook the dust off their feet, and quickly turned toward the *Beis Din*.

"Remember not to touch other Jews, so that they will not become *tamei*," Naftali reminded his friend. They were allowed to enter the *Har HaBayis*(1) area in spite of their being *teme'ei meisim*;[2] even a dead body could be brought there.

The boys continued walking, and eventually the building which served as the seat of the Minor Sanhedrin(44) [*Sanhedrin HaKetanah*][3] became visible. They stopped at the entrance next to the *Beis Din* attendant.

"We'd like to pass this letter on to the *dayanim*," Naftali said respectfully. Chananya, who was more timid, stood next to him in total silence. They waited a little while until the attendant motioned for them to enter. They entered and passed the letter on to the *dayanim*, taking extreme care not to touch them. While the members of the Sanhedrin were busy discussing the issue, Naftali and Chananya waited on the side. Eventually, the scribe of the *Beis Din* wrote the halachic ruling and passed the letter, sealed with the seal of the *Beis Din*, to the children.

The excited boys hurried to return to the *metzora*'s house. They were in such a hurry that they didn't notice that they had broken into a run. They reached the house panting for breath and handed the letter to Reb Yitzchak.

Reb Yitzchak skimmed the short lines quickly, and sat down

---

1. Mishnah *Middos* 1:3.

2. *Pesachim* 67a.

3. *Sanhedrin* 86b.

for a while lost in deep thought. Then he said, "The letter that I sent with you contained a very serious question on *lashon ha-ra*. Now that it has been ruled upon, I can tell you all about it. Then I'll send you on an additional mission."

He shifted in his chair and started his account.

"This morning after you left, I went to seclude myself in a little cave which I frequently use for such purposes. I sat there for a few minutes and eventually dozed off. I was awakened by the voices of some people who were talking outside very close to the mouth of the cave. One of the voices sounded familiar to me. I strained my ear and was amazed at myself: how could I have failed to recognize the venomous voice of the evil man, Chanan, the head of the Yerushalayim Tzedokim.

"'We've got to do something to take revenge on the *Kohen Gadol* and the Sanhedrin for the great evil that they have done to us,' I heard him say determinedly. 'I'm sure you remember what happened several months ago after Yishmael ben Piyachi, the *Kohen Gadol*, had prepared a *Parah Adumah*.[4] The cow was rendered *pasul* by the Sages, because it had been mistakenly prepared by a pure person, in accordance with our view, instead of a *tevul yom*, according to the view of the Sages.'"

Naftali could not keep from interrupting Reb Yitzchak. "Reb Shmuel told us about that!" he said.

"Shh!" Chananya silenced him. "I want to hear the story!"

"I realized that Chanan and his friends were plotting together against the Kohanim. They were trying to figure out how to cause the Kohanim who would be taking care of the upcoming burning of the *Parah Adumah*, to become *tamei*. They knew that the *Beis Din* and the Kohanim would spare no effort to burn the cow in purity [*taharah*], so therefore they planned to take their revenge on the *Chachamim* — known as the Perushim — by

---

4. Mishnah *Parah* 3:5, *Tiferes Yisrael* #45.

"I was awakened by the voices of some people who were talking outside"

causing them to make a blunder."

"Why do they want to take revenge specifically in this way?" Chananya could not figure out.

"I'll explain," said Reb Yitzchak. "Since the previous *Parah Adumah* had been rendered *pasul* because it was prepared according to the Tzedokim's view, their popularity has diminished. The incident has become known throughout the land, and this has caused a tremendous spiritual reawakening. Many, many Jews have repented, and begun to observe all the *Chachamim's* decrees and enactments more stringently, as well as all the laws of the Oral Torah. People concluded, 'If a stringent ruling [*chumrah*] of the Tzedokim has not been accepted by the *Chachamim*, then we most certainly must reject their lenient rulings [*kulos*] as well!'

"After the Tzedokim found out all this, their anger knew no bounds. They felt they had to cause the Perushim to stumble. When I heard them, I was shocked. Their venomous hatred — the traditional hatred of the ignorant for *talmidei chachamim* — revealed itself quite clearly in all its ugliness. Just by hearing their words, anyone would immediately know exactly who is right and who is wrong.

"In the end, Chanan and his friends unanimously decided to hide the body of a dead child, who had died the day before, in one of the upper pillars of the bridge. They figured it would be discovered only after the burning of the *Parah Adumah*, so they rubbed their hands together with great satisfaction in anticipation of their sure success.

"'When it is discovered that the *Kohen Gadol* burned the cow in a state of *tum'as meis*, everybody will conclude that the deeds of the Perushim are not favored by Heaven. Consequently, our popularity will rise again,' Chanan said, while his gang of Tzedokim laughed evilly."

Reb Yitzchak smiled at the boys' gaping mouths and continued telling the story. "You may have noticed that the bridge is built in a special way.[5] Pillars are stuck into the soil of the mountain, with spaces in between. The pillars are connected on top by dome-like roofs [*kippos*]. Fixed on top of each of these *kippos* is another pillar, and all these pillars are also connected on top by *kippos*. The bridge rests upon this second layer of *kippos*. This special kind of structure prevents those who walk along the bridge from becoming *tamei* from corpses buried underground, beneath the bridge.

"A dead body that may be buried under the lower set of *kippos* will not be of any significance. Its *tum'ah* will not rise to the surface of the bridge, because the arch of the lower *kippos* will block the *tum'ah*. And even if the body is buried under a lower pillar, exactly between two *kippos* — so that neither blocks the rising *tum'ah* — the upper *kippos* will stop it from rising above the bridge.

"The Tzedokim, however, in all their wickedness, plan to hide the dead body inside one of the upper pillars, connected to the bridge itself, the pillar having no *kippah* on top to block the *tum'ah*. Thus they hope to cause all the passers-by to become *tamei*.

"There is only one thing they did not take into consideration: me!" Reb Yitzchak exclaimed. "I sat in the cave and managed to overhear all the details of their vicious plot. It was real *siyata diShmaya*, because I even know the exact spot where the wicked Tzedokim are planning to hide the dead body. The spot can be recognized easily, because there is a very high tree growing three hundred *amos* from here. One of its branches almost touches the pillar into which they are planning to hide the dead body.

"Hashem sent you to me today, as if you were heavenly angels sent at the right moment. I had intended to ask the *Beis Din*

5. Mishnah *Parah* 3:6.

if I was allowed to reveal the Tzedokim's plot, because it would involve speaking *lashon ha-ra*. I've suffered enough because of all the *rechilus* and *lashon ha-ra* that I've spoken in my life, so I didn't feel like committing those grave sins all over again, *chas ve-shalom*. I knew that it is permissible to speak *lashon ha-ra* about wicked people,[6] but I wanted to make sure that the Tzedokim fall into this category.

"The *dayanim* confirmed my assumptions. They wrote to me that all those who after being exposed to a Torah way of life, negate the Torah, even the Oral Law only, and even a single rabbinic ruling, fall into the category of *apikorsim* (heretics), and one is permitted to speak *lashon ha-ra* about them.[7] And now, children, I'll write a letter describing all the details of the plot. Please pass it on to the *Beis Din* quickly."

After Reb Yitzchak finished writing his letter, he gave it to Naftali and Chananya. The children ran down the mountain with the swiftness of light-footed gazelles, jumping over rocks and pits, and running through groves. It took them only a few minutes to reach their destination. They approached the seat of the *Beis Din* breathing heavily. The *dayanim* opened the letter and expressed their amazement at its contents.

"Kindly leave the room, children," one of the *dayanim* requested.

As they sat outside they saw the *Beis Din* messenger leaving the seat of the *Beis Din* hurriedly. He returned after a short while accompanied by venerable looking Kohanim. From the bits of the conversation that they overheard, the two boys understood that the members of the *Sanhedrin HaGedolah* who sat in *Lishkas HaGazis*(53) — the Chamber of Hewn Stone — were involved in the

---

6. Chafetz Chayim, *Hilchos Lashon HaRa* 4:5.
7. Ibid., 8:7.

matter. The *Kohen Gadol*, Rabbi Yishmael ben Piyachi, had also been informed.

After a short while—which seemed like an eternity to the children— a group of people emerged from the inner room and spoke to the children. "Can you show us the way to the *metzora's* dwelling?"

They were so excited that they couldn't utter a word, so they nodded their heads silently.

Needless to say, Reb Yitzchak could not be invited to come to the *Beis Din* to testify about the plot, because a *metzora* is forbidden to enter Yerushalayim.

"Let's go, then!" the one who gave the impression of being the most distinguished of the group commanded. They covered the short distance quickly and reached the place. During the time when the members of the group questioned Reb Yitzchak, hearing all the details of his evidence, the excited Chananya and Naftali waited on the side. After the messengers of the *Beis Din* had left, Reb Yitzchak returned to his house. The children entered and saw him standing in the living room with his arms lifted up in fervent prayer.

As they looked at him silently, it suddenly seemed to Naftali that his afflicted arm looked darker.

"Maybe I am mistaken," he thought doubtfully.

"Chananya, do you see his arm?" he whispered to his friend.

They examined his arm carefully, and then noticed that the white hairs had fallen out in addition to the change in the color of the skin.

They waited patiently until Reb Yitzchak finished praying. As soon as he finished, they burst out, "They have fallen out! We saw, we saw—your arm is brown! There are no white hairs!"

When Reb Yitzchak managed to understand the meaning of their excited shouting, he glanced at his arm quickly, and a smile flashed onto his face. He was beside himself with surprise and happiness.

"Run quickly and tell the Kohen to come here. He lives next to the city gate, and his name is Yochanan," he said after he had calmed down.

Naftali and Chananya ran down the mountain happily for the third time that day. This time they were headed for the house of Yochanan the Kohen. When the Kohen heard the news he hurried to Reb Yitzchak's house together with the boys, accompanied by his son.

"I hope I'll manage to check him before the ninth hour of the day,"[8] Yochanan muttered to himself.

After he had examined Reb Yitzchak's arm closely he declared triumphantly, "I am happy to bring you good tidings: your *tzara'as* is gone! You are *tahor*.[9] Your affliction [*nega*] has healed!"[10]

Reb Yitzchak burst into tears of joy, and words of gratitude to HaKadosh Baruch Hu came out of his mouth:[11]

> Go and hearken, and I will recount,
> all you who fear God,
> what He has done for my soul.
> Unto Him with my mouth did I call,
> and exaltation was under my tongue.
> Had I beheld iniquity in my heart,
> the Lord would not have heard.

---

8. Mishnah *Nega'im* 2:2: "When are they (the *nega'im*) seen (examined)? In the fourth and the fifth, and the seventh, and the eighth, and the ninth (hours)." See also Rambam, *Hilchos Tum'as Tzara'as* 9:6.

9. Rambam, *Hilchos Tum'as Tzara'as* 9:3.

10. It is possible to be purified of *tzara'as* if either the white color becomes dark or the white hairs fall out. In Yitzchak's case both phenomena occurred, which was a clear sign that the *metzora* had become healed of his affliction (*Sifra* 14:3).

11. *Tehillim* 66:16–20.

But God did hear,
He hearkened to the voice of my prayer.
Blessed is God, Who has neither turned
away my prayer, nor His kindness from me.

"Go to town and bring all that is necessary for the purification of the *metzora*," the Kohen commanded his son.

"May we call our friends to witness the rite of purification?" Naftali and Chananya requested. The overjoyed Reb Yitzchak immediately agreed, and Naftali and Chananya proceeded to class. The afternoon session was well underway when they entered, and Reb Shmuel looked at them sternly.

"Where were you?" he demanded.

Naftali and Chananya burst into an excited recount of the afternoon's events. The rest of the pupils listened with rapt attention.

"All right then," Reb Shmuel agreed in the end. "Your coming late was for a legitimate reason. Let's all go to *Har HaZeisim* now."

Chapter Sixteen

Two Birds

When the children reached *Har HaMishchah* (*Har HaZeisim*) they saw that Shimon, the son of Yochanan the Kohen, had not yet returned with the things necessary for the *taharah* (purification).

Reb Yitzchak welcomed them with great joy and a radiant face, saying, "Blessed is God, Who has neither turned away my prayer, nor His kindness from me.[1] Only a few hours ago I was in such bad shape, as you saw, and now I am the happiest man in the world! I will be *tahor* soon! I'll be able to rejoin my family soon!"

While they waited, Reb Shmuel learned the details of *taharas ha-metzora* with his students.

"Tell me please, what items are required for *taharas ha-me-tzora*?" he asked.

"Two ritually pure living birds, a piece of cedar wood, a thread of scarlet wool (*shni ha-tola'as*) and a bunch of *eizov*,"[2] Naftali quoted fluently.

---

1. *Tehillim* 66:20.
2. *Vayikra* 14:4.

"You left out two things," Yehoshua reminded him. "The next verse mentions an earthenware vessel and spring water [*mayim chayim*]."[3]

"A knife for the slaughter of one of the birds is also needed," Binyamin added.

"That is correct," Reb Shmuel confirmed.

"Why is a *shechitah* knife necessary? Isn't it possible to cut the back of its head with a thumbnail [*melikah*] the way one slaughters birds of *kodashim*?" Reuven asked.

"Notice that the verse says, '*ha-tzippor ha-shechutah*'[4] (the ritually slaughtered bird). The word 'slaughtered' seems to be superfluous here, because it already features in the previous verse: '*ve-shachat es ha-tzippor*' (and he shall slaughter the bird). From this seeming redundancy, the *Chachamim* derived that one must specifically slaughter the bird with a knife, and not through *melikah*."[5]

"What else is needed for the purification of a *metzora*?" Reb Shmuel asked.

The boys frowned, deep in though.

"A razor!" Bo'az exclaimed a few moments later. "To shave off the *metzora*'s hair."[6]

"How long does it take to bring all these things?" asked Chananya impatiently. Yochanan the Kohen smiled.

"It's not so easy to obtain all the necessary things," he told the children. "I'll explain why. The earthenware vessel must be brand new.[7] This is derived by our Sages from the verse, '*el keli cheres al*

3. *Vayikra* 14:5.

4. *Vayikra* 14:16.

5. *Sifra*.

6. *Vayikra* 14:8.

7. Mishnah *Nega'im* 14:1.

mayim chayim'[8] (over spring water in an earthenware vessel). Just as the water must not have been previously used for any purpose, so must the vessel be absolutely new.[9] Therefore, my son went to a store that sells earthenware vessels. It's not difficult to obtain spring water. It can be drawn from the spring that flows here, on the mountain. The most difficult article to obtain is the two birds.

"The Torah commands us to bring two *tzipporei deror*.[10] The nature of the *deror* bird is that it does not recognize authority,[11] and is therefore hard to catch. Besides that, the two birds have to be identical:[12] they must be the same color and size, have the same value, and be bought or taken at the same time.[13]

"I sent my son Shimon to the man who lives in the western corner of town," Yochanan summed up. "He sells *tzipporei deror*, cedar wood, *eizov* and scarlet-dyed wool. By the way, the last three items must also be of the proper *shiur* (halachic size).[14] The cedar wood must be an *amah* long,[15] and a quarter of the thickness of a bed leg. This is determined by breaking the leg into half lengthwise, and then into half again. The size of the *eizov* branch plucked from the ground must be at least a *tefach*,[16] and the scarlet-dyed wool must weigh at least one *shekel*."[17]

---

8. *Vayikra* 14:5.

9. *Sotah* 15b.

10. Mishnah *Nega'im* 14:1.

11. *Beitzah* 24a.

12. Mishnah *Nega'im* 14:5.

13. Mishnah *Yoma* 6:1, *Tiferes Yisrael*.

14. Rambam, *Hilchos Tum'as Tzara'as* 11:1.

15. Mishnah *Nega'im* 14:6.

16. *Niddah* 26a.

17. *Yoma* 42a.

As soon as Yochanan finished his explanation his son Shimon arrived, sweating profusely and carrying a whole load of things. Yochanan took them all and laid them on stones. The children stepped aside in order not to disturb him. They then formed a circle and stood around him.

"Shimon, please go down to the spring and fill this vessel with a *revi'is* of water,"[18] Yochanan requested, handing his son an earthenware vessel. Shimon ran down to the spring and quickly returned with the vessel full of *mayim chayim*. In the meantime, the Kohen carefully examined the birds and let Reb Shmuel hold the healthier and stronger of the two.[19]

He then checked whether the knife was sharp enough according to halachah, whereupon he took the bird from Reb Shmuel and held it in his hand. The Kohen pronounced the blessing, "Blessed are You… Who sanctified us with His commandments and commanded us concerning the ritual slaughter."[20] Then he slaughtered the bird over the vessel with the *mayim chayim*.[21] Blood started running from the bird into the vessel. The Kohen squeezed the bird's body so that enough blood would enter the water and affect its color.[22] Then he dug a small pit in the ground and buried the bird in it.[23]

"The slaughtered bird is *assur be-hana'ah*[24] [forbidden for any kind of use]. Therefore it must be buried, in case one forgets and

---

18. Mishnah *Nega'im* 14:1.

19. Mishnah *Nega'im* 14:1, *Tiferes Yisrael* #5; Rambam, *Hilchos Tum'as Tzara'as* 11:1.

20. Rambam, *Hilchos Berachos* 11:15 — heard from Rabbi Chayim Kanievsky *shlita*.

21. *Vayikra* 14:5.

22. Rambam, *Hilchos Tum'as Tzara'as* 11:1

23. Mishnah *Nega'im* 14:1.

24. *Kiddushin* 57a.

derives some benefit from it,"[25] Reb Shmuel explained to the children.

The Kohen took the piece of cedar wood, the *eizov* and the scarlet thread into his hand, wound part of the thread around the cedar wood and the bunch of *eizov*, and then added the living bird to them. He then dipped all four into the vessel that contained the spring water mixed with the blood of the slaughtered bird, and took them out. Then he sprinkled some of the mixture seven times on the back of Reb Yitzchak's hand,[26] whereupon he took the bird and carried it to town.

"The Kohen is going to town to release the bird," Reb Shmuel explained, "as it says in the verse, 'and then release the living bird toward the open field.'"[27]

"He could have released it here; why did he have to go to town?" Yechezkel was surprised.

"Concerning purification from *nega'im*, the verse says, 'He shall then release the living bird toward the outside of the city, toward the open field.'[28] From this we learn that the Kohen must stand in the city and release the bird from there toward the outside of the city.[29] We also learn that the bird must be released toward the open field, and not toward the sea or the desert."[30]

"Everything that concerns the purification of a *metzora* is highly symbolic and contains profound meaning," Reb Yitzchak told the children. "For instance, the two birds symbolize a man who has twittered too much,[31] and 'released' his tongue, like one

---

25. Mishnah *Nega'im* 14:1, Bartenura.
26. Mishnah *Nega'im* 14:1.
27. *Vayikra* 14:7.
28. *Vayikra* 14:53.
29. *Kiddushin* 57b.
30. Mishnah *Nega'im* 14:2.
31. *Arachin* 16b.

The Kohen sprinkled seven times on the back of Reb Yitzchak's hand

releases a bird. The cedar wood, the *eizov* and the scarlet wool thread (called *shni ha-tola'as*) are utilized in order to demonstrate that the *tzara'as* has been caused because of haughtiness: a haughty man's heart is as proud and high as a cedar tree. And how can he fix it? By humbling himself as low as an *eizov* branch and a worm (which is also called *tola'as*)."[32]

"But why must the bird be slaughtered specifically over an earthenware vessel?" Gamliel wanted to know.

"Our *Chachamim* have an explanation for this too. An earthenware vessel that becomes *tamei* can only be restored to purity by breaking it.[33] The same is true for a person whose fault is hating others for no reason — the main cause of *lashon ha-ra*. He can only rid himself of it by total repentance, which is as hard as breaking his body."[34]

Reb Yitzchak paused and then continued.

"One of the birds is slaughtered, while the other is released toward the outside of the city. This symbolizes the positive and negative aspects of speech.[35] Speech is a gift when it is used for Torah study and prayer, whereas it can be used improperly if one speaks *lashon ha-ra* and *rechilus*. Therefore, one of the birds is slaughtered as a symbol of our desire to 'slaughter' the evil aspect of speech and to refrain from it. We let the second bird live, to show that man can and must use his mouth for a good purpose.

"We dip the bird and the other three objects in spring water to show that through Torah study, which is life-giving like water,

---

32. *Vayikra* 14:4, Rashi.

33. *Shabbos* 84a.

34. *No'am Elimelech* (a Chassidic commentary on the Torah by Rabbi Elimelech of Lizhensk), *Parashas Metzora*.

35. *Keli Yakar, Vayikra* 14:4.

a person is able to rectify and purify himself of his sin, and see to it that he does not stumble again.

"In the end we release the bird toward and open field, to express to the *metzora* that if he repents properly and sincerely, his *tzara'as* will fly away from him and will never afflict him again.[36]

"And pay attention to this," Reb Yitzchak added. "If that bird returns to the purified *metzora* on the same day, it is a sign that his *tzara'as* will come back to him again in the future."[37]

"I have just thought of an interpretation of the act of releasing the bird," Bo'az said. "This bird is caught by man and kept in captivity.[38] Then it is released and freed to return to its friends and join them. This is exactly what happens to the *metzora*. He sits all alone, outside the city, until he is cured and he can return and live a normal life in human society."

The entire group was visibly impressed by Bo'az's clever remark.

The Kohen returned from town, and Reb Yitzchak warmly parted with the boys. Together with Reb Shmuel they returned to Yerushalayim, while the Kohen entered a small house together with Reb Yitzchak, to shave off his hair.

On their way back to Yerushalayim, Reb Shmuel explained, "Only after all the hair of the *metzora*'s entire body has been shaved off, and the *metzora* has immersed himself in the *mikveh*, will he be able to return home.[39] Also, the clothes which he wore during his period outside the city will have to be immersed in a *mikveh*.

---

36. *Midrash Tanchuma, Parashas Metzora.*

37. *Targum Yonasan, Vayikra* 14:7.

38. *Chizkuni, Vayikra* 14:7.

39. *Vayikra* 14:8–10.

"On the seventh day of his purity, he will shave off all his hair again, immerse himself and his clothes in the *mikveh*, and then fall into the category of a regular *tevul yom*. He will then be permitted to eat *ma'aser sheini* produce.[40] If the *metzora* is a Kohen, he'll be able to eat *terumah* when the stars come out in the evening. The next (eighth) day, the former *metzora* will offer the special *korbanos* he must bring. Then he will finally become absolutely *tahor*, and will be able to eat *kodashim*."

"I once heard something interesting," Alexander offered. "The medical experts claim that *tzara'as* is caused by sadness and depression, and in order to cure it, the afflicted person must engage in some joyous activity to improve his mood.[41] But we Jews, who live according to Torah, know that *tzara'as* is caused by *lashon ha-ra*, and the *metzora* who desires to be cured must seclude himself in a desolate place, outside the city area. According to the opinion of medical doctors, this will only intensify the *tzara'as*, but we know that only in this way, which leads to repentance, will the *nega* be cured."

---

40. Mishnah *Nega'im* 14:3.
41. *Ohr HaChayim, Vayikra* 14:2.

Chapter Seventeen

The Heichal and the Kodesh HaKodashim

A group of boys stood quietly in a corner of the *Ezras Yisrael*(4). These were, of course, the pupils of Reb Avraham's class. The day before, on the seventh day of their impurity, they were sprinkled with *mei niddah*, according to the requirements of halachah. Afterwards they immersed in the *mikveh*,[1] and toward evening they became entirely purified of their *tum'as meis*.

This morning, for the sake of their forthcoming visit to the *Azarah*, the children immersed again. Now they were finally standing in the *Ezras Yisrael*, after a long week during which they were forbidden to enter the Beis HaMikdash. The past week had not been boring at all, but the boys were anxiously and impatiently looking forward to returning to the *Azarah*.

The majestic building of the Beis HaMikdash towered over the surroundings in all its splendor before their very eyes. It was a hundred *amos* high[2] (about 164 feet or fifty meters) — as high as an eighteen-story building!

---

1. *Bemidbar* 19:19.
2. Mishnah *Middos* 4:6.

187

"The building of the Beis HaMikdash is divided into three large halls, one following the other,"[3] Reb Shmuel explained to his pupils. "The first hall is called the *Ulam*(10) (Antechamber), the second one is called the *Heichal*(11) (Sanctuary) or the *Kodesh* (Holy). The third one is known to us as *Kodesh HaKodashim*(12) (the Holy of Holies). Besides these halls, there are forty smaller rooms: thirty-eight *Ta'im*(69)[4] (Compartments) around the *Heichal* and the *Kodesh HaKodashim*, and two(68) on the sides of the *Ulam*.[5]

"The *Ulam*(10) is the first hall one encounters upon entering the building. It actually serves as the antechamber to the *Heichal*(11). Twelve Steps(22)[6] lead from the *Azarah*(6) to the Entrance to the *Ulam*(41). The gate of this entrance differs from the other gates in the Beis HaMikdash. All the other gates are twenty *amos* high and ten *amos* wide.[7] The Entrance to the *Ulam* is twice the size and four times the area: It is forty *amos* high and twenty *amos* wide. Another difference: all the entrances and gates of the Beis HaMikdash have doors, along with curtains; the Entrance to the *Ulam* has no doors. The *paroches* (curtain) hanging in the entrance also serves the purpose of a door,"[8] concluded Reb Shmuel as he pointed at the magnificent *paroches*.

"Wow, what a gigantic *paroches*!" Chananya expressed his awe. "Forty by twenty *amos*! Eight hundred square *amos*! Who can weave such a large *paroches*?"

"Well, the people working in *Lishkas HaParoches*(74) (Curtain

---

3. Mishnah *Middos* 4:7.

4. Mishnah *Middos* 4:3.

5. Mishnah *Middos* 4:7.

6. Mishnah *Middos* 3:6.

7. Mishnah *Middos* 2:3.

8. *Yoma* 54a.

The Ulam (Antechamber),
Heichal (Temple Chamber),
and Kodesh HaKodashim (Holy of Holies)

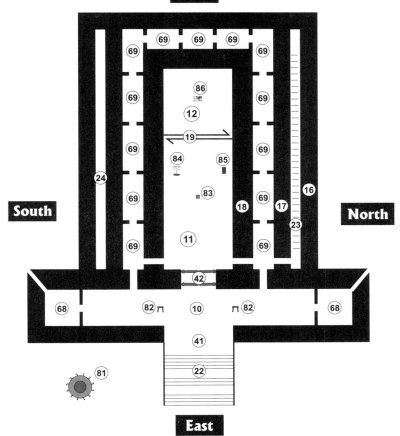

West

South

North

East

10. *Ulam*
11. *Heichal*
12. *Kodesh HaKodashim*
16. Wall of *Ulam*, Staircase, and Drainage Channel
17. Wall of Compartments (*Ta'im*)
18. Wall of *Heichal*
19. *Ama Teraksin* (two curtains and the passage between them that divided the Heichal from the *Kodesh HaKodashim*)
22. 12 Steps ascending to *Ulam*

23. Staircase
24. Drainage Channel
41. Entrance to *Ulam*
42. Entrance to *Heichal*
68. Knives Chamber
69. Compartments
81. *Kiyor* (Washing Basin)
82. Two Tables in *Ulam*
83. The Golden (Incense) Altar
84. Menorah
85. Showbread Table
86. *Ehven HaShesiyah* (Location of the Ark in the First Temple)

Chamber) are appointed to do this job.[9] The thirteen curtains needed for the different entrances are woven there."[10]

"And what does the *Ulam* itself contain?" one of the boys asked.

"Two Tables(82) are standing in the *Ulam*.[11] One of them is made of marble, and the new Showbread [*lechem ha-panim*] is put on top of it, before it is placed on the Table(85) inside the *Heichal*. The second Table in the *Ulam* holds the previous week's *lechem ha-panim* on it, after it has stood in the *Heichal* for a week. This Table is made of gold, and the *lechem ha-panim* is kept on it until it is distributed to the Kohanim. The two *leshachos* (chambers) on either side of the *Ulam* are called *Beis HaChalifos*(68)[12] (Knives Chamber).

The term *chalifos* surprised Alexander, and he wondered, "What? Another chamber for clothes? Didn't we learn that the *bigdei kehunah* are kept in *Lishkas Pinchas HaMalbish*(52)?" Alexander's mistake was understandable, as *chalifah* means a suit of clothing.

"The root of the word *chalifos*, in this sense, is *chalef* and not *chalifah*," Reb Shmuel replied. "Who knows, what *chalef* means in the language of Rome?"

"*Chalef* means knife,"[13] Yechezkel from Rome answered. The word was familiar to him.

"Good!" Reb Shmuel praised him. "The *shechitah* knives are kept in the *Beis HaChalifos*. There are many small compartments (*chalonos*) in the wall of the *Lishkah*, and each *mishmar* (division of

---

9. Mishnah *Middos* 1:1.

10. *Yoma* 54a.

11. Mishnah *Shekalim* 6:4.

12. Mishnah *Middos* 4:7.

13. Ibid., Bartenura.

priests) has its own *chalon*.[14] That's where each *mishmar* keeps the knives which it uses during the week of its service in the Beis Ha-Mikdash. Do you remember the story about Bilgah's *mishmeres*?"

"Ah, those were the ones who were punished by having their *shechitah* ring in the *Beis HaMitbechayim*(8) locked!" — Yonasan remembered.

"Correct, very good. Bilgah's *mishmeres* was also punished in the *Beis HaChalifos*. Their *chalon* was blocked off.[15]

"We learned that Yisraelim are forbidden to enter the *Ulam* and the *Heichal*,"[16] Reb Shmuel continued. "As a matter of fact, Kohanim are not allowed to enter it either, except when there is a need.[17] Because we won't be able to visit it, we'll have to content ourselves with a description only." The children were all ears.

"An Entrance(42) (*pesach*) separates the *Ulam* from the *Heichal*. It has four doors."[18]

"What? Four doors in one entrance?" Naftali wondered.

"Yes, indeed. Let us now figure out its width. The length[19] of the *Heichal* is forty *amos*, and its width — twenty *amos*. Its entrance is located in its width, right in the middle. Please, figure out the length of the part that remains over on each side, between the Entrance and the corner of the *Heichal*."

A thoughtful silence ensued. Then Binyamin raised his hand. He presented his answer well.

"There remain five *amos* on each side of the Entrance," Binyamin said. "It's as simple as this: The width of the *Heichal* is

---

14. Ibid., *Tiferes Yisrael* #72.
15. *Sukkah* 56a.
16. Mishnah *Keilim* 1:8.
17. *Menachos* 27b.
18. Mishnah *Middos* 4:1.
19. Mishnah *Middos* 4:7.

The Four Gates of the Heichal

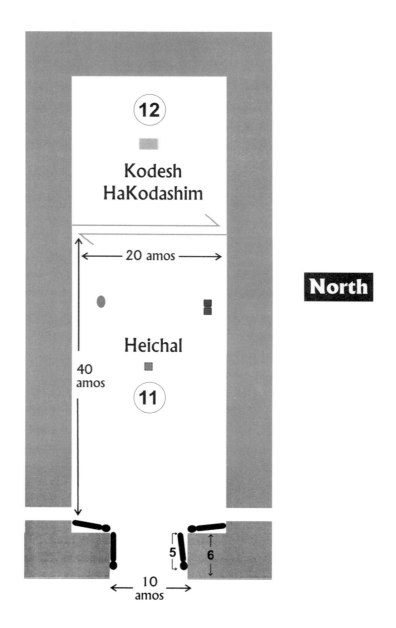

South

North

12

Kodesh
HaKodashim

20 amos

Heichal

40
amos

11

5

6

10
amos

twenty *amos*, and we learned that the width of the entrances of the Beis HaMikdash is ten *amos*[20] — which means that we remain with another ten *amos*. We then divide this in two, which gives us five *amos* on each side."

"Well done!" Reb Shmuel exclaimed, impressed by Binyamin's clear explanation. "And now listen to another detail: the Wall(18) of the *Heichal* is six *amos* thick.[21] Now, there are two doors in each regular gate, right?"

The boys nodded their heads.

"What is the width of each door of the Entrance to the *Heichal*(42)?"

"The width of the entrance is ten *amos*, so each door is five *amos* wide," Binyamin the mathematician answered on the spot. Both he and his friends were so engrossed in the lecture that they didn't notice the small crowd that had formed around them. People who passed through the *Ezras Yisrael*(4) stopped to listen to this special lecture.

Reb Shmuel also did not appear to notice the spectators, and continued. "Listen carefully. The first two doors were hung one *amah* deep into the interior of the six-*amah*- deep Entrance.[22] Then they proceeded further into the Entrance and hung another two doors at the very end of the Wall(18). Now tell me, how wide is the space between these two pairs of doors?"

"Five *amos*!" Also this time it was Binyamin who answered first. "Six *amos* minus one. As the *rebbi* just said, the first pair was hung one *amah* into the interior of the Entrance. So we have to subtract one *amah* from the six-*amah* total depth of the Entrance."

---

20. Mishnah *Middos* 2:3.
21. Mishnah *Middos* 4:7.
22. Mishnah *Middos* 4:1.

"Correct. Thus, when the first doors are opened inwards they completely cover the remaining five *amos* of the depth of the entrance. The second pair of doors also open inwards, turning 180 degrees, so that they also both completely cover the thickness of the wall of the *Heichal*."

The explanation made a very deep impression on the children.

"Didn't the *rebbi* say that the height of the building is one hundred *amos*?"[23] Bo'az asked.

"I did."

"And what is the height of the *Heichal*(11)?" Bo'az continued to ask.

"The height of the *Heichal* is forty *amos*. A second floor is built over it, which is called the *Aliyah*(70) (Attic). The *Aliyah*'s height is the same as the *Heichal*'s," Reb Shmuel concluded.

"Two times forty equals eighty. The height of the building is one hundred *amos*. What happened to the missing twenty *amos*?" Bo'az was confused.

Reb Shmuel, however, was not confused. "You remember the Twelve[24] Steps(22) leading from the *Ezras Kohanim*(6) to the Beis HaMikdash?" The boys nodded their heads. "Well, the height of each step is half an *amah* — in other words, six *amos* altogether. This is the foundation of the building. The roof of the *Heichal*, which is actually the floor of the *Aliyah*, is five *amos* thick, and so is the roof of the *Aliyah*.[25] So how many *amos* do we have so far?"

"Six plus five plus five — sixteen," the boys answered in chorus.

---

23. Mishnah *Middos* 4:6.
24. Mishnah *Middos* 3:6.
25. Mishnah *Middos* 4:6.

Measurements of the
Height of the Beis HaMikdash

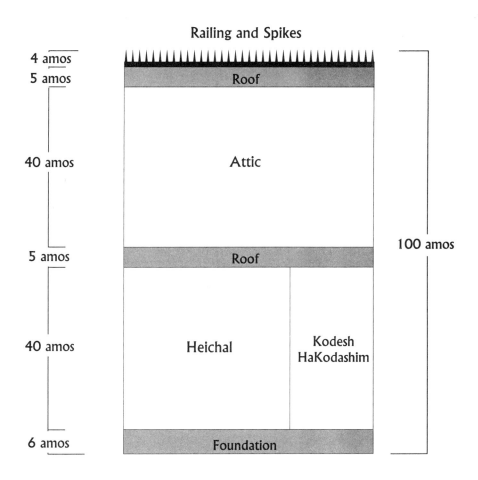

Railing and Spikes

4 amos

5 amos — Roof

40 amos — Attic

5 amos — Roof

40 amos — Heichal | Kodesh HaKodashim

6 amos — Foundation

100 amos

"The *ma'akeh* (railing) and the *kalya oreiv* make up another four *amos*. Thus we have come up with the height of one hundred *amos*," Reb Shmuel summed it up.

"What's a *kalya oreiv*?" Reuven asked.

"Spikes of iron, sharp as a knife, are fixed on the roof and *ma'akeh* of the Beis HaMikdash.[26] Their sharpness drives away birds from the roof. The word *kalya* comes from the root *kalah*, which means to finish or destroy, and *oreiv* means crow."

The boys lifted up their eyes toward the roof, trying to discern the *kalya oreiv*, but they couldn't because the building was too high.

"You'll be able to see it at a distance, when we walk farther away from here," Reb Shmuel promised. Then he continued. "The First Beis HaMikdash also had a *kalya oreiv*, but there was no need for it because the very holiness of the building prevented the birds from approaching.[27]

"And now let's get back to the description of the *Heichal*(11). The length of the *Heichal* is forty *amos*, and its width is twenty *amos*. Three holy objects are kept there: *Mizbach HaZahav*(83) [the Golden Altar], the Menorah(84), and the *Shulchan*(85) [the Showbread Table]. The Golden Altar is used to burn incense [*ketores*] on every day: in the morning and in the evening. The Menorah is used for lighting the seven lamps, and the *Shulchan* to place the *lechem ha-panim* on it, from Shabbos to Shabbos.[28] Do you know on which side of the *Heichal* the Menorah and the *Shulchan* are standing?"

"The Torah tells us, 'You shall place the Table on the outer side of the *paroches*, and the Menorah opposite the Table, on the

---

26. Ibid., *Tiferes Yisrael* #59, *Bo'az* #4.

27. *Arachin* 6a, Tosafos (ד"ה כגון).

28. *Shemos* 40:22–27.

south side of the Dwelling; you shall therefore place the Table on the north side,'" Yonasan quoted expertly.[29]

"Yes, exactly! Since the Menorah is standing in the south and the *Shulchan* in the north, our Sages said:[30] '*Ha-rotzeh she-yachkim—yadrim*'—He who desires to become wise shall move southwards; '*ve-she-ya'ashir—yatzpin*'—and if he wants to get rich—northwards. The Menorah, which symbolizes wisdom, is in the south, and the *Shulchan*, which symbolizes wealth, is in the north."

"What do *yatzpin* and *yadrim* really mean? Does it mean that such a person must settle either in the north or in the south?" Gamliel asked.

"No, it means that he should turn to the north or to the south when he prays."[31]

"What about a person who desires to be both wealthy and wise?" Reuven asked.

"Looks like wealth and wisdom don't go together," Chananya quipped. Yehoshua supported his remark: "Our Sages say, 'Not every person is privileged to two *Shulchanos* (tables).'[32] They meant that not everyone is privileged to attain both wisdom and wealth."

Suddenly, the boys were surprised to hear an unfamiliar voice of a grown-up, who entered into their conversation. It was one of the people who was standing next to them, and he made a pithy observation:

"There is a way to face both directions—through *anavah* (humility)![33] A person who is an *anav* thinks of himself as nothing.

---

29. *Shemos* 26:35.
30. *Bava Basra* 25b.
31. Ibid., Rashi.
32. *Berachos* 5b.
33. *Siach Sarfei Kodesh*, in the name of the Maggid of Mezritch.

It's as if he takes up no space. With such an attitude he is not bound by the laws of nature, and can face opposite directions at the same time!" The children smiled, pleased with such an original idea.

Reb Shmuel continued.

"Two Curtains(19) are hanging between the *Heichal*(11) and the *Kodesh HaKodashim*(12).[34] The outer one is folded open on the south side, and the inner one on the north side,[35] so as to make room for entering without exposing the *Kodesh HaKodashim*. There is a space of one *amah* between them. On Yom Kippur, the *Kohen Gadol* passes through this space on his way to enter the *Kodesh HaKodashim*.

"There weren't two Curtains in the First Beis HaMikdash,[36] but there was a wall that had an entrance in the middle.[37] There was a curtain hanging over the entrance, and the poles [*badim*] of the Ark protruded into it so that they were noticeable in the *Heichal*."

"Is the *rebbi* referring to the verse, 'They extended the poles so that the shape of the ends of the poles were seen from the Sanctuary, facing the Inner Sanctuary [*Dvir*], but the poles themselves were not seen on the outside'?"[38] Yonasan the Tanach expert quoted.

"Exactly!" Reb Shmuel confirmed, and continued. "During the final period of the First Beis HaMikdash, King Yoshiyahu hid the Ark,[39] and now only the *Ehven HaShesiyah*(86) (*Shesiyah*

---

34. *Yoma* 51b.

35. *Yoma* 52b.

36. *Yoma* 51b.

37. *Yoma* 54a, Rashi (ד"ה ויוצאין).

38. *I Melachim* 8:8.

39. *Yoma* 52b.

Stone) is behind the Curtain, within the *Kodesh HaKodashim*. The *Shesiyah* Stone, or Foundation Stone, rises three fingers above the surface of the earth.[40] It is from this stone that HaKadosh Baruch Hu began to create the world.[41]

"We forgot to describe the rooms that surround the *Heichal* and the *Kodesh HaKodashim*," Reb Shmuel remembered. "As I mentioned earlier, these thirty-eight rooms are called *Ta'im*(69) (Compartments). Fifteen are built on the north side on three levels, five *Ta'im* on each level. There are fifteen *Ta'im* on the southern side as well, and they are also arranged in the same way — on three levels, or stories. There are eight *Ta'im* on the west side — three on the first floor, three on the second, and two on the third. Now, who can tell me why there aren't any *Ta'im* on the east side?"

"The entrance to the *Heichal* is on the east side," Yehoshua said.

"The *Ulam* is on the east side," Bo'az added.

"Good, boys," Reb Shmuel praised them. "Now, are there any other questions?"

"Is there anything in the *Aliyah*(70) above the *Heichal* and *Kodesh HaKodashim*?" Yechezkel wondered.

"There is nothing there besides two Curtains separating the space of the *Aliyah* that is above the *Heichal* from the space that is above the *Kodesh HaKodashim*,"[42] Reb Shmuel answered.

"Does anyone enter the space that is above the *Kodesh HaKodashim*?" Chananya asked.

"Only Kohanim do, once every seven years, in order to check if there are any repairs to be done.[43] In this the *Aliyah* is more

---

40. *Yoma* 53b.

41. *Yoma* 54b.

42. *Yoma* 54a.

43. *Pesachim* 86a.

strict than the *Kodesh HaKodashim* itself! The *Kohen Gadol* enters the *Kodesh Hakodashim* once a year, on Yom Kippur, but the Kohanim enter the *Aliyah* that is above it only once every seven years!

"The book of *Melachim* relates the story of Asalyahu, the daughter of King Achav, who wanted to reign over the kingdom Yehudah. With this aim she murdered all the offspring of the House of David, and only Yo'ash, the baby, survived, because they had managed to smuggle him out.[44] Yonasan, please quote the verse that deals with this incident," Reb Shmuel requested.

Yonasan did not disappoint his *rebbi*: "Then Yehosheva, the daughter of King Yoram, the sister of Achazyahu, took Yo'ash... and stole him from among the king's sons, who were murdered, him and his nursemaid, into the bed chamber, and they hid him from Asalyahu, so that he was not murdered."

Reb Shmuel concluded, "Our Sages say that the bed chamber mentioned in the verse was actually the *Aliyah*.[45] That's where Yo'ash remained hidden for six years, until he was taken out of there and made king of Yehudah."

---

44. *II Melachim* 11:1–3.
45. Ibid., Rashi.

Chapter Eighteen

The Purification of the Metzora

S halom, dear children! How are you?" A strange-looking man addressed Naftali and his friends as they walked in the street.

The children looked at him in amazement. The man was completely bald, without even eyebrows or *payos*! "He looks like a real pumpkin,"[1] Naftali thought. The strange-looking man led three sheep along with him.

"Well, are you still careful to avoid speaking *lashon ha-ra* and *rechilus*, as you once took upon yourself?" the man asked in the tone of an old friend.

He sounded very familiar

"Oh, it's our friend Reb Yitzchak from *Har HaZeisim*!" Bo'az shouted excitedly.

"Right! It's him! It's Reb Yitzchak!" all the rest joined Bo'az in a chorus of greetings.

"Don't shout like that in the street," Reb Shmuel chided them. "How are you, Reb Yitzchak?"

"I'm on my way to the Beis HaMikdash," Reb Yitzchak answered. "Yesterday was the seventh day of my *taharah*, and the Kohen shaved off my hair for the second time. I immersed in the

---

1. *Sotah* 16a.

mikveh, and became a *tevul yom*. After the sun set, I became al-most entirely pure.[2] Now I am going to the Beis HaMikdash in order to complete the process of my purification."

Reb Yitzchak seemed to hesitate for a moment, and then of-fered, "Perhaps you want to accompany me? I feel I owe a signifi-cant part of my *taharah* to you. It could very well be that I became pure in the merit of delivering that *mussar* talk to you, as well as in the merit of the improvements in your behavior that you took upon yourselves following it."

Reb Shmuel willingly agreed. "Children, let's hurry and im-merse ourselves in the nearby *mikveh* before we enter the Beis HaMikdash," he said.

When the excited children and their *rebbi* returned, Reuven asked Reb Yitzchak, "Why didn't you have to immerse just now?"

"Because I will immerse in *Lishkas HaMetzora'im*(48)," Reb Yitzchak answered. "By the way, I have already immersed twice," he continued. "The first time was after I had my hair shaved off, as the verse says, 'The priest shall shave off all his hair, and he shall then bathe himself in ritual water and will thus become pure. After that he may enter the camp...,'[3] and the second time was yesterday, as the Torah says, 'Then, on the seventh day, the priest shall shave off all the person's hair — of his head, his beard and his eyebrows; he shall shave off all his hair. The person shall then wash his clothes and bathe his body in ritual water, and will thus become pure.'"[4]

They entered the Temple Mount through the Chuldah Gates(25) and turned to the right. They went all the way around the eastern

---

2. *Vayikra* 14:9, Rambam, *Hilchos Tum'as Tzara'as* 11:2.

3. *Vayikra* 14:8.

4. *Vayikra* 14:9.

The strange-looking man led three sheep along with him

side of the Beis HaMikdash, continuing past the Eastern Gate(29) and reaching the Pyre Hall(56) [*Beis HaMoked*] — which was located in the northern wall of the *Azarah*. They crossed the *Soreg*(14) and entered the *Cheil*(2). There they climbed the Twelve Steps(20) and reached the *Sha'ar Beis HaMoked*(32) [Pyre Hall Gate].

"Is Reb Yitzchak permitted to be here?" Gamliel whispered in Reb Shmuel's ear, so that Reb Yitzchak could not hear, "Didn't we learn that a *mechusar kippurim* is forbidden to enter the *Azarah* prior to bringing his offering?"[5]

Reb Shmuel answered back in a calming whisper, "Don't worry, Gamliel. The northern half of the Pyre Hall does not have the same sanctity as the *Azarah*.[6] Reb Yitzchak has to get to *Lishkas HaChosamos*(59) (Chamber of the Receipts, or Seals), which is located in a non-sacred area. There he has to purchase a receipt for oil, called a *chosam shel choteh* ['sinner receipt']."

While they were whispering, they saw Reb Yitzchak turn left and enter *Lishkas HaChosamos*, which was located in the north-eastern corner of the Pyre Hall.[7]

Reb Shmuel raised his voice and said to his pupils, "We can discuss *Lishkas HaChosamos* until Reb Yitzchak returns. Because some *korbanos* must be accompanied by *nesachim* (poured-offerings), which require different amounts of fine-quality wheat flour, oil and wine, there is a system for purchasing them. There are four types of receipts sold here: 'CALF,' 'RAM,' 'GOAT-KID' and 'SINNER,' each one representing a different type of *nesech*.[8] These receipts are pieces of parchment that attest that the bearer

---

5. Mishnah *Keilim* 1:8.

6. Mishnah *Middos* 1:6.

7. Ibid., Bartenura.

8. Mishnah *Shekalim* 5:3: "There were four seals in the Temple and on them were written CALF, RAM, GOAT-KID and SINNER."

paid for his *nesech*. A *metzora* has to buy a 'sinner receipt.' Reb Yitzchak will get his receipt in *Lishkas HaChosamos*, which is located in the Pyre Hall(56). He will then present it in order to get his *nesachim* — in *Lishkas HaShemanim*(49) [Oil Chamber], which is located in the *Ezras Nashim*(3)."

Chananya was shocked. "Reb Yitzchak's receipt will bear the inscription '*sinner*'?! Aren't we concerned about shaming him?"

"The honor of a person who sins with his tongue is not spared.[9] *Lashon ha-ra* is a grave sin, and the person who speaks it deserves to be called a sinner. On the contrary, it is preferable that such a person be publicly shamed, so that he may humble his heart and atone for his sin."

The children looked around and saw the four chambers(57)(58)(59)(60) located in the four corners of the *Beis Ha-Moked*(56).[10] They watched the big fire burning in the center and saw wide stone steps on the sides.[11]

"These are the steps that the Kohanim of the *mishmeros* sleep on at night. The old Kohanim sleep on the steps, and the young ones sleep on the floor," Reb Shmuel said in anticipation of their question.

Reb Shmuel noticed Naftali surveying the ends of beams sticking out from the upper part of the wall, about halfway into the room.[12] "These beams indicate the limits of the sacred area and the beginning of the non-sacred area," the *rebbi* explained.

Reb Yitzchak emerged from *Lishkas HaChosamos* with a flushed face. "Here's my receipt. I also had the privilege to hear some words of reproof from the Kohen," he added, still shaken by

---

9. Chafetz Chayim, *Shemiras HaLashon* II:16.
10. Mishnah *Middos* 1:6.
11. Mishnah *Tamid* 1:1.
12. Mishnah *Middos* 1:6.

the rebuke that he had received. "The Kohen said to me, 'The whole advantage a human being has over an animal is his gift of speech.[13] As long as a person uses this gift for good purposes, such as for learning Torah and praying, he retains his superiority over an animal. But as soon as he pollutes his mouth by forbidden talk, he deteriorates much lower than an animal, because his gift of speech is harmful whereas an animal's tongue is harmless.'"

The group left the Pyre Hall(56) for the *Ezras Nashim*(3). Once they got there, they went to its southwestern corner, where *Lishkas HaShemanim*(49) was.[14] Reb Yitzchak received fine-quality wheat flour [*soles*], oil and wine in exchange for his receipt: "...three-tenths [of an *eifah*] of fine-quality [wheat] flour mixed with oil [as] a meal-offering, and one *log* of [olive] oil."[15] These were to accompany the three *korbanos* which the *metzora* had to offer: one male sheep for a guilt-offering, one female sheep for a sin-offering, and another male sheep for a burnt-offering. Each *korban* was accompanied by a meal-offering of one-tenth of an *eifah* of *soles* mixed with a quarter of a *hin* (three *log*) of oil, and a poured-offering of a quarter of a *hin* of wine to pour onto the *Mizbeach*. Besides all this, one more *log* of oil was needed for the purification of the *metzora*.[16]

The Kohen in charge of *Lishkas HaShemanim* gave Reb Yitzchak some good advice: "Sometimes one Jew happens to hurt another Jew's feelings for no reason at all. As a result, the hurt Jew fumes inside, burning with a desire for revenge. He knows that the

---

13. Chafetz Chayim, *Shemiras HaLashon, Sha'ar HaZechirah*, chap. 3.

14. Mishnah *Middos* 2:5.

15. *Vayikra* 14:10.

16. *Vayikra* 14:10–20, *Menachos* 91a, Rambam, *Hilchos Ma'aseh HaKorbanos* 2:6.

The Path Taken by the Metzora

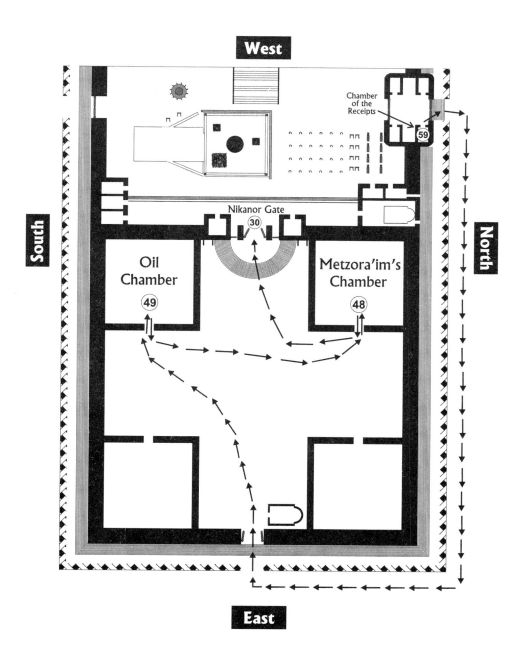

Torah prohibits revenge, but finds it extremely difficult to forgive his fellow, and each time he remembers his hurt ego, he feels like telling everybody about his fellow's evil behavior. How can he conquer his *yetzer ha-ra* (evil inclination)? There is a solution.

"Imagine a person walking quietly along his way. All of a sudden he knocks his own right foot against his left foot, trips, falls, and gets injured. Will it occur to him to hit his own left foot for the evil that it has caused him? Of course not! It's a part of his own body!

"This is precisely the way a Jew must treat his fellow Jew. All of Yisrael is but one soul divided into parts, just like a body consists of several parts. Just as a person never feels a desire to take revenge on a part of his own body that may have harmed him — because it would mean taking revenge upon himself — so must he be careful not to take revenge on his fellow Jew."[17]

They left *Lishkas HaShemanim*(49), and Reb Yitzchak turned to Reb Shmuel with a request. "Could you please keep an eye on the *nesachim* for me until I return? And you, children, please look after these three sheep. I have to go and immerse myself in the *mikveh* of *Lishkas HaMetzora'im*(48) that is located in the north-western corner.[18] I'll be right back."

"There is a difference of opinion about the reason for the *metzora*'s immersion today, because he already immersed yesterday," Reb Shmuel explained. "Some say it is because every person who comes to the Beis HaMikdash has an obligation to immerse.[19] Others argue that the reason for immersion is due to 'serach tum'ah' (being 'accustomed' to impurity).[20] We are afraid

---

17. Chafetz Chayim, *Shemiras HaLashon, Sha'ar HaTevunah*, chap. 6.

18. Mishnah *Middos* 2:5.

19. Mishnah *Middos* 2:4, *Tosfos Yom Tov*.

20. Rambam, *Hilchos Mechusarei Kippurim* 4:1.

that the *metzora* might have gotten used to being *tamei* during his period of impurity. Because of this, he might have been careless and accidentally become *tamei* again, even though he just immersed the day before."

When Reb Yitzchak returned, Yechezkel asked if he had been told more advice about avoiding *lashon ha-ra*.

"Yes," Reb Yitzchak replied with a smile, "and I really appreciated every single word of it. I just hope all my sins will be atoned for, and I'll never sin again!" he heaved a heartrending sigh. "From now on I'll be careful about every word that comes out of my mouth. I'll think very carefully before I speak!"

The children climbed the Fifteen Steps(21) ascending to Nikanor Gate(30). Reb Yitzchak stood in the entrance and asked the gate-keeper to call one of the Kohanim from the *Ezras Kohanim*(6) to come. He himself was forbidden to enter because he was still a *mechusar kippurim*.[21] Two Kohanim came promptly to Nikanor Gate.

"I have to bring a *korban Metzora*," Reb Yitzchak told them humbly.

"And who are these children?" One of the Kohanim wanted to know.

"They joined me because they wanted to watch the sacrificing of the offerings," Reb Yitzchak said.

"You are still very young," the Kohen told them, "but you must be very careful in avoiding the grave sin of *lashon ha-ra* already now, at your young age, because, as they say, habit becomes second nature.[22] If you don't get used to watching your speech properly, you'll find it very difficult to kick the bad habit of speaking *lashon ha-ra* when you grow up."

---

21. Mishnah *Keilim* 1:8.
22. Chafetz Chayim, *Hilchos Lashon HaRa* 9:5.

The children nodded their heads.

Reb Yitzchak dedicated one of the male sheep for the guilt-offering (*asham*). Both sheep were in their first year. The Kohen had Reb Yitzchak and his sacrificial animals stand facing west,[23] and took Reb Yitzchak's *asham* sheep and the *log* of oil. He then led the sheep to the *Azarah*, picked it up it together with the *log* of oil, and moved them up and down and sideways to each of the four directions.[24] This was in accordance with the verse, "The Kohen shall then take one of the male sheep and bring it near as a guilt-offering, with the *log* of oil, and wave them as a wave-offering before the Eternal."[25] Then he returned them to the entrance.

Reb Yitzchak put both his hands through the gate, into the area of the *Ezras Yisrael*(4), leaned them on the sheep's head with all his might, and confessed through bitter tears.[26] His brokenhearted cries and wailing motivated the children to solemnly promise to guard their mouths from *lashon ha-ra* — much more than a thousand words of rebuke would have done. After Reb Yitzchak had finished, the guilt-offering was taken to the north side of the gate — where *kodshei kodashim* could be slaughtered[27] — and was slaughtered there.

"The blood of the *asham* is received by two Kohanim," Reb Shmuel said.[28] "One Kohen receives the blood in a vessel, in order to splash it onto the *Mizbeach*, and the second receives some of the blood in his right palm."

---

23. *Vayikra* 14:11, *Sifra*.
24. Rambam, *Hilchos Mechusarei Kippurim* 4:2.
25. *Vayikra* 14:12.
26. Mishnah *Nega'im* 14:8.
27. Rambam, *Hilchos Beis HaBechirah* 5:16.
28. Mishnah *Nega'im* 14:8.

The Kohen with the vessel approached the *Mizbeach* and splashed the blood against it twice, one splash each against the northeast and southwest corners, according to the law of a guilt-offering — so that all four sides of the *Mizbeach* were daubed.[29] The second Kohen transferred the blood from his right palm into his left palm, and returned to the gate.[30] Reb Yitzchak stretched out his neck and stuck his head into the space of the *Ezras Yisrael*(4).[31] The Kohen dipped the finger of his right hand in the blood,[32] and put some of it on the middle part of Reb Yitzchak's right ear. Then Reb Yitzchak stretched out his hand, and the Kohen put some blood on the thumb of Reb Yitzchak's right hand, whereupon Reb Yitzchak stuck his right foot into the space of the *Ezras Yisrael* and the Kohen put some blood on his big toe.[33]

Reb Shmuel hurried to explain before the boys started asking questions. "The *metzora* is not allowed to enter the *Azarah* because he is a *mechusar kippurim*.[34] On the other hand, it is forbidden to take out the blood from the *Azarah* so that it won't become *pasul*. Therefore, the Kohen stands in the *Azarah* with the blood in his hand, while the person being purified stands outside, and only sticks in the necessary limbs."

Now the Kohanim took the female sheep of the sin-offering (*chatas*) and the male sheep of the burnt-offering (*olah*),[35] and brought them as sacrifices according to all the requirements of

---

29. *Zevachim* 54b.

30. Rambam, *Hilchos Mechusarei Kippurim* 4:2.

31. Mishnah *Nega'im* 14:9.

32. Rambam, *Hilchos Mechusarei Kippurim* 4:2.

33. *Vayikra* 14:14.

34. Mishnah *Nega'im* 14:9, Bartenura.

35. Rambam, *Hilchos Mechusarei Kippurim* 4:2.

The Kohen put some blood on Reb Yitzchak's thumb

halachah. Then they returned to the entrance again. One of them poured[36] some of the *log* of oil into the palm of another Kohen's left hand[37] and then dipped his right forefinger into the oil and sprinkled it toward the *Kodesh HaKodashim*(12).[38] This was repeated seven times; each sprinkling requiring another dip into the oil.[39] From the oil that was left in the palm of the other Kohen's left hand, the first Kohen put some on the the middle part of Reb Yitzchak's right ear, on the thumb of his right hand, and on the big toe of his right foot—right where the blood of the guilt-offering had been placed. The remainder of the oil he put on Reb Yitzchak's clean-shaven head.

Reb Shmuel explained, "The Kohen sprinkled the oil seven times toward the *Kodesh HaKodashim*, as a hint that he who sins with his evil tongue affects the most sacred spot in the world—the one which faces the Throne of Glory. Therefore, in his atonement, he needs to face the *Kodesh HaKodashim*.[40]

On their way back home, their minds full of the images they had seen, Reb Yitzchak told them, "Here's a thought that just came to me: The *metzora* sins with his head—that is to say, his brain—by treating other people with contempt, assuming himself to be wiser than they; therefore, the remainder of the oil is poured onto his head."[41]

When they reached the crossroads, they parted. Reb Yitzchak turned his steps toward his house. He was in a pensive mood, and softly repeated to himself, with feeling, all the way to his

---

36. *Vayikra* 14:15.
37. Mishnah *Nega'im* 14:10.
38. *Vayikra* 14:16–18.
39. Mishnah *Nega'im* 14:10.
40. Chafetz Chayim, *Shemiras HaLashon* 2:5.
41. Ibid., 2:16.

house, "Grant our hearts (i.e. our minds) to discern, each one of us, the virtues of our fellowmen, and not notice their flaws, and that each one of us should speak with his fellowman honestly, the way that pleases You."[42]

---

42. Supplication before prayer, composed by Rabbi Elimelech of Lizhensk.

Chapter Nineteen

A Very Special Festive Meal

O n Thursday afternoon the boys heard exciting news.

"This coming Friday night we're going to have our Shabbos meal at the house of our mutual friend, Reb Yitzchak, the former *metzora*," Reb Shmuel announced, with a flicker of amusement in his eyes. The children welcomed the announcement with exclamations of joy and excitement. They couldn't think of a more pleasant experience than spending a Shabbos in the company of the kindhearted Reb Yitzchak. Seeing their outburst of joy, Reb Shmuel thought to himself: "It's amazing how people can change. Until recently, Reb Yitzchak was loathed by everybody because of his arrogance. Nobody liked him. The *tzara'as* with which he was afflicted and the months spent outside the city seem to have changed him completely."

"It'll be interesting to see a luxurious house in Yerushalayim," Yechezkel said. "I saw magnificent houses in Rome, but I haven't yet had a chance to see any in Yerushalayim."

"It'll be much more interesting to participate in this meal, the likes of which you've never participated in before," commented Reb Shmuel.

"Why, is Reb Yitzchak going to treat us with roast ducks or fattened geese?" Alexander asked only half-seriously.

"It'll be a festive meal in honor of Pesach Sheini," Reb Shmuel replied.

215

"Oh, how could we forget?! This coming Friday is the 14th of Iyar, which is when the Pesach Sheini sacrifice is offered. It'll be eaten that night."

"Just a moment," Gamliel said, "but why does Reb Yitzchak have to eat the Pesach Sheini lamb?"

"When the regular *korban Pesach* was sacrificed in Nisan, Reb Yitzchak was a *metzora* and therefore forbidden to eat *kodashim*.[1] Didn't he tell us he'd spent months upon months on *Har HaZeisim*?" Yehoshua gave a logical answer.

"Wow, it sounds exciting," Chananya exclaimed. "Are we also going to partake of the *korban Pesach*?"

Reb Shmuel suppressed a smile. "What do you think, boys, are we going to partake of the *Pesach*?"

"How can we partake of the *Pesach* if we are not part of a *chavurah* [group]? We have to be members of a *chavurah* who sacrifice the *korban Pesach* together if we want to eat it," Bo'az replied. "The *Pesach* lamb is eaten only *li-menuyav* — by those registered for it!"[2]

"How about matzos? Can we eat matzos?" Naftali wondered.

"Oh yes, it's permitted to eat matzos the whole year, except for the day before Pesach,"[3] Reb Shmuel reassured him. "Tomorrow afternoon I'd like to take you to the Beis HaMikdash to see the offering of the Pesach Sheini sacrifice."

"Is the Pesach Sheini sacrifice also slaughtered in three shifts [*kitos*]?" Binyamin queried.

"Is Hallel recited?" Reuven added his own question.

"What a moving experience it was to hear the Hallel recited

---

1. Yevamos 74b.

2. *Zevachim* 56b.

3. Talmud Yerushalmi, *Pesachim* 10:1.

last month!" Chananya HaLevi reminisced.

"*B'ezras Hashem*, we'll be able to see everything tomorrow afternoon," Reb Shmuel said.

*   *   *

The next day the children, ready to witness the holy service, stood silently on the Wall of the *Azarah*(15), opposite the *Mizbeach*(7). Tens of thousands of people crowded the *Azarah* with their *korbenos Pesach*, male lambs in their first year.[4] The Leviyim sang the Friday psalm during the final stage of the offering of the afternoon *korban Tamid*.

"The Kohanim must hurry up today," Reb Shmuel said. "Time is short, and there's a lot of work to be done. It's Friday today, and everyone must hurry to roast the *Pesach* lambs before Shabbos, because the roasting of the *korban Pesach* does not override the prohibition to cook on Shabbos — not even the *Pesach* sacrificed in Nisan, not to mention Pesach Sheini."[5]

"How about *shechitah* when Pesach Sheini occurs on a Shabbos? Does it override the prohibition of slaughtering like the *shechitah* of the *korban Pesach*?" Reuven asked incisively.

"Yes, the *shechitah* of Pesach Sheini overrides (*docheh*) Shabbos,"[6] Reb Shmuel answered quickly.

"Do all these thousands of people belong only to the first shift?" Naftali wondered.

"The truth is that only the *korban Pesach* in Nisan is slaughtered in three shifts,[7] whereas the Pesach Sheini offering is not,"[8]

4. *Shemos* 12:5.
5. *Pesachim* 65b.
6. *Pesachim* 95a.
7. *Pesachim* 64a.
8. Tosefta, *Pesachim* 8:3.

Reb Shmuel replied. He continued by posing a question:

"Tell me, children, who are obligated to offer the Pesach Sheini sacrifice?"

"Those who were far from Yerushalayim and did not manage to reach it on time for the regular Nisan offering, and also someone who was *tamei*. This is what the Torah says: 'If any man is impure... or is on a journey of some distance... he shall carry out the service of the *Pesach*-sacrifice for the Eternal... in the second month, on the fourteenth day of the month, in the afternoon,'"[9] Yonasan answered immediately.

"There are other cases," Reb Shmuel said. "Sick people who could not offer the *korban Pesach*, or prisoners, or people who were prevented by other factors[10]—even those who had not offered the regular *korban Pesach* deliberately.[11] All these can offer their *korban Pesach* on the 14th of Iyar."

Reuven summed it up: "If I understand correctly, anybody who has not offered the *korban Pesach* in Nisan can do it in Iyar. So then why does the Torah mention only those who are on a journey of some distance or are impure?"

"The two cases mentioned in the Torah are unique," Reb Shmuel explained. "You see, there are three categories of people who did not bring the Pesach Sheini sacrifice. The first category consists of people who deliberately did not offer in Nisan, and failed to do so in Iyar—even inadvertently. Nevertheless, their deliberate sin in Nisan makes them liable for the *kares* punishment. The second category comprises those who failed to offer the *korban Pesach* inadvertantly in Nisan. If in Iyar they fail to bring—also by accident—they are exempt from *kares*. However,

9. *Bemidbar* 9:10–11.

10. Rambam, *Hilchos Korban Pesach* 5:1.

11. *Pesachim* 92b, Rambam, *Hilchos Korban Pesach* 5:2.

if they deliberately didn't offer the *korban Pesach* in Iyar, they are liable for *kares*. The two cases mentioned in the Torah make up the third category. If a person did not bring the *korban Pesach* in Nisan due to his being *tamei* or having been too far away, he is exempt from *kares* even if he failed to offer the *korban* in Iyar deliberately.[12]

"How far is 'too far away'?" Alexander asked.

"The verse says,[13] 'On a journey of some distance,' which our Sages say means being at least fifteen *mil*[14] away from the *Azarah* on the 14th of Nisan at sunrise.[15] In such a case, it becomes impossible to reach the Beis HaMikdash on foot by the time they start to slaughter the *korban Pesach*."

The Leviyim finished their singing with the verse, "Your testimonies are most trustworthy, concerning Your House, the Holy Dwelling, O Eternal, for a length of days."[16] After a short pause they began to recite Hallel, and the magnificent sight of the offering of the *korban Pesach* immediately riveted the boys' attention.

They were already well versed in the *halachos* of the *korban Pesach*, as they had all offered it a month before. This extremely moving experience was still very vivid in Naftali's memory. He could still see himself standing next to his father in the *Azarah*, squeezed among millions of Jews. The recitation of Hallel thundered in the air, capturing the souls of the *olei regel* and stirring up their most sacred emotions. Naftali remembered how he had joined the singing with every fiber of his being, thanking HaKadosh Baruch Hu

---

12. Rambam, *Hilchos Korban Pesach* 5:2.

13. *Bemidbar* 9:10.

14. Approximately nine and a half miles, or about sixteen kilometers.

15. *Pesachim* 93b, Rambam, *Hilchos Korban Pesach* 5:9.

16. *Tehillim* 93:5.

for all His boundless acts of loving-kindness.[17]

When the sacrificing was finished, the *Azarah* emptied out quickly. It was Erev Shabbos, and the people hurried to roast their *korbenos Pesach*. The boys descended from the Wall(15) and marched off to the house to get ready for the holy Shabbos.

*   *   *

The wealthy Reb Yitzchak's servants stood at the entrance of his house and they welcomed the children affably. These formerly unfriendly servants also had been compelled to change their attitude following the affliction that had affected their master. After he had returned from *Har HaZeisim* he announced determinedly, "Starting from today, *no lashon ha-ra is to be spoken* in my house. We must judge every person favorably, speak nicely to everybody and avoid hurting anybody's feelings!" The servants complied with the new decrees; at first it was out of lack of choice, but afterwards they began to do so willingly, and the entire atmosphere of the house changed completely.

The children walked along the lengthy vestibule on the thick soft carpets that covered the floors. Exquisitely dressed servants were everywhere. The children stopped at the entrance to the banquet hall, astounded by what they saw. Long tables were being arranged in the magnificent room. There were fifteen members in Reb Yitzchak's *chavurah*. Among them was a man who was completely bald like Reb Yitzchak. The boys understood that he was also a former *metzora* who had been unable to sacrifice the *korban Pesach* in Nisan.

Alexander observed the participants, and all of a sudden he exclaimed, "Hey, look, it's Yoel! He's from Tzippori just like me!"

---

17. For more about Naftali's experiences in the Beis HaMikdash during the month of Nisan, see *Three Special Days* (Jerusalem: Feldheim Publishers, 2003).

Yoel noticed Alexander and greeted him. After they had exchanged a few words, Yoel told Alexander, "I was on my way to Yerushalayim on Erev Pesach. In the middle of the journey, my horse suddenly collapsed and died. He must have been overtired from the long trip. I reached the *Azarah* after sunset."

Naftali was surprised that there were only fifteen people in Reb Yitzchak's *chavurah*, because he remembered that his own *chavurah* on Pesach had numbered more than thirty people. He asked Reb Shmuel about it.

"Last month you offered the special *korban Chagigah* brought on the 14th of Nisan, right?" Reb Shmuel began with a question that sounded like a statement. Naftali nodded.

"Well, the *korban Pesach* must be eaten on a full stomach. Because you brought the *korban Chagigah* also, this helped satiate everyone so that you could have many people in your *chavurah*.[18] On Pesach Sheini, however, the *korban Chagigah* is not offered,[19] so the people fill up on the *korban Pesach* itself. Therefore, the *chavuros* must be smaller," Reb Shmuel explained.

The children sat quietly, watching what was going on at the second table.

The members of the *chavurah* made Kiddush over wine according to the regular Friday night version. Then they washed their hands and ate matzah, *maror* (bitter herbs) and the *korban Pesach*, as the halachah prescribes.[20]

"I see that you don't read the Haggadah on Pesach Sheini,"[21] Naftali observed.

---

18. *Pesachim* 70a.

19. Tosefta, *Pesachim* 8:3.

20. *Bemidbar* 9:11: "They shall carry out [its service] in the second month on the fourteenth day [of the month] in the afternoon; they shall eat it with *matzos* and bitter herbs."

21. Sefas Emes, *Pesachim* 95a.

The *chametz challos* and the *matzos* were lying on the same table, in startling contrast to each other. Reb Shmuel explained to the boys that the prohibition of owning *chametz* on Pesach in Nisan[22] does not apply to Pesach Sheini, and anything leavened as well as sourdough may be seen in one's domain.[23] In fact, the members of the *chavurah* are allowed to eat *chametz* right after the matzah![24]

"The general rule is that every halachah that applies directly to the *korban Pesach* itself must be observed on Pesach Sheini as well. For instance, the prohibition of breaking any of its bones and the commandment to eat it with *matzos* and *maror* apply to Pesach Sheini. However, other *halachos*, such as the prohibition against owning *chametz* when the *Pesach* is slaughtered or eaten, do not apply on Pesach Sheini," Reb Shmuel explained.

"Why don't the members of the *chavurah* recite Hallel?" Bo'az asked.

"The verse says, 'You shall have a song [of praise to sing to Hashem, just] like on the night [when the Pesach] Festival was sanctified.'[25] Our Sages elucidated this verse in the following way: On the night sanctified as a Festival (i.e. the Festival of Pesach) Hallel must be recited, and on the night not sanctified as a Festival (i.e. the 15th of Iyar) Hallel does not need to be recited,"[26] Reb Shmuel replied.

"If so, why is Hallel recited during the offering of the Pesach Sheini sacrifice, on the 14th of Iyar?

"Good question! There are two answers. The first one is that

---

22. *Shemos* 13:7.

23. *Pesachim* 95a.

24. *Sukkah* 47b, Rashi (ד"ה ופנית בבקר).

25. *Yeshayahu* 30:29.

26. *Pesachim* 95b.

the verse relates to the night and not to the day, so that during the offering of the *korban Pesach* — which is carried out during the daytime — Hallel is not limited and is indeed recited. The second answer is —" at this point Reb Shmuel felt a wave of emotion and inspiration — "how is it possible *not* to recite Hallel when Yisrael bring their *Pesachim*?! The Hallel bursts out all by itself then!"

Chapter Twenty

The Children Who
Grew Up on the Rock

During the late morning hours the next Wednesday, excitement was in the air as everyone got ready to leave the classroom. They were going to see the children who grew up on the rock, and then walk down to *Ma'ayan HaShilo'ach* [the Spring of Shilo'ach].

Reb Shmuel gave them the last few explanations before they left.

"The Kohen who takes care of the burning of the *Parah Adumah* leaves his family a week before the ritual. Our Sages learn this by interpreting a verse from the Torah[1] and coming to the following conclusion: Just as during the building of the *Mishkan* (Tabernacle), Aharon and his sons left their houses and spent seven days in the Courtyard of the *Ohel Mo'ed*,[2] so, too, must there be a seven-day separation by both the Kohen who performs the burning of the red cow and the *Kohen Gadol* who per-

---

1. *Vayikra* 8:34: "Just as [I have] done today, so the Eternal has commanded [me] to do [for seven days], to make an atonement for you."
2. *Vayikra* 8:33–36.

forms the Yom Kippur service.[3]

During the week prior to the burning of the cow, the Kohen sits in *Lishkas Beis HaEhven*(43) [Stone Chamber],[4] at the northeast corner of *Har HaBayis*. This chamber was given such a name because it does not contain any vessels that can become *tamei*. It only contains stone vessels or vessels made from earth and not hardened in an oven, which are always *tahor*.[5] This is in order for the Kohen to achieve a high state of purity. He has to stay *tahor* until the time of the burning, and because it is feared that he might have become *tamei* from a dead body in the past,[6] he is sprinkled six times with the ashes of the *Parah Adumah* during that seven-day period.[7] Thus, even if he did become *tamei*, he will be purified on the third and the seventh day of his separation period."

"Must he be sprinkled six times? Isn't twice enough — on the third and the seventh days?" Yechezkel wondered.

"Remember what we learned on *Har HaZeisim*, boys? In matters dealing with the burning of the *Parah Adumah* we observe as many *chumros* as possible,[8] because causing the Kohen to become *tamei* before the burning of the cow is a big leniency (*kulah*). As we learned, on the day of the burning we cause the Kohen to become *tamei*,[9] whereupon he immerses himself in a *mikveh*. This is done in order to publicize our rejection of the heretical view of the Tzedokim, who claim that a *tevul yom* is forbidden to burn the cow," Reb Shmuel reminded his students.

---

3. *Yoma* 2a.

4. Mishnah *Parah* 3:1.

5. Mishnah *Keilim* 10:1.

6. *Yoma* 43b.

7. Mishnah *Parah* 3:1, Bartenura.

8. Rambam, *Hilchos Parah Adumah* 2:4.

9. Mishnah *Parah* 3:7.

"So why is he sprinkled six times, and not seven?"

"Because he needs to be sprinkled on every day of his separation except the fourth day. It's very simple. If the Kohen became a *temei meis* three or more days before he left his house, then the first day of his seven-day period of seclusion will actually be at least the third day of his state of impurity. Then he will also need to be sprinkled on the fifth day of his seclusion — which would be the seventh day of his impurity.

"If the Kohen became *tamei* two days before seclusion, then if we sprinkle him on the second and sixth days of his separation period, he will become *tahor*. If he became *tamei* one day before seclusion, then we purify him by sprinkling him on the third and seventh days of his seclusion. The Kohen certainly did not become *tamei* on his first day of seclusion, in *Lishkas Beis HaEhven*, so there is nothing to gain by sprinkling him on the fourth day.[10]

"As a result, the Kohen leaves his house on a Wednesday so that the fourth day of his separation period may occur on Shabbos,[11] when the sprinkling of *mei chatas* is forbidden.[12] Therefore, the day of the burning of the cow will also occur on a Wednesday."

Reb Shmuel added the following: "Another *chumrah* our Sages instituted was that each of the six different sprinklings were performed with the ashes of a different *Parah Adumah*.[13] You see, each time a red cow was burned, part of its ashes was not used by the general public but was set aside.[14] That's how the Beis HaMikdash ended up today with eight jars of ash that remained

---

10. Rambam, *Hilchos Parah Adumah* 2:4

11. Ibid., 2:5.

12. *Pesachim* 65b.

13. Mishnah *Parah* 3:1.

14. Mishnah *Parah* 3:11.

over from the eight cows that have been burned up until now.

"The person who sprinkles the Kohen during the six days has to be *tahor*,[15] because if he is *tamei*, the sprinkling will not purify the Kohen at all. In order to be perfectly sure that the person who sprinkles is *tahor*, another *chumrah* is practiced: children who have never become *tamei* are used for this purpose."[16]

"Why can't they use a man who was purified on the third and the seventh days?" Chananya asked.

"Because it's very possible that the person who sprinkled *him* was not *tahor*!" Yehoshua gave a brilliant answer.

"Wonderful!" Reb Shmuel praised him generously.

"Concerning other cases of *tum'as meis*, we always rely on the *taharah* of the one who is doing the sprinkling. But with the *Parah Adumah*, the Sages thought it necessary to be as stringent as possible."

*   *   *

"Look," Reb Shmuel cried, "these special children are raised in these houses."

The children inspected the place with great interest. They saw a number of houses built on a big rock surrounded by a high stone fence.

"The children are born here," Reb Shmuel said, "and they grow up here until they turn eight. This rock on which the houses are built is located above a hollow site, which protects the young dwellers of the houses from *tum'ah* by blocking the *tum'ah* of dead bodies that may be buried beneath them. The children live in this pure place."[17]

---

15. *Bemidbar* 19:18.
16. Rambam, *Hilchos Parah Adumah* 2:7.
17. Mishnah *Parah* 3:2.

"Do they live here alone? Who is taking care of them? Who cooks for them? Who teaches them Torah?" The boys asked sympathetically.

"They have a special *melamed* who teaches them. It's even possible to come and visit them. Even if the *melamed* or the visitors are *teme'ei meisim* and accidentally touch them, the children can become *tahor* from such *tum'ah* by the evening.[18] Purification from such *tum'ah* does not require the ashes of the *Parah Adumah*; it is enough for them to immerse themselves in a *mikveh* and wait for nightfall. However, no metallic utensils ever enter the house, because if they came into contact with a *meis*, their *tum'ah* is similar to that of the dead body itself!"[19]

The group waited outside for a short while, and suddenly the gate of the courtyard opened and little children passed through it, sitting on doors that had been placed on oxen.[20] Strong Kohanim led the oxen toward *Ma'ayan HaShilo'ach*. The group of curious pupils joined the procession. The oxen marched slowly into the spring. Then they stopped and the children dismounted from the oxen with stone cups in their hands. The water was quite shallow, reaching up to their knees. They filled the cups with cool spring water. Then they mounted the oxen, and the procession turned toward *Har HaBayis*.

Naftali and his friends followed in back of the children, listening to their *rebbi's* words.

"There's no way the children can become *tamei* while riding the oxen. The broad bellies of the oxen,[21] and also the doors, separate the children from the ground, so that even if there is a

---

18. *Bava Kamma* 2b.
19. Mishnah *Ohalos* 1:3.
20. Mishnah *Parah* 3:2.
21. Ibid., Bartenura.

The children sitting on the oxen looked around with great interest

tum'ah on the way it does not affect them. The *tum'ah* is blocked from rising and making the children *tamei*.[22] The children never dismount from the oxen while riding on them, and it is only after the oxen have walked into the Spring of Shilo'ach that they dismount. There can certainly be no dead bodies buried in the spring, because nobody buries the dead in a river."[23]

The children riding on the oxen looked around with great interest because they had never seen a street in Yerushalayim before. The curious glances of the passers-by caused them great pleasure.

"They really deserve their pleasure," Naftali thought to himself. "They sacrifice several years of their lives living like prisoners, just for the sake of fulfilling our Sages' *chumrah*."

After the children had reached *Har HaBayis*(1) they dismounted from the oxen.[24] They could not become *tamei* on the Temple Mount from some unknown grave below, because the whole of it is located on a hollow site. There was a little jug full of the ashes of the *Parah Adumah* standing next to the entrance of the *Ezras Nashim*(29). The children took some of it and mixed it with the water in their cups.[25] Then one of them took a bunch of *eizov* into his little hands, dipped it in the water and sprinkled the *Kohen Gadol* with it.

"Take a good look at the *eifer ha-parah* (ash of the cow)," Reb Shmuel said. "I heard from one of the Kohanim that nowadays they still use the *eifer ha-parah* that was prepared by Elazar Ha-Kohen in the days of Moshe Rabbeinu — about thirteen hundred years ago."

---

22. Ibid., *Tosfos Yom Tov*.
23. Ibid., Bartenura.
24. Mishnah *Parah* 3:3.
25. Rambam, *Hilchos Parah Adumah* 2:7.

They watched the *Kohen Gadol* return to *Lishkas Beis Ha-Ehven*(43). In the ensuing silence, Reuven came up with an insightful and challenging question.

"We learned that a *Kohen Gadol* has two chambers where he is separated from his home: *Lishkas Parhedrin*(54), where he is sequestered for seven days before Yom Kippur,[26] and *Lishkas Beis HaEhven*, where he is sitting at the moment before the burning of the *Parah Adumah*. What's the need for two chambers? Isn't *Lishkas Beis HaEven* enough?"[27]

"I have just thought of a possible answer," Yechezkel declared. "The service of Yom Kippur is performed inside the *Azarah*. Therefore before Yom Kippur, the *Kohen Gadol* sits in *Lishkas Parhedrin*, which is open to the *Azarah*. However, prior to the burning of the *Parah Adumah*, which is done outside, on *Har HaZeisim*, the *Kohen Gadol* sits in the *Lishkas Beis HaEhven*, which is outside of the *Azarah* on *Har HaBayis*(1), a site of lesser holiness."

"Excellent!" Reb Shmuel exclaimed, "Who has more ideas on the subject?"

"This chamber is called *Beis HaEhven*," Alexander said, "because only stone utensils are used there in order to observe as many *chumros* as possible. If the *Kohen Gadol* sits here before Yom Kippur as well, there'll be less publicity of the *chumros* enacted by our Sages."

"Wonderful!" Reb Shmuel marveled. "Both answers are beautiful!"

Bo'az added, "Perhaps the reason why *Lishkas Parhedrin* is also called *Lishkas HaEitzim*[28] is because we want to distinguish

---

26. *Yoma* 2a.

27. Ibid., Tosafos (ד"ה ומאי שנא).

28. Mishnah *Middos* 5:4.

between the two chambers.[29] As we know, the word *eitz* can mean either "tree" or "wood." *Lishkas Beis HaEhven* contains stone vessels only, whereas in *Lishkas Parhedrin*(54) there is no obligation to use only stone vessels. Therefore it's also called *Lishkas HaEitzim* — a hint that also wooden vessels can be used there."

---

29. Ibid., *Tosfos Yom Tov*.

Chapter Twenty-One

The Burning of the Parah Adumah

A week later, the ten excited pupils of the study group walked in the crowd of thousands of people who were on the way out of the city, turning their steps toward *Har HaZeisim*. The sponsor of the group, Reb Avraham, had arrived in Yerushalayim the day before together with a delegation of venerable elders from Tiveriah. Jews streamed to Yerushalayim from all over the land to participate in the ceremony.

The news about the Tzedokim's sinister conspiracy shocked the faithful Jews who followed the path of Torah. They were determined to sanctify Hashem's Name publicly by demonstrating their derision and mounting anger toward the heretic Tzedokim. The wickedness and arrogance of the Tzedokim seemed to know no bounds. They had the nerve to try to cause the *Kohen Gadol* and his assistants who took care of the *Parah Adumah* to become *tamei*! What a vicious sect they were! Jews came to watch the burning of the *Parah Adumah* in order to prove that the heretics' plot to undermine the interpretation of the Torah, according to the Oral Tradition, was to no avail.

The mountain was a sea of people. Crowds of excited Jews waited impatiently. Thanks to Reb Avraham, who was held in high esteem, the boys and their teacher were privileged to watch the ceremony from a perfect spot, standing right behind the Elders of Yisrael. These venerable members of the Sanhedrin usually traveled in wagons, but this time they walked all the way to *Har HaZeisim* to demonstrate their love of this mitzvah.[1] Reb Yitzchak, the former *metzora*, whom Heaven merited to inform the *Beis Din* about the plot of the Tzedokim, was standing right next to them, beaming with undisguised joy.

From the bits of conversation that the boys overheard they understood that Chanan, the leader of the Tzedokim, had fled the city together with his clique of friends, as soon as their disgraceful scheme became public. But many of the Tzedokim had decided to return to the tradition of the Sages: transmitted from Mount Sinai, and passed down through every generation, to our time.

The Tzedokim who remained dedicated to their fallacy preferred to hide in their homes, rather than show their faces in public on a day when the *Chachamim* performed a special act that denounced and rejected the false views of the heretics.

The boys stood waiting for the appearance of the *Kohen Gadol* leading the *Parah Adumah* through Shushan Gate(26).[2] In the meantime they enjoyed availing themselves of Reb Shmuel's wisdom.

"I heard that the *Kohen Gadol* will be burning the *Parah Adumah*," Yonasan said. "Didn't you tell us that any Kohen can do it?"

"That's true. The Torah says, 'You shall give it to Elazar the Priest,'[3] which our Sages elucidate as follows: 'It' had to be given to Elazar,[4] who was a deputy (*segan*) *Kohen Gadol*, but the cows that were burned after it didn't have to be burned specifically by the *segan*.

---

1. Mishnah *Parah* 3:7, *Tosfos Yom Tov.*

2. Mishnah *Middos* 1:3.

3. *Bemidbar* 19:3.

4. *Yoma* 42b.

"The burning of the red cow is perfectly kosher if carried out by either a common priest [*kohen hedyot*] or the *Kohen Gadol*,"[5] Reb Shmuel continued. "However, because this mitzvah is so important and so dearly cherished, it became customary to honor the *Kohen Gadol* with this special privilege,[6] because he is holier than the other Kohanim."[7]

"Is the *Kohen Gadol* going to wear his eight garments?" Chananya HaLevi asked hopefully.

"Sorry to disappoint you, but he'll wear only four garments," answered his teacher.[8] "This is learned by means of a *gezerah shavah*[9] (an analogy between two laws established on the basis of identical expressions in the text of the Torah). The Torah says about the *Parah Adumah*: 'This shall be for the Children of Yisrael and for the proselytes who live among them as an everlasting statute [*chukkas olam*].'[10] The Torah uses the same expression about the Yom Kippur service: 'This shall be for you as an everlasting statute [*chukkas olam*], to make atonement for the Children of Yisrael.'[11] Just as the service of Yom Kippur is carried out by the *Kohen Gadol* dressed in four garments, so is the burning of the *Parah Adumah* carried out by the *Kohen Gadol* wearing four garments."

"So when is the cow finally going to come out through the gate?" Yehoshua burst out impatiently, turning his eyes longingly toward the gate.

"It looks like they want to finish sacrificing the *Tamid shel*

---

5. Rambam, *Hilchos Parah Adumah* 1:11.

6. Mishnah *Parah* 3:8, Rambam.

7. Mishnah *Parah* 3:8, *Tiferes Yisrael*.

8. Mishnah *Parah* 4:1.

9. Ibid., Bartenura.

10. *Bemidbar* 19:10.

11. *Vayikra* 16:34.

shachar first," Binyamin suggested.

"Even after they come out of Shushan Gate, it may take them a long time to reach the spot where the burning is supposed to take place," Reb Avraham said.

"But why? It shouldn't take them more than about a quarter of an hour to walk there, should it?" queried Naftali.

"What do you think they'll do if the cow decides to take its time and walk there slowly, or decides to stop and rest for a while?" Reb Shmuel replied with a question.

"And it's impossible to put a harness on it and pull it, because the Torah says, '…a completely red cow that has no blemish on it, nor was any burden ever upon it,'"[12] Yonasan remarked.

"So what do they do if the cow doesn't want to come out?"

"I've got an idea," Reuven suggested on the basis of his village-life experience. "Once I wanted to take a stubborn cow out of the barn and it wouldn't budge, so my father took another cow out, and the stubborn one joined it. Perhaps it's possible to do the same in this case, if need be."

"Your father certainly acted wisely," Reb Avraham intejected, "but it is forbidden to do this in the case of a *Parah Adumah*."

"Why?" the children wondered.

"If a cow of a different color is taken out together with the red one, people may later mistakenly assume that the non-red cow has been slaughtered."[13]

"So what do they do if the cow gets stubborn and refuses to move?" Gamliel piped up.

"It ought to *run* along the ramp, if you ask me," Alexander interrupted excitedly. "Just think of the great *zechus* it has! Millions of Jews are going to be purified of their *tum'ah* by means

---

12. *Bemidbar* 19:2.
13. Mishnah *Parah* 3:7.

of its ashes! Ought not the cow sing and dance all the way to the slaughterhouse?"

"You expect the cow to sing?" Chananya chuckled.

"You'll be surprised to hear that once upon a time there were cows that sang. Who knows when that was?" Reb Avraham asked smilingly.

Nobody answered.

"Try to remember what it says in Tanach about the cows that brought back the Ark of God from the Pelishtim's land."

"And the cows went straight ('*Vayisharna*') along the way, on the road to Beis Shemesh, walking on the highway,"[14] Yonasan quoted.

"Exactly! Our Sages elucidate the verse, saying that the cows that brought the Ark turned their faces to the *Aron* and started singing.[15] The word *Vayisharna* can be understood as 'singing.'"

"Which song did they sing?" Naftali wondered.

"Our Sages' opinions differ on this issue,"[16] Reb Shmuel answered. "But according to one opinion, the cows sang eighteen verses from *Divrei HaYamim*,[17] starting with the passage, 'Offer thanks to the Eternal, declare His Name; make His deeds known among the nations.'"[18]

"Once there was an animal that was endowed with intelligence," Reb Avraham related to his attentive young audience. "It refused to come forward when they wanted to use it for a sinful act. During the bitter dispute between the prophet Eliyahu and the prophets of the idol Ba'al that took place on Mount

---

14. *I Shemuel* 6:12.
15. *Avodah Zarah* 24b.
16. Ibid.
17. *I Divrei HaYamim* 16:35, Rashi.
18. *I Divrei HaYamim* 16:8–36.

Carmel,[19] it was decided that each rival party would erect an altar and offer a bullock on it as a burnt-offering. The party upon whose altar the heavenly fire descended and consumed the sacrifice offered on it, would be considered the bearer of truth and favored by God.

"The prophets of Ba'al chose a bullock for their sacrifice, but the bullock refused to move.[20] They tried to pull it forcefully, but it wouldn't budge. Then the bullock opened its mouth and said to Eliyahu: 'The bullock you have chosen and I grew up together, and we fed from the same trough. Why must my lot be worse than his? Why must he ascend to Heaven as a burnt-offering to Hashem, thereby sanctifying His Name, while I must comply with the will of the prophets of Ba'al and vex my Creator?'

"'Go with the prophets of Ba'al,' Eliyahu told him, 'and just as HaKadosh Baruch Hu's Name is going to be sanctified through my bullock, it will also be sanctified through you, because everyone will see the fallacy of idol-worship.'

"The bullock obeyed Eliyahu's command and let himself be taken by the false prophets from Eliyahu's arms. This is what the verse means by, 'And they took the bullock which he had given them.'"

As soon as Reb Avraham finished his story, a large group of Kohanim emerged from Shushan Gate(26). They ascended the bridge and examined it very thoroughly, to make sure there was nothing impure lying on it. Some of the Kohanim descended from the bridge and joined their fellow Kohanim who were standing around the place of the *sreifah* (burning). It was built on a dome-like "*kippah*" in order to prevent the danger of *tum'ah*.[21]

---

19. *I Melachim* 18:19 ff.
20. Ibid., Radak on v. 26.
21. Rambam, *Hilchos Parah Adumah* 3:1.

A distinguished procession was then seen emerging from Shushan Gate. Those were the *Kohen Gadol*, all of his assistants, and the *Parah Adumah*.[22] One of the assistants was carrying a piece of cedar wood, *eizov*, and scarlet wool thread. The cow was walking slowly, with dignity, as if realizing the honorable and significant role it would play in the lives of millions of Jews. It took the procession about half an hour to reach the spot designated for the *shechitah*.

A big pile of wood was lying ready in a pit.[23] There were several kinds of wood in the pile: cedar, oak, cypress and fig-tree. The wood was arranged in the shape of a tower with window-like empty spaces in it for the circulation of air, so that it could burn well. The Kohanim took the red cow up to the top of the tower of wood and tied it with a rope made of *megeg*, a type of reed which does not become *tamei*.[24] The cow's head pointed to the south, but its face was turned to the west.

In the presence of the whole congregation, Rabbi Yishmael ben Piyachi, the *Kohen Gadol*, caused himself to become *tamei* by touching a dead *sheretz*,[25] which had been prepared in advance. Before the *Kohen Gadol* entered the cave where the *mikveh* was, the members of the Sanhedrin rested their hands on his head,[26] and said to him: "*Ishi Kohen Gadol*—My highly esteemed *Kohen Gadol*, immerse yourself once!" The *mikveh* was also built on a "kippah."

---

22. Mishnah *Middos* 1:3.

23. Mishnah *Parah* 3:8.

24. Mishnah *Parah* 3:9.

25. Rambam, *Hilchos Parah Adumah* 1:14. A *sheretz* here refers to any of the eight teeming animals mentioned in *Vayikra* 11:29–30, i.e. a mouse.

26. Mishnah *Parah* 3:8.

The cow was walking slowly, with dignity

While the *Kohen Gadol* was immersing himself, the assistant Kohanim examined the cow very thoroughly to make sure it had no blemishes on it.[27]

After a short while Rabbi Yishmael appeared in the entrance to the cave, having finished immersing himself properly, as required by halachah. The assistant Kohanim then took the vessels that were to be filled with the ashes of the *parah* and caused them to become *tamei* through contact with the *sheretz*, whereupon they were also immersed.[28]

Rabbi Yishmael ascended the wooden tower and turned his face to the west.[29] With his right hand he slaughtered the cow, and with his left hand he gathered the blood that gushed out of its throat.[30] Rabbi Yishmael could see[31] the Entrance to the *Heichal*(42) from where he was. He dipped his right forefinger in the blood that was in his left hand and sprinkled it toward the *Kodesh HaKodashim*.

The *Kohen Gadol* sprinkled seven times in the direction of the Beis HaMikdash,[32] and after each sprinkling, wiped the blood that had remained on his finger on the cow's body and dipped his finger anew into the blood in his left hand.[33] After the seventh sprinkling he wiped his hands on the cow's body.[34] Naftali asked about this, and Reb Shmuel answered.

---

27. *Bemidbar* 19:2.

28. Rambam, *Hilchos Parah Adumah* 1:14.

29. Mishnah *Parah* 9:9.

30. Rambam, *Hilchos Parah Adumah* 3:2.

31. Mishnah *Middos* 2:4.

32. *Bemidbar* 19:4: "Elazar the priest shall then take [some] of its blood with his [fore]finger, and sprinkle [some] of its blood seven times directly toward the front of the Tent of Meeting."

33. Rambam, *Hilchos Parah Adumah* 3:2.

34. Mishnah *Parah* 3:9.

"The verse says, 'The cow shall be burned in his sight; its hide, flesh and blood, together with its excrement shall be burned.'[35] Therefore, the Kohen wipes the blood on the cow's body, so that this blood gets burned together with the cow."

Rabbi Yishmael descended the tower cautiously and, using small pieces of wood, set it on fire.[36] The flames quickly grew in size and power and started licking the flesh of the cow, until all of it was engulfed in flames. The heat was so intense that the *Kohen Gadol* had to distance himself from the burning tower, his eyes paying close attention to the burning cow.[37] When he saw how its belly burst from the heat of the fire,[38] he took the piece of cedar wood into his hand and raised his voice, asking:

"*Eitz erez zeh*? (This piece of cedar wood?)"

"*Hein!* Yes!" those present replied. The question and the answer were repeated twice afterwards.

Then the Kohen lifted up the *eizov* and asked:

"*Eizov zeh*? This hyssop?"

"*Hein!* Yes!" he was answered, whereupon the question and the answer were repeated twice.

The questions and the answers about the scarlet wool thread (*shni ha-tola'as*) were also repeated three times. Then the *Kohen Gadol* wound the thread around the piece of cedar wood and the *eizov*, and threw all three of them directly into the cow's belly.[39]

The sight of *ketziras haOmer* — the reaping of barley for the *Omer*-offering — crept into Naftali's memory. "The reaper also

---

35. *Bemidbar* 19:5.

36. Mishnah *Parah* 3:9

37. Rambam, *Hilchos Parah Adumah* 3:2.

38. Mishnah *Parah* 3:10.

39. Mishnah *Parah* 3:11.

asked a number of questions before reaping," Naftali thought to himself. Then he turned to Reb Avraham and asked him, "Have these questions been asked in order to eliminate all hope from the hearts of the Tzedokim concerning the validity of their distorted views?"

"No, the questions are asked for a different reason," Reb Avraham replied. "There are different kinds of cedar wood, *eizov* and scarlet wool.[40] The Kohen poses a question and gets an answer in order to demonstrate to the public that he intends to take the kind that the Torah commanded."

After the fire had gone out, the Kohanim beat the charred remains of the cow and the wood with sticks and gathered the ashes into vessels.[41] The ashes were divided into three parts:[42] One part was given to the priestly divisions for the purification of the Kohanim; the second part was stored for the purpose of purification of the entire *klal Yisrael*, and the third part was placed in the *Cheil*(2) for safekeeping, as the Torah commands, "and [they, i.e. the ashes] shall be for the community of the Children of Yisrael for safekeeping, as sprinkling water; it is a purifier."[43]

The pupils of the study group left *Har HaZeisim* awed and very happy at having had the privilege to see, at least once in their lifetime, the rite of the burning of the *Parah Adumah*. They streamed back to Yerushalayim squeezed in among the massive crowd of Jews. The noise was powerful, but Binyamin's voice was clearly heard above the humming throng:

"The burning of the *Parah Adumah* actually atones for the

---

40. Rambam, *Hilchos Parah Adumah* 3:2.
41. Rambam, *Hilchos Parah Adumah* 3:3.
42. Rambam, *Hilchos Parah Adumah* 3:4.
43. *Bemidbar* 19:9.

sin of the Golden Calf.[44] This is reflected in the *gematria* of the words '*Parah Adumah*' (341), which equals the *gematria* of the phrase '*zeh al avon eigel* — this is for the [atonement] of the sin of the calf.'"[45]

---

44. *Bemidbar* 19:22, Rashi quoting Rabbi Moshe Darshan.

45. *Bemidbar* 19:2, *Ba'al HaTurim*.

Chapter Twenty-Two

In the Middle of the Night*

At two o'clock in the morning, Reb Shmuel woke the boys from their sweet slumber. Naftali rubbed his eyes after washing his hands three times. He was very tired because he had been unable to fall asleep from excitement, although he had gone to bed early the night before. How could he fall asleep when he kept thinking about what he was about to see in a very short time: the removal (separation) of the ashes [*terumas hadeshen*], the offering of the *korban Tamid*, and other details of the Divine service in the Beis HaMikdash?

They walked along the quiet streets of Yerushalayim, shivering from the chilliness of the night. Reb Shmuel spoke in a low voice.

"Usually the gates of the Temple Mount are closed at night.[1] Only Tadi Gate(27) remains open,[2] and we'll be able to enter the

---

* Due to the great number of opinions concerning the order of the morning service in the Beis HaMikdash, and the difficulty in deciding upon which to base this chapter, the description of the service is presented here according to the view of Rabbi Yaakov Emden, *zt"l*, in his work, *Ezras Kohanim*, which features in *Siddur Beis Yaakov*.

1. Mishnah *Tamid* 3:7, *Tiferes Yisrael* #48.
2. Mishnah *Yoma* 1:8, *Tiferes Yisrael* #46.

Temple Mount area(1) through it."

They immersed in the *mikveh*, and then went through the northern gate, the Tadi Gate. A Levi stood on guard at the entrance. Reb Shmuel greeted him, and he reciprocated by a friendly nod of his head. Then they removed their shoes and entered *Har HaBayis*.

"Who is this guard?" Yechezkel wondered. "I've never seen a guard at the gate of *Har HaBayis* before!"

"The Leviyim carry out several important duties in the Beis HaMikdash," Reb Shmuel answered. The first one is to sing on the *Duchan*(5) (Platform),[3] as the Torah says, 'He shall serve in the Name of the Eternal, his God.'[4] When the Leviyim sing hymns in service to Hashem, they mention His Name. Their second task is to serve as attending officers in the Beis HaMikdash.[5] And in the desert they had another task to fulfill — to be responsible for the dismantling of the *Mishkan*,[6] for transporting it[7] and for assembling it in the place where Yisrael camped.[8]

"Besides all of these duties, the Leviyim were appointed to take care of opening and locking the gates of the Beis HaMikdash and standing on guard.[9] The Leviyim carry out the service of standing on guard at the gate at night only.[10] Whether ene-

---

3. *Arachin* 11a.

4. *Devarim* 18:7.

5. *Bemidbar* 18:2,6. Rashi says in both verses that the Leviyim served as managers and treasurers.

6. *Bemidbar* 10:17, Rashi.

7. *Bemidbar*, chap. 4.

8. *Bemidbar* 10:21: "... and the sons of Gershon and the sons of Merari had set up the Dwelling by the time they arrived."

9. *Arachin* 11b.

10. Rambam, *Hilchos Beis HaBechirah* 8:1.

mies or robbers threaten to attack or not, the Sanctuary must be guarded because this adds to its glory and honor. In this way, the Leviyim are like honor guards. A palace that is not guarded can't compare with a guarded one!"[11]

"If that's the case, then why do they guard the House only at night, and not in the day?" Reuven asked.

"In the day the Kohanim's service in the Beis HaMikdash is itself a way of honoring it, whereas at night, when no service is performed, guarding remains the only way to honor it,"[12] Reb Shmuel explained. "And furthermore, this *shemirah* (guard duty) is not an option; it is a duty[13] that is mentioned in the Torah: 'You shall safeguard the duties of the Sanctuary.'"[14]

Yehoshua wanted to know more details. "How many Leviyim carry out guard duty in the Beis HaMikdash?"

"You'd be surprised to know that there are also Kohanim who serve as guards,"[15] Reb Shmuel surprised them. There are twenty-four guard posts. *Kohanim* guard in three of them, and Leviyim are stationed in all the rest."

"I don't understand," Naftali said. "There aren't twenty-four gates in the whole Beis HaMikdash. There are only thirteen gates in the *Azarah*,[16] and five on *Har HaBayis*,[17] so why do they need twenty-four guards?"

"Well, the guard posts are not always located at gates, and not every gate is guarded," Reb Shmuel said. "We can discuss

---

11. *Sifrei Zuta* 4 (ד"ה ונלוו).

12. Mishnah *Tamid* 1:1, *Tiferes Yisrael* #1.

13. Rambam, *Hilchos Beis HaBechirah* 8:3.

14. *Bemidbar* 18:5.

15. Mishnah *Middos* 1:1.

16. Mishnah *Middos* 2:6.

17. Mishnah *Middos* 1:3.

all these guard posts during the next half hour that we have at our disposal.

"We just saw a guard stationed at Tadi Gate(27). Besides this guard, there are another four Leviyim guarding at the other four gates of *Har HaBayis*.[18] Another four Leviyim are stationed in the four inner corners of the Temple Mount Wall(13): that makes nine altogether. Let's go and see where the other guards are stationed."

They turned to the right and began to circle the Wall of the *Azarah*(15). There was another *shomer* (guard) standing at the outer corner of the *Azarah*.

"Four more *shomrim* (guards) stand outside one of the four corners of the *Azarah*," Reb Shmuel said. "Now we have thirteen altogether."

Binyamin calculated. "Let's look for the other eleven then!"

"There's a Kohen stationed in the upper chamber above *Sha'ar HaNitzotz*(35) [Gate of the Spark]," Reb Shmuel pointed out to the left.

"So we've come up with thirteen Leviyim and one Kohen so far," Binyamin said.

The boys turned the corner and reached the Temple Mount area right behind the *Kodesh HaKodashim*. There, besides the two Leviyim guarding at the corners whom the boys had already counted, they came across another Levi, at about the middle of the back wall of the *Azarah*. That made fourteen Leviyim. Then they turned the corner again and greeted a *shomer* guarding one of the gates leading into the *Azarah*.

"Five of the *Azarah* gates are also guarded by Leviyim," Reb Shmuel remarked.

"Nineteen Leviyim and one Kohen," Binyamin kept track.

---

18. Mishnah *Middos* 1:1.

Guard Posts in the Beis HaMikdash

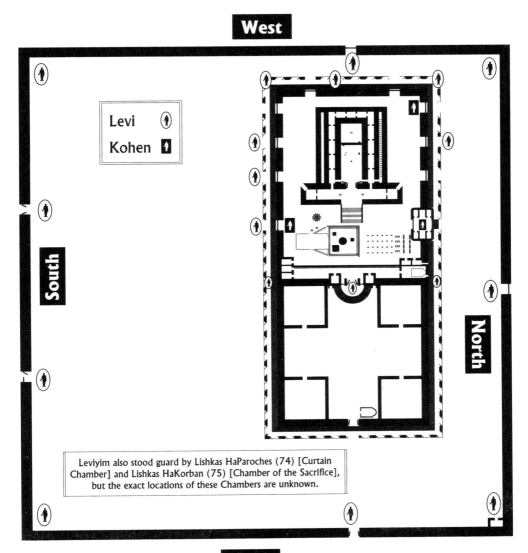

West

Levi 🚹
Kohen 🚹

South

North

Leviyim also stood guard by Lishkas HaParoches (74) [Curtain Chamber] and Lishkas HaKorban (75) [Chamber of the Sacrifice], but the exact locations of these Chambers are unknown.

East

As they stood near the *shomer*, a man came by brandishing a staff.[19] When the man approached them, the Levi stood up and said, "*Ish Har HaBayis, shalom aleicha!* — Peace be unto you, officer of the Temple Mount!"

The explanation for this curious occurrence came promptly from Reb Shmuel:

"This is the *memuneh* (the official in charge) of the *shomrim*, nicknamed "*Ben Beivai*." [20] Either he, or one of the men he supervises, patrols the guard posts at night.[21] A *shomer* who is careless enough to doze off at his guard post in the course of his *shemirah* will fail to greet the *memuneh*, and faces punishment.[22] The *ish Har HaBayis* has the right to hit him with the staff."

"To hit him with the staff?" Gamliel cried. "To hit a Jew?!"

"Picture yourself a *shomer* dozing off in the middle of carrying out his task in the palace of an earthly king. Such a *shomer* would be fined at best and executed at worst. How much more so a person who serves as a guard in the House of Hashem! If a *shomer* falls asleep, it is a sign that he has let himself be distracted from his task of honoring Hashem Yisbarach! They have the right even to burn his clothes!"

When they passed *Sha'ar HaMayim*(40) [Water Gate], Reb Shmuel said, "Here, in *Lishkas Beis Avtinas*(65) [Avtinas Family Chamber], which is built just above the gate, another Kohen is stationed."[23]

"We're still short two Leviyim and one Kohen," Binyamin could not keep from announcing.

---

19. Mishnah *Middos* 1:2; Rambam, *Hilchos Beis HaBechirah* 8:10.
20. Mishnah *Shekalim* 5:1.
21. Ibid., *Tiferes Yisrael* #11.
22. Mishnah *Middos* 1:2.
23. Mishnah *Middos* 1:1.

"One Levi guards *Lishkas HaParoches*(74), and the second one, *Lishkas HaKorban*(75)."[24]

"And what about the last Kohen?" Binyamin wondered.

"The third Kohen guards *Beis HaMoked*(56), where the Kohanim sleep," Reb Shmuel declared. "Did you notice that because of their exalted position, the Kohanim guard inside the *Azarah*?[25] They are stationed by *Lishkas Beis Avtinas*(65), *Beis HaNitzotz*(61) and *Beis HaMoked*(56). Due to the Kohanim's higher station, they guard up in *Lishkas Beis Avtinas*, [26] which is located above *Sha'ar HaMayim*(40); in the upper chamber above *Sha'ar HaNitzotz*(35),[27] and in *Beis HaMoked*(56), which is a large and spacious room.[28] The Leviyim, whose station is lower, are appointed to guard the outer gates and the Temple Mount area, places located on the ground and not above it."

Reb Shmuel's words were suddenly interrupted by a tremendously loud and powerful call:

"Arise *Kohanim* to perform your service, and Leviyim to sing on your Platform and Yisrael to stand at your post![29]

The children's hearts almost skipped a beat from the blast

---

24. Ibid. It is apparent from the *Tiferes Yisrael* commentary that it is *Lishkas Tela'ei Korban*(57) (Chamber of Sacrificial Lambs), which was situated in the *Azarah*. However, Rambam, in *Hilchos Beis HaBechirah* 8:4, seems to maintain that the Leviyim guarded outside the Sanctuary, and the Kohanim inside it — which would negate identifying *Lishkas HaKorban* with *Lishkas Tela'ei Korban*, which was inside the Sanctuary. Consult also the commentary "*Mefaresh*" on Tractate *Tamid* 26b, which states that the "*Lishkas Tela'ei Korban*" was outside the *Azarah*.

25. Rambam, *Hilchos Beis HaBechirah* 8:4.

26. *Middos* 1:5.

27. *Tamid* 1:1.

28. *Middos* 1:8.

29. *Yoma* 20b.

of this powerful voice. Reb Shmuel spoke to them soothingly, "Were you stunned? That was Gvini, the herald of the Beis HaMikdash.[30] The residents of Jericho, who are ten *parsaos* away from Yerushalayim,[31] hear his call![32] Let's get closer to the *Beis HaMoked* now. I'm sure it'll be interesting there."

They reached the gate of *Beis HaMoked*(32) and waited outside. They didn't have to wait long. The *memuneh* appeared almost immediately and knocked gently on the door, which was promptly opened by one of the Kohanim.[33] Now the boys could vividly see what was going on inside.

All the Kohanim were awake. Most of them had gotten up at dawn and had already immersed themselves in the *mikveh*. They were ready to perform the day's service. There were those among them who hadn't been able to fall asleep from excitement and eagerness to do the *avodah*, knowing that each Kohen gets the privilege of offering *korbanos* only two days a year. This is how it can be figured out: There were twenty-four *mishmeros*, or divisions, of Kohanim, serving in rotation, one week at a time. In other words, every *mishmar* went up to Yerushalayim once every twenty-four weeks.[34] A *mishmar* is made up of seven *batei av* (clans, households),[35] each *beis av* carrying out the service in the *Beis HaMikdash* a different day of the week. This means that each Kohen got a chance to serve only two days a year. This did not include the service in the Beis HaMikdash during the Festi-

---

30. Mishnah *Shekalim* 5:1.

31. Ibid., Bartenura.

32. Mishnah *Tamid* 3:8.

33. Mishnah *Tamid* 1:2. See also *Tosfos Yom Tov* ad loc.

34. *Ta'anis* 27a.

35. *Ta'anis* 15b, Rashi (ד"ה אנשי בית אב); Rambam, *Hilchos Klei HaMikdash* 3:9.

vals, when all the *mishmeros* served equally.[36]

The children stood looking at the Kohanim, some of whom were young men. This was their first opportunity to have the privilege of participating in the holy Divine service. They were beaming with joy and enthusiasm. Naftali came closer and peeked through the big gate that was half open. Most of the Kohanim present in the room were already wearing priestly garments [*bigdei kehunah*]. Others were running to *Beis HaMoked HaKatan*(60) [Small Pyre Chamber], which had a tunnel in it leading to the *mikveh*.[37]

Preparations for the Divine service were at their height. A group of Kohanim was standing on the side, pouring their hearts out in recitation of *Tehillim*. One of them, an elderly looking man, exclaimed pleadingly, "Master of the world! You know that we desire to do Your Will, but what is holding us back? The *se'or she-be'issah*[38] and our enslavement under the rule of the heathen kingdoms. May it be Your will to save us from them, so that we return to You and fulfill Your statutes with a perfect heart!"[39]

Another, younger Kohen pleaded, "Cause Your Divine Spirit to influence us, so that we cleave to You and always yearn for You more and more. Lift us up from one spiritual level to the next so that we may have the merit to reach the spiritual level of our saintly *Avos*, Avraham, Yitzchak and Yaakov!"[40]

Another Kohen was standing next to the entrance, covering his face with his hands, his shoulders shaking from crying. His

---

36. *Sukkah* 55b.

37. Mishnah *Middos* 1:6.

38. Lit., "leaven in the dough," an allusion to the *yetzer ha-ra* (evil inclination).

39. *Berachos* 17a.

40. Prayer composed by Rabbi Elimelech of Lizhensk.

voice sounded faint and broken through his hands. "May it be Your will that Your mercy conquer Your anger, and Your mercy prevail over all Your Attributes, so that You treat Your sons with Your Attribute of Mercy, dealing with them better than they deserve according to the letter of the law."[41]

"I know I don't deserve to stand before You, O Master of the world," another Kohen's voice trembled. "I am not worthy enough to sacrifice *korbanos* before You, but all that I desire is to please You, so please, in Your great mercy, help me receive a worthy service today, for I wish to serve You!"

"Whoever has immersed may come and participate in the *payis*!"[42] the *memuneh* shouted.

Reb Shmuel whispered an explanation to them. "All the Kohanim who have immersed have the right to participate the *payis*[43] that will take place shortly. The first *payis* will determine which Kohen will carry out *terumas ha-deshen*, which is the removal of part of the ashes from the *Mizbeach*."

"Will we be able to see how the *payis* is performed?" Chananya asked hopefully.

"We won't be able to see the first and the second ones," Reb Shmuel was compelled to disappoint him. "They are performed in *Lishkas HaGazis*(53)[44] when the gates of the *Azarah* are still locked. However, we may be able to see the third *payis*, which decides who will have the privilege of burning the *ketores* (incense). Come, the Kohanim will start inspecting the *Azarah* in a few minutes. Let's get going!"

---

41. *Berachos* 7a.

42. Mishnah *Tamid* 1:2.

43. *Payis* — allotment of rights to carry out Divine Service by means of a sort of lottery.

44. Rambam, *Hilchos Temidin u'Musafin* 6:1.

Chapter Twenty-Three

Who Stole the Kiyor?

T he members of the study group stood on the Wall of the
Azarah(15) breathing heavily from the strained effort of the
ascent. They had just climbed about one hundred steps in a
matter of a few minutes! They managed to arrive just before the
Kohanim started inspecting the *Azarah*.

The cool breeze of Yerushalayim, so characteristic of the early
morning hours in the Holy City, was blowing in their faces. They
stood leaning on the railing, looking toward the *Azarah*.

"The Kohen in charge is responsible for opening a small
door, called a *Pishpesh*, which is built into one of the gates of *Beis
HaMoked*(32) that opens into the *Azarah*,"[1] Reb Shmuel began explaining. "He takes the key from where it is kept in *Beis HaMoked*
and opens the *Pishpesh* for the Kohanim."

A minute later the door opened, and a group of Kohanim
wearing *bigdei kehunah* marched out one after the other on their
way into the *Azarah* area. They were holding burning torches.

They arranged themselves in two groups. One group turned
to the right, walked along the northern wall of the *Azarah*, turned
toward the west, continued behind the *Kodesh HaKodashim*(12),
and then turned again and walked past the southern side, ending

---

1. Mishnah *Tamid* 1:3.

up at the eastern wall. On their way around, the Kohanim inspected the *Azarah* to make sure nothing was amiss there.[2] They
finished their inspection at the *Lishkas Osei Chavitin*(51) [Chamber
for the Preparation of the *Kohen Gadol*'s flour-offering].

The second group turned to the left and covered a shorter
distance. They began to walk along the northern wall and soon
reached the northeastern corner of the *Azarah*. From there they
turned eastward and walked until they also reached the *Lishkas
Osei Chavitin*. When the two groups met each other opposite the
Lishkas Osei Chavitin they said, at the same time, to each other:
"*Shalom! Ha-kol shalom!*" (Shalom! Everything is fine!). They meant
to say that all the holy vessels and objects were in their proper
places, and it was possible to start the service of the day.

A small group of Kohanim entered the *Lishkas Osei Chavitin*(51). There they began to prepare the flour-offering that is offered by the *Kohen Gadol* every day.[3] The rest of the Kohanim
hurried to *Lishkas HaGazis*(53),[4] looking forward nervously to the
first *payis*, in which one of the Kohanim was destined to be al-
lotted the fulfillment of a precious mitzvah — *terumas ha-deshen*.[5]
Needless to say, the children who were standing on the wall
could not see how the *payis* was done.

While they were waiting, Reb Shmuel told them about the
Kiyor, the copper washing urn. "We all know that a Kohen who
wishes to serve in the Beis HaMikdash must first sanctify his
hands and feet by washing them, for the Torah explicitly states,
'You shall make a copper urn for washing, with its copper stand,
and place it between the Tent of Meeting and the Altar, and put

---

2. Mishnah *Middos* 1:7.

3. *Vayikra* 6:15.

4. Rambam, *Hilchos Temidin u'Musafin* 6:1.

5. *Yoma* 22a.

The Path Followed by the Kohanim Patrolling the Azarah

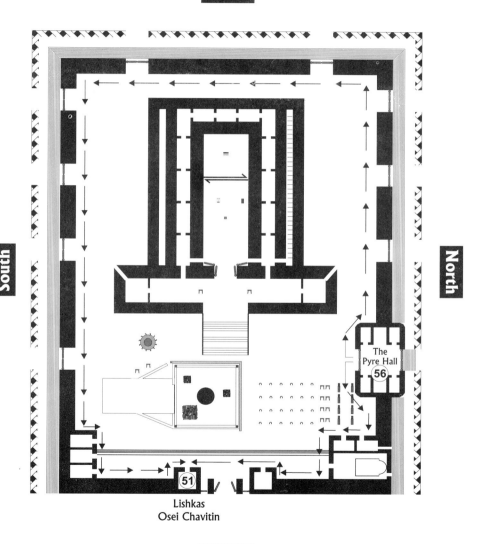

West

South

North

East

The Pyre Hall
56

51

Lishkas
Osei Chavitin

water in it. Aharon and his sons shall wash their hands and feet from it.'[6] This washing is essential for a Kohen who serves in the Beis HaMikdash, as it says, 'They shall wash with water when entering the Tent of Meeting, and thus they will not die, or when drawing near to the Altar to serve, to burn up a fire offering for the Eternal. They shall wash their hands and feet and thus not die.'[7] These verses teach us that if they do not wash their hands and feet, their punishment is death."[8]

The boys were silent as Reb Shmuel continued his fascinating lecture. "The hands and feet are washed with the *Kiyor*(81), from the faucets attached to its sides. It is actually a huge water tank. It stands between the Main Ramp of the *Mizbeach* [*HaKevesh HaGadol*](92) and the *Ulam*(10), as stated in the Torah, 'And place it between the Tent of Meeting and the Altar.'"[9]

"So why isn't it further north, directly Between the *Ulam* and the Altar(9), instead of just between the Main Ramp and the *Ulam*?" Alexander asked.

"It says, 'He placed the sacrificial Altar near the entrance of the Dwelling, the Tent of Meeting.'[10] The site of the *Mizbeach*(7) itself must be directly opposite the Entrance to the *Ulam*(41), with nothing blocking; therefore, the *Kiyor* is placed a bit to the south of the entrance, between the Ramp and the *Ulam*."[11]

"There is a *gemat...*" Binyamin started saying, but was abruptly interrupted by Yehoshua, who asked, almost in a scream:

"Where is the *Kiyor* supposed to be?!"

---

6. *Shemos* 30:18,19.

7. *Shemos* 30:20,21.

8. Ibid., Rashi.

9. *Shemos* 30:18.

10. *Shemos* 40:29.

11. Mishnah *Middos* 3:6; *Zevachim* 59a.

"Between the Main Ramp and the *Ulam*," Reb Shmuel repeated in surprise.

"But *it's not there*!" Yehoshua cried.

"What do you mean it's not there?"

The children and their *rebbi* looked closely at the place where the *Kiyor* was supposed to stand. It wasn't there.

"Woe to us! The *Kiyor* is stolen!" Naftali moaned. "How is it possible? All the gates are closed, the entrances are guarded by *shomrim*, and even so, it was stolen! How is it possible that the Kohanim who patrolled the *Azarah* didn't notice that it was missing?"

"What, are there thieves in the area?!" Gamliel's frightened voice was heard. "Let's get out of here. I'm scared!"

"To steal a holy vessel from the Beis HaMikdash! What a disgrace!" Chananya exclaimed.

"I wonder who did it! Maybe those Tzedokim did it — those who always want to harm us," Yechezkel added.

Reb Shmuel wanted to say something, but the shocked and upset children didn't pay any attention. Bo'az tried to be logical. "The gates were closed the entire night, and in the daytime Kohanim run around the place. It would be quite logical to assume that it was stolen by one of the Kohanim, whose *yetzer ha-ra* got the better of him."

Alexander rushed to defend the members of his native tribe: "It is utterly impossible that a Kohen, who serves in the holiest place on earth, would debase himself to become a thief!" he said heatedly.

"I once heard that if a Kohen steals one of the holy vessels, a zealot can even kill him!"[12] Bo'az persisted in maintaining his opinion. "I only wonder how he managed to take out the *Kiyor* through the gates without getting caught. The *Kiyor* is not so

---

12. *Sanhedrin* 81b.

small — it's impossible to hide it in your pocket."

The sudden silence that ensued permitted Reb Shmuel to finally put in a few words.

"Boys, boys, *the Kiyor has not been stolen!*" he said. "It's wasn't stolen," he repeated. It is simply below the surface of the ground. Every night it is lowered underground by means of a special pulley-type device called a *muchni*, and kept there until the morning, so that its water will not become *pasul* overnight.[13]

"As you know, each holy vessel sanctifies whatever is placed in it, so that it becomes holy, as the Torah says, 'Whatever comes into contact with them (the holy vessels) will be sanctified.'[14] Thus, if the water is kept in the *Kiyor* overnight, it would become *pasul*[15] — just like the *emurim* of a *korban* that are kept overnight and not burned.

"The *muchni* was manufactured by a *Kohen Gadol* named Ben Katin.[16] By means of this machine, the *Kiyor* is lowered beneath the surface of the earth into a deep well, so that the water that the *Kiyor* contains becomes one with the water of the well. This prevents it from becoming *pasul*. In the morning the *Kiyor*, which is now full of water from the well, is lifted up and returned to its place, and the Kohanim can use it again for sanctifying their hands and feet."

Reb Shmuel stopped for a moment to take a deep breath and continued. "There is another innovation ascribed to Ben Katin's merit. He added more faucets to the *Kiyor*.[17] You see, the *Kiyor* that was made at the time of Moshe Rabbeinu had only two

---

13. *Yoma* 37a.

14. *Shemos* 30:29.

15. *Sukkah* 50a, Rashi (ד"ה ואי).

16. *Yoma* 37a, Rashi (ד"ה בן קטין).

17. *Yoma* 37a.

faucets. One was in the upper part, used only in the morning when the *Kiyor* was full, and one was lower down and thus used in the late afternoon, when the water level fell below the opening of the upper faucet. Ben Katin attached ten additional faucets to the *Kiyor,* and since then all the Kohanim who have won the *payis* have been able to sanctify their hands and feet simultaneously, without having to wait.

"By the way, boys," Reb Shmuel concluded, "because of Ben Katin's brilliant innovations for the sake of the service in the Beis HaMikdash, they say about him,[18] *'Zecher tzaddik li-verachah'*[19] (May the memory of a righteous person be for a blessing)."

In the meantime, the Kohanim left *Lishkas HaGazis*(53). One of them was the Kohen who had won the *payis* for performing *terumas ha-deshen.*[20] He walked toward the site of the *Kiyor*(81) with fear and awe. The Kohanim who were standing near *Lishkas HaGazis* turned to him with the following words: "Beware! Be careful not to even touch the shovel for *terumas ha-deshen* before you sanctify your hands and your feet with the water of the *Kiyor!*"[21]

The children watched the Kohen attentively from the Wall(15) in the dim light of the Great Pyre(88) [*HaMa'arachah HaGedolah*] that was smoldering on the *Mizbeach* from the day before. The Kohen stood behind the Main Ramp(92). Then all of a sudden, a powerful noise was heard, and the children jumped and gasped in panic.

"It's all right, children, don't worry!" Reb Shmuel calmed them. "This is the sound of the *muchni's* wheel. It is lifting up

---

18. *Yoma* 38a.

19. *Mishlei* 10:7.

20. *Yoma* 22a.

21. Mishnah *Tamid* 1:4.

the *Kiyor*. The noise is extremely powerful, and is heard as far as Jericho."[22]

Gamliel suddenly remembered the powerful noise that had woken him up, in the wee hours of the morning, on many occasions back in his native village of Nov. Now he understood what it meant.

The *Kiyor* ascended majestically, until it assumed its spot. The copper shone in the light of the fire that burned on the *Mizbeach*. Gamliel heaved a sigh of relief. In spite of Reb Shmuel's story about the *muchni* and its purpose, he couldn't feel calm until he saw the *Kiyor* with his own eyes...

---

22. Mishnah *Tamid* 3:8.

Chapter Twenty-Four

Terumas HaDeshen

The Kohen washed his hands and feet under the faucet of the *Kiyor*, and then disappeared somewhere behind the Main Ramp(92) of the *Mizbeach*(7).

"The Kohen has disappeared! Where is he?" The children wondered.

"At the moment he is on his way to fetch the silver shovel, which is a type of fire pan. It is lying in the corner between the western part of the Main Ramp and the *Mizbeach*,"[1] Reb Shmuel explained.

The Kohen climbed the Ramp, holding the shovel in his hand. After he reached the roof of the *Mizbeach* he turned to the right and began to circle it, walking along the Kohanim's Footpath(91), until he reached the Great Pyre(88).[2] He then bent toward the heap of burned coals. He moved away the upper layer, so that he could gather some completely burned ash from the center of the fire into his shovel.[3] The Kohen then walked further along the Footpath, carrying the ashes, until he completed the circle.

---

1. Mishnah *Tamid* 1:4.

2. *Yoma* 43b, Rashi (ד"ה בכל יום).

3. Mishnah *Tamid* 1:4.

When he reached the Ramp he walked down onto the floor of the *Azarah* again.

The children watched every step the Kohen took and every movement he made. They saw him walk toward the southeastern corner of the Ramp, from where he turned northwards, parallel to the eastern side of it. There he measured ten *amos* and put down the spent coals onto the floor of the *Azarah*, three *tefachim* away from the eastern side of the Ramp.

The boys were enthralled by the procedure, although they couldn't make heads or tails of it. They decided to save their questions until the end of the service, in order not to miss out on any detail now.

The moment the Kohen put down the ashes,[4] the other Kohanim started running in the direction of the *Kiyor*(81). They washed their hands and feet together in the way the halachah mandated, with the left hand on top of the left foot and right hand on top of the right foot. Afterwards, they ascended the Main Ramp with flat shovels and pitchforks in their hands. Their purpose was to clean the Great Pyre of the parts of the burnt-offerings (*olos*) and the coals that had remained there from the night before, and to prepare it for the service of the new day.

They moved the parts of the *olos* that had not yet been burned to the sides of the *Mizbeach* with the help of the pitchforks, and removed the ash to the *Tapuach*(87) with the shovels.[5] (The *Tapuach* is a big pile of ashes located in the center of the *Mizbeach*.) They shoveled part of the ash from the *Tapuach* into a large vessel that had two chains attached to its sides.[6]

"That vessel is called a *pesachter*," Reb Shmuel explained.

---

4. Mishnah *Tamid* 2:1.

5. Mishnah *Tamid* 2:2.

6. Mishnah *Tamid* 5:8.

Terumas HaDeshen

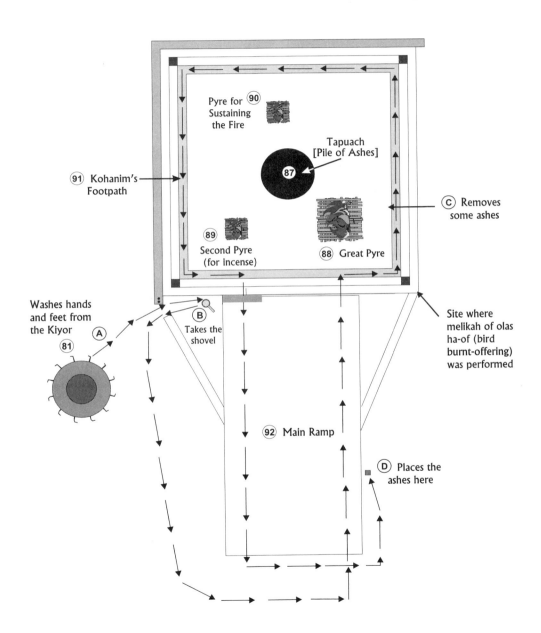

Pyre for ⁹⁰ Sustaining the Fire

Tapuach [Pile of Ashes]

⁸⁷

⁹¹ Kohanim's Footpath

Ⓒ Removes some ashes

⁸⁹ Second Pyre (for incense)

⁸⁸ Great Pyre

Washes hands and feet from the Kiyor

Ⓐ

⁸¹

Ⓑ Takes the shovel

Site where melikah of olas ha-of (bird burnt-offering) was performed

⁹² Main Ramp

Ⓓ Places the ashes here

"Its volume is fifteen *se'ah*, and the ashes of the *Tapuach* are placed in it."

"What are these two chains for?" Yehoshua asked.

"You'll see in a minute," Reb Shmuel answered mysteriously.

Kohanim pulled the *pesachter*, which was full of ashes, toward the Main Ramp(92) in the following way: one of them pulled at one chain, causing the *pesachter* to start sliding down the Ramp, and another held on to the other chain to prevent the *pesachter* from sliding too quickly.

> Abbaye ordered the daily service of the Altar on the basis of tradition and in accordance with the view of Abba Shaul: The Great Pyre was arranged on the Altar before the Second Pyre, [from which fire was taken] for the incense-offering; the Second Pyre, for incense, was arranged before the placing of the two logs of wood [on the Great Pyre]...

In the meantime, some other Kohanim had brought up logs of wood onto the *Mizbeach*.[7] The Kohen who had merited to perform *terumas ha-deshen*[8] arranged them in a pile on the eastern part of the *Mizbeach*[9] — the site of the Great Pyre(88). Afterwards, the Kohanim arranged the Second Pyre for the incense-offering(89) [*HaMa'arachah HaSheniyah shel ketores*] in the southwestern corner of the *Mizbeach*.[10] They took the unburnt parts of the *olos* that had been moved away to the sides of the *Mizbeach* and placed them upon the wood of the Great Pyre. Then the Kohen who had won the first *payis* drew near and lit the two pyres (piles of wood) with awe and trepidation.[11]

---

7. Mishnah *Tamid* 2:3.

8. *Yoma* 22a.

9. Mishnah *Tamid* 2:4.

10. Mishnah *Tamid* 2:5.

11. Rabbi Yaakov Emden, *Ezras Kohanim*.

"How fortunate this Kohen is to have won the *zechus* to perform so many *mitzvos!*" Naftali thought to himself. "He raised the *muchni* from the well, performed *terumas ha-deshen*, arranged the Great Pyre and, in the end, lit both fires on the *Mizbeach!*"

While he was thinking all this, he watched the same Kohen go down the Ramp. The Kohen took two big logs of wood and climbed the Ramp again.[12] He then put them into the fire of the Great Pyre(88).[13]

This reminded Naftali of the verse, "And each morning the Kohen shall burn wood upon the wood-pyre."[14] This was also his privilege!

The Kohanim turned their steps toward *Lishkas HaGazis*(53). As they entered, they waited with bated breath to see who would win the *payis* this time.[15] Those chosen would have the privilege of carrying out the offering of the *Tamid shel shachar*, which entailed thirteen types of service.

The children started asking questions:

"Why did the Kohanim warn their fellow Kohen, who had won the *mitzvah* of *terumas ha-deshen*, not to touch the vessel before washing his hands and feet?" Alexander asked.

"Our Sages were concerned that out of his yearning to fulfill the mitzvah, the Kohen might start doing the *avodah* before he washed.[16] Therefore, they forbade the Kohanim to even touch the

---

12. *Yoma* 22a.

13. *Ezras Kohanim*. See also *Tiferes Yisrael* #24 on *Tamid* 2:4, which suggests that the wood was placed before the lighting of the fire.

14. *Vayikra* 6:5.

15. *Ezras Kohanim*. Rambam, in *Hilchos Temidin u'Musafin* 6:1, maintains that the first *payis* and the second *payis* were drawn simultaneously. However, the wording of the *mishnayos* in *Tamid*, at the end of chapter 2 and the beginning of chapter 3, seems to support the view of *Ezras Kohanim*.

16. Mishnah *Tamid* 1:4, *Tiferes Yisrael*, *Bo'az* #3.

The Kohen lit the fires on the Mizbeach

holy utensils before they wash their hands and feet."

"I noticed that the Kohanim ascended the *Mizbeach* from the eastern side of the Main Ramp(92) and descended it from its western side,"[17] Yehoshua said. "Is there any special reason for that?"

"According to the established principle that all directional moves one makes in the Beis HaMikdash should favor the right side,[18] the Kohen ascends the Ramp from his right, which is to the east when he faces the *Mizbeach*. After he has circled the *Mizbeach* he also descends it from his right, which then, facing away from the *Mizbeach*, is to the west," Reb Shmuel answered.

Naftali hastened to ask before someone else got ahead of him, "Is the *deshen* always placed in the same spot?"

"Yes it is," Reb Shmuel confirmed. "There is indeed a special spot where the *deshen* is placed: about ten *amos* away from the bottom of the Main Ramp."

"Why there in particular?" Chananya asked.

"I know! Because it has to be near the *Mizbeach*, as the verse states,[19] 'The Kohen shall... then separate some of the ash that remains from the burnt-offering which the fire consumed, and place it next to the Altar,'" Yonasan responded.

"But it is possible to place the *deshen* closer to the *Mizbeach*. There is a twenty-*amah* space between the spot where the *deshen* is placed and the *Mizbeach*, because the Main Ramp(92) is thirty *amos* long,"[20] Chananya insisted.

Reb Shmuel stepped in. "The Torah says about the bird burnt-offering [*olas ha-of*]: 'He shall remove its crop together with

---

17. *Yoma* 43b.

18. *Yoma* 45a.

19. *Vayikra* 6:3.

20. Mishnah *Middos* 5:2, *Tiferes Yisrael* #11.

its entrails, and cast them beside the eastern side of the Altar, to the prescribed place of the ashes.'[21] The Torah means to say that the place to which the crop with its entrails must be thrown is the spot where the *deshen* must be placed.[22] *Melikah* (slitting the back of the neck) of the *olas ha-of* is done on the *Sovev*(96),[23] in the Southeastern Corner(97). From there the bird's crop with its entrails must be thrown to the place of *terumas ha-deshen*.

"The term '*hashlachah*,' or throwing, never implies a distance of less than twenty *amos*.[24] The place of *terumas ha-deshen* is, therefore, twenty *amos* from the *Mizbeach*. It must also be three *tefachim* away to the side from the Main Ramp[25] so that the ash does not blacken the white ramp."[26]

"I think it is removed toward the end of the day," Yechezkel said knowingly.

"What is removed? From where?" Reb Shmuel failed to understand.

"The *deshen*," Yechezkel replied, as if taking it for granted. "It is proved by the fact that the place was absolutely empty today, when the Kohen put the *deshen* there."

Reb Shmuel smiled. "Did you know that besides the *deshen* and the crop with its entrails, the ashes[27] of the Incense or Golden Altar(83) [*Mizbach HaKetores/Mizbach HaZahav*] are also placed there, as well as the ashes of the Menorah(84)? One of the miracles of the Beis HaMikdash occurs there regularly: they are

---

21. *Vayikra* 1:16.
22. Mishnah *Tamid* 1:4.
23. *Zevachim* 64b.
24. *Tamid* 28b, *Mefaresh* (ד"ה צבר).
25. Mishnah *Tamid* 1:4, *Tiferes Yisrael* #63.
26. Mishnah *Middos* 3:4.
27. Mishnah *Tamid* 1:4.

all absorbed by the earth there.''[28]

"Wh... what happens to them?" Chananya asked in disbe-
lief.

"Yes, yes, all the ashes are 'swallowed' in that particular
spot," Reb Shmuel repeated, enjoying the boys' sincere amazement. "And another miracle occurring in the Beis HaMikdash is
the 'swallowing' of the earthenware utensils in the *Azarah*. The
Kohanim cook the meat of the *kodshei kodashim* in earthenware
pots in order to eat the meat in the *Azarah*, whereupon they
break the pots,[29] as stated in the Torah, 'And the earthenware
vessel in which it is cooked shall be broken.'[30] They must be broken in a holy place[31] — that is to say, in the *Azarah*. If the broken
vessels were not swallowed by the floor of the *Azarah*, it would
be filled with piles and piles of broken pottery."

"What is the *shiur* (halachic amount) of ash required to be removed for *terumas ha-deshen*?" Bo'az asked.

"Not less than a three-finger fistful [*kometz*] and not more
than a firepan-full,"[32] Reb Shmuel replied expertly.

It was Alexander's turn to pose a question. "Where do the
Kohanim carry the ashes that they take from the *Tapuach*(87) and
put into the *pesachter*?"

"I'd like *you* to answer that," Reb Shmuel said. "The Torah
mentions it very clearly."

---

28. *Yoma* 21a. Tosafos (ד"ה נבלעין) questions whether only the *terumas ha-
deshen* ashes were miraculously absorbed, or other ashes as well. Rashi
(*Vayikra* 1:16) maintains that they were all swallowed by the earth there.

29. *Yoma* 21a.

30. *Vayikra* 6:21.

31. *Zevachim* 93b. The earthenware vessels must be broken because their
walls absorb sacred food, which inevitably becomes *nosar* at dawn. *Nosar*
must be destroyed, and earthenware vessels cannot be kashered.

32. *Yoma* 24a; *Ezras Kohanim*.

"He shall then... take the ash outside the camp to a ritually pure place,"[33] Yonasan, Naftali and Alexander quoted together.

"But who would be willing to carry out a task like that? Maybe *ba'alei mumin* (Kohanim with bodily blemishes) who are barred from performing all other kinds of Divine service in the Beis HaMikdash do it," Yehoshua conjectured.

"Well, you make two mistakes," Reb Shmuel answered. "Although *hotza'as ha-deshen* (taking the ash outside) is not defined as a kind of Divine service, it is not *ba'alei mumin* who do it.[34] And although *hotza'as ha-deshen* is not regarded as a very honorable task, no Kohen was ever too lazy to carry it out.[35]

"The Kohen who takes the *deshen* outside the camp must change into more worn-out clothing, as it says in the Torah: 'He shall remove his garments and put on other garments and take the ash outside the camp.'[36] Our Sages offer the following interpretation: When one serves his master a glass of wine, he should not wear the same clothes that he wears when cooking for him in the kitchen![37] Nevertheless, no Kohen has ever said he wasn't willing to take out the *deshen*."

Reb Shmuel then continued. "As you can see, the site of the Great Pyre(88) [*HaMa'arachah HaGedolah*] is in the eastern part of the roof of the *Mizbeach*.[38] The Second Pyre, for incense [*HaMa'arachah HaSheniyah shel ketores*](89), is located in its western part, closer to the *Heichal*(11), because the Kohanim take coals from there to burn the incense on the Golden (Incense) Altar(83)

33. *Vayikra* 6:4.
34. Rambam, *Hilchos Temidin u'Musafin* 2:15.
35. Mishnah *Tamid* 2:2.
36. *Vayikra* 6:4.
37. *Shabbos* 114a.
38. Mishnah *Tamid* 2:4.

in the *Heichal*.[39] This Pyre is located at the distance of four *amos* from the southern border of the *Mizbeach,* so that it may face the Entrance to the *Ulam*(41). No specific site is designated for the Third Pyre(90) [*HaMa'arachah le-Kiyum HaEish*].[40] The Kohanim may light it on the *Mizbeach,* in any spot they like."

"So what's this Pyre for? Aren't two Pyres enough?" Reuven wondered.

"The holy Torah commanded us to light three Pyres on the *Mizbeach.*[41] Our Sages derived the Great Pyre(88) from the words, '...upon the wood-pyre which is on the Altar,' and the Second Pyre, for the incense(89), from the continuation of the verse: '...and the fire of the [incense] Altar shall be lit with [the fire of the wood-pyre].'[42] They derived the need for the third one from the verse, 'The fire on the Altar shall be lit on the Altar itself.'[43] This Pyre sustains a constant fire."

"So what is the real purpose of the Third Pyre?" Chananya still found it difficult to understand.

"According to one opinion, it is used to strengthen the fire of the Great Pyre when it begins to subside.[44] According to other opinions, its purpose is just to fulfill the Torah's command: 'The fire on the Altar shall be lit on the Altar itself,' and there is no other special reason to have it.[45] As a matter of fact, this Third Pyre is called *HaMa'arachah le-Kiyum HaEish,* the Pyre for Sustaining the Fire."

---

39. *Zevachim* 58b.
40. Rambam, *Hilchos Temidin u'Musafin* 2:9.
41. *Yoma* 45a.
42. *Vayikra* 6:2.
43. *Vayikra* 6:5.
44. *Yoma* 45a, Rashi (ד"ה קיום האש).
45. Rambam, *Hilchos Temidim u'Musafin,* chap. 2; *Lechem Mishneh* ad loc.

"I can see that the fire is already burning there," Yehoshua said. "When was it lit? Is there a special time for lighting?"

"Just as there is no special spot for it on the *Mizbeach*, there is no special time for it to be lit, either,"[46] answered Reb Shmuel.

"What kind of wood do they burn on the Pyre?" Naftali wanted to know.

"Fig-tree wood,[47] nut-tree wood and olive-tree wood are types of wood that burn well. None of them burns down immediately[48] or raises a lot of smoke.[49] They are burned on the Great Pyre(88). Only fig-tree wood is burned on the Second Pyre, though.[50] There is a profound reason for this: After Adam Ha-Rishon was punished for accepting *lashon ha-ra* from the Serpent, he made a *tikun* for his sin by covering himself with fig leaves. Therefore, because the incense atones for the sin of *lashon ha-ra*, the Second Pyre for incense burns only fig-tree wood. Just as fig leaves were used as a *tikun* for *lashon ha-ra*, so fig-tree wood is used for burning the incense, which atones for the same sin."[51]

---

46. Ibid.
47. Mishnah *Tamid* 2:3.
48. Ibid., Bartenura.
49. Ibid., *Tiferes Yisrael* #23.
50. Mishnah *Tamid* 2:4.
51. Mishnah *Tamid* 2:5, *Tiferes Yisrael* #31.

Chapter Twenty-Five

The Offering of the Tamid Shel Shachar*

The boys continued to shower Reb Shmuel with questions.

"How many *payis* drawings are there every morning?"

Reb Shmuel was only too happy to answer. "There are four different *payis* drawings every morning.[1] As we learned, the first *payis* determines who will do the *terumas ha-deshen*. The second is being drawn at this moment. It will entitle thirteen fortunate Kohanim to carry out all the *avodah* connected with the offering of the morning *Tamid*-sacrifice.[2] The Kohen who wins the third *payis* will burn the incense [*ketores*], and the fourth *payis* will determine who will bring up the sacrificial parts of the animal from the Ramp (*Kevesh*) to the *Mizbeach*.[3] We may be able to witness the third or the fourth *payis*, because they are drawn when the gates of the *Azarah* are already open.

---

* The early-morning regular burnt-offering.

1. *Yoma* 22a.

2. Ibid., 25a.

3. Ibid., 26a.

"Let me describe to you what is won in the second *payis*,"[4] Reb Shmuel offered. "One of the Kohanim wins the privilege of slaughtering the *korban Tamid*. Another Kohen gathers the blood and throws it onto the *Mizbeach*. A third and a fourth remove the ashes from the Golden *Mizbeach*(83) [*dishun ha-Mizbeach ha-penimi*] and from the Menorah(84) [*dishun ha-Menorah*]. These *avodos* are not directly connected with the *korban Tamid*, but are performed during the time of the *shechitah*.

"Another six Kohanim bring up the parts of the *korban* onto the Main Ramp(92). The next Kohen brings up the *soles* (fine-quality wheat flour) and the oil for the meal-offering onto the Ramp. The twelfth Kohen brings up the *chavitin* (the *Kohen Gadol*'s flour-offering), which is now being prepared in *Lishkas HaChavitin*(51),[5] and the last Kohen carries the wine."

After the above detailed account, Reb Shmuel proceeded to discuss another subject. "Dear pupils! We have already learned about the twenty-four *Taba'os*(77) [Rings] into which the heads of the sacrificial animals are inserted just before the *shechitah*. The *shechitah* of the *Tamid*, however, is carried out in the *Taba'as* specifically designated for it only.

"The Torah states about the *korban Tamid*: 'Two sheep in their first year per day, as a regular burnt-offering.'[6] Our Sages elucidated the words of this verse in the following way:[7] The word *yom*, day, in the verse is an allusion to the sun. Therefore, the *Tamid* must be slaughtered toward the sun. Accordingly, when the sun rises in the east, the *Tamid*-offering's head is inserted in a western *Taba'as*, which is not shaded by the Wall of the *Azarah*(15).

---

4. Mishnah *Tamid*, 3:1; *Yoma* 25a.

5. Mishnah *Tamid* 1:3.

6. *Bemidbar* 28:3.

7. *Tamid* 31b.

Tamid-Offering Slaughter Area

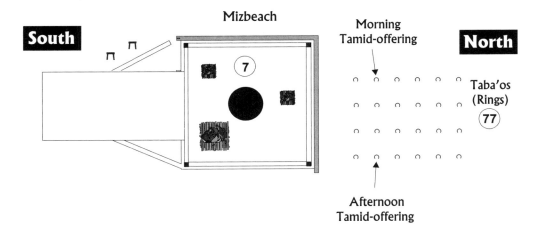

West

South

North

East

Mizbeach

Morning
Tamid-offering

Taba'os
(Rings)

Afternoon
Tamid-offering

Toward the evening, when the sun sets in the west, the *korban's* head is inserted into one of the eastern *Taba'os*."

"Is it possible to slaughter the *korban* in any of the six *Taba'os* in the eastern and western rows? My father told me that only one of them is used," Yonasan said.

"Listen well," Reb Shmuel replied. "The second *Taba'as* from the *Mizbeach* is chosen for this purpose. The early morning *Tamid*[8] is slaughtered in the second *Taba'as* in the western row, and the afternoon *Tamid* is slaughtered in the second *Taba'as* on the eastern side. The Sages did not choose the first *Taba'as*, which is closest to the *Mizbeach*, out of respect for this holy site, because the sacrificial animal may relieve itself there.[9] That would be an insult to the *Mizbeach's* honor. Another reason for it was because the *Mizbeach* itself would shade the area of the *shechitah* of the *korban Tamid*."[10]

The first Kohanim emerging from *Lishkas HaGazis*(53) appeared in the entrance to the room.

"Go and see if the time to slaughter has arrived,"[11] the *memuneh* commanded. The Kohanim promptly climbed the steps up to the Wall of the *Azarah*. In no time at all they stood next to the boys. They looked toward the east and then shouted to the *memuneh*:

"The east has not entirely lightened up yet. The time of the *shechitah* has not yet arrived."

"It is permissible to slaughter the *Tamid* at dawn [*alos hashachar*].[12] But once it happened that the Kohanim looked to-

---

8. Mishnah *Tamid* 4:1.

9. Ibid., *Tosfos Yom Tov*.

10. Ibid., Bartenura.

11. Mishnah *Tamid* 3:2.

12. *Megillah* 20b; *Berachos* 12a, Tosafos (ד"ה משום).

ward the east, and when it appeared to them that it had started to lighten up, they slaughtered the *korban Tamid*.[13] However, they had made a mistake; dawn had not arrived yet, and it was the light of the moon that they had seen. From then on, they have been careful to wait patiently until the horizon lightens up entirely, and only then do they slaughter the *korban Tamid*," Reb Shmuel related.

In the meantime, the eastern side of the horizon was gradually lightening up, until its blackness had entirely dissipated. One of the Kohanim standing on the Wall declared loudly: "*He'ir penei kol ha-mizrach!*"[14] ("The entire face of the east has lightened up.")

The children pushed closer to the Wall's railing [*ma'akeh*]. They didn't want to miss out on anything, even the smallest detail of the Divine Service. Naftali had secured a good spot for himself, next to his *rebbi*, and made the most of it for his favorite occupation — asking questions.

"My father once told me that the Kohen on the Wall who declares the light on the horizon is asked whether the light has spread as far as Chevron, in order to mention the *zechus Avos* (merit of the Patriarchs). Why didn't the *memuneh* ask him this question?"

"This question is asked only on Yom Kippur,[15] when there's a special need to mention the merit of the *Avos* — Avraham, Yitzchak and Yaakov — who are buried in Chevron."

At this point the voice of the *memuneh* was suddenly heard. "Go and bring a lamb from the *Lishkas Tela'ei Korban*(57) [Chamber of Sacrificial Lambs]!"[16]

---

13. *Yoma* 28a.
14. Mishnah *Tamid* 3:2; Rambam, *Hilchos Temidin u'Musafin* 1:2.
15. *Menachos* 100a, Rashi, Tosafos (ד"ה מתתיא בן שמואל).
16. Mishnah *Tamid* 3:3.

"The *Lishkas Tela'ei Korban* is located in the southwestern corner of *Beis HaMoked*(56) [Pyre Hall],"[17] Naftali tried to revive his memory. "At least six lambs, checked for blemishes, are regularly kept there."[18]

Naftali saw that the Kohanim who were in the *Azarah* took out ninety-three silver and golden utensils, which were needed for the service of the day.[19] They placed them onto a silver Table(80)[20] that was hidden behind the Main Ramp(92).

One of the Kohanim led in a gigantic sheep, the size of which the boys had never seen.[21] It was difficult to see in the poorly lit *Azarah*, and Naftali hesitated whether it was a sheep or a bull. The animal was taller than the priests who led it, and was very fat. Only when it was examined for blemishes by the light of torches[22] did Naftali become convinced that it was indeed a sheep. It was given water to drink from a golden cup.

"The sheep is given water to drink, to make it easier to flay it after slaughtering," Reb Shmuel's explanation preceded the question.

"But why from a golden cup?" Naftali asked, greatly surprised.

"Because of the principle, '*Ein aniyus be-makom ashirus*' — 'There is no show of poverty in a place of wealth,'"[23] Reb Shmuel solved the riddle. "In a place like the House of Hashem, so awesome and honorable, only precious utensils are used, as it befits the King of all kings."

---

17. Mishnah *Middos* 1:6.

18. *Arachin* 13a.

19. Mishnah *Tamid* 3:4.

20. Mishnah *Shekalim* 6:4.

21. *Menachos* 87a, Tosafos (ד"ה שגובהן); *Bereishis Rabbah* 65:17.

22. Mishnah *Tamid* 3:4.

23. *Tamid* 29a.

The Kohen who won the privilege of slaughtering the *Tamid* led the sheep toward the *Taba'os*(77).[24] Naftali noticed two Kohanim going up[25] the Steps(22) leading to the *Ulam*(10). They were carrying utensils and were followed by other Kohanim.

Reb Shmuel continued to explain to Naftali what was going on before his eyes. "These two Kohanim have won the privilege of removing the ashes from the Golden *Mizbeach* and the Menorah. The Kohen who removes the ashes from the Golden *Mizbeach* will open the Entrance to the *Heichal*(42), assisted by other Kohanim. Twenty Kohanim are needed to open the heavy gates of the *Heichal's* entrance![26] I'll tell you how this is done.

"Kohanim enter the *Ulam*, turn to the right, toward the northern small Side Door [*Pishpesh*][27] and, once through there, enter the *Heichal* through one of the Compartments(69) [*Ta'im*], located on the northern side of the *Heichal*. They open the *Pishpesh* with two keys.[28] One unlocks an internal lock, which the Kohen who won the *payis*, entitling him to open the Entrance to the *Heichal*, can reach only by inserting his entire arm through a hole in the wall near the door. The other key opens a standard lock. When the *Pishpesh* is open, the Kohanim enter[29] the first Compartment, turn to the left (southward), enter the *Heichal*(11) and reach the Entrance to the *Heichal*, and there..."

Reb Shmuel suddenly stopped. A powerful noise had cut him off. The noise was accompanied by the blowing of a shofar — *tekiyah, teru'ah, tekiyah*[30] — and by Gamliel's frightened yelp.

---

24. Mishnah *Tamid* 3:5.

25. Mishnah *Tamid* 3:6.

26. *Yosiphon,* chap. 93.

27. Mishnah *Tamid* 3:7.

28. Mishnah *Tamid* 3:6.

29. Mishnah *Tamid* 3:7.

30. *Sukkah* 53b.

The Kohanim's Entrance into the Heichal

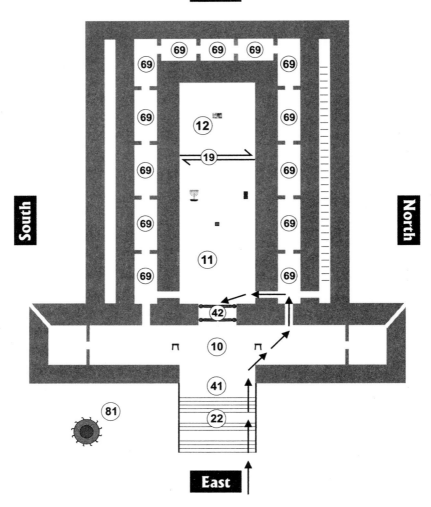

10. *Ulam* (Antechamber)

11. *Heichal* (Temple Chamber)

12. *Kodesh HaKodashim* (Holy of Holies)

19. Two Curtains and the one-cubit passage between them, which divided the *Heichal* from the *Kodesh HaKodashim*

22. 12 Steps ascending to *Ulam*

41. Entrance to *Ulam*

42. Entrance to *Heichal*

69. Compartments

81. *Kiyor* (Washing Basin)

After the blowing of the shofar had ceased, Reb Shmuel continued in a calming tone, "This is the noise made by the doors of the *Heichal* when they are being opened. It is heard as far as Jericho.[31] I'm sure you still remember what we learned about the four doors of the *Heichal*."[32]

> The placing of the two logs of wood come before the removing of the ashes from the inner (Golden) *Mizbeach*...

The children nodded their heads.

"It is forbidden to slaughter *korbanos* before these doors are opened,[33] as it says, '...and slaughter it [the offering] at the entrance of the Tent of Meeting.'[34] Our Sages interpret this verse to mean that it is permissible to slaughter only when the Tent of Meeting—and thus, the *Heichal*—is open and not when it is closed."

As their rebbi was speaking, the gates of the *Azarah* were opened wide.[35] The children wanted to go down immediately, but their *rebbi* convinced them that they'd better stay on top of the Wall, because from there they would continue having a clear view of the offering of the *Tamid*.

> The removal of the ashes from the inner (Golden) *Mizbeach* precedes the cleaning of the five lamps of the Menorah...

The children complied, and continued to watch the Kohanim's service. Reb Shmuel explained to Naftali that after the Entrance to the *Heichal*(42) was opened, one of the *payis*-winning Kohanim was supposed to enter and remove the ashes [*deshen*] of the

---

31. Mishnah *Tamid* 3:8.

32. Mishnah *Middos* 4:1.

33. *Zevachim* 55b.

34. *Vayikra* 3:2.

35. Mishnah *Tamid* 3:7, *Tiferes Yisrael* #58.

The Morning Tamid-Offering

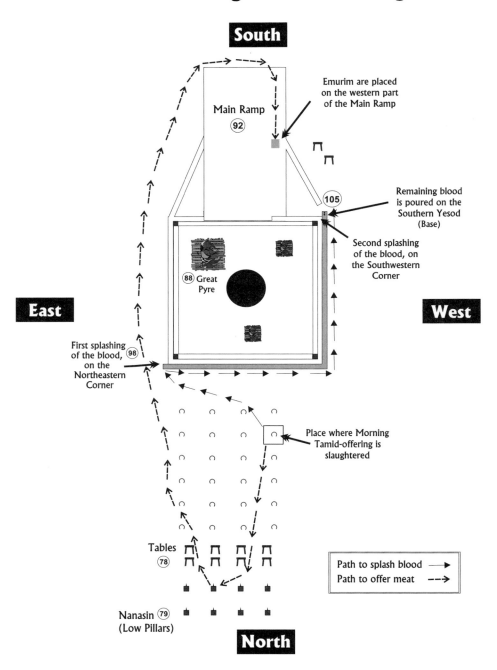

South

Emurim are placed on the western part of the Main Ramp

Main Ramp
92

105

Remaining blood is poured on the Southern Yesod (Base)

Second splashing of the blood, on the Southwestern Corner

East

West

88 Great Pyre

First splashing of the blood, 98 on the Northeastern Corner

Place where Morning Tamid-offering is slaughtered

Tables
78

Path to splash blood ⟶
Path to offer meat ⤏

Nanasin 79
(Low Pillars)

North

previous day from the Golden *Mizbeach*(83) into a vessel called a *teni*, leave it there and then exit from the *Heichal*(11).[36] The other Kohen would then enter after him and clean out five of the seven lamps of the Menorah, in order to prepare it for that evening's lighting.

"But why only five?" Naftali thought to himself. "Why not clean out all seven lamps?" But he held back his question. He saw the two Kohanim walk out of the *Heichal* empty-handed, without the *deshen*. He wanted to ask about that also, but that's when the Kohanim started to slaughter the *korban Tamid*, so he gave up the idea.

With the combined effort of several Kohanim, the sheep's huge head was placed into the proper ring.[37] The sheep's forelegs were then bound to its hind legs, and the Kohanim who had won the privilege of transfering its limbs and organs to the *Mizbeach*, held the *Tamid* down.

The Kohen who had won the privilege of slaughtering the sheep uttered the blessing, "Blessed are You, Hashem, our God, King of the world, Who sanctified us with His commandments and commanded us concerning the slaughtering"—whereupon he slaughtered the sheep with a firm hand.[38]

Another Kohen made the blessing on collecting the blood—"...Who sanctified us with the sanctity of Aharon and commanded us to receive the blood"[39]—whereupon he caught the blood into a sprinkling bowl. He

> The cleaning of the five lamps of the Menorah precedes the sprinkling of the blood of the *korban Tamid...*

---

36. Mishnah *Tamid* 3:9.

37. Mishnah *Tamid* 4:1.

38. Rav Chayim Kanievsky *shlita*, based on Rambam, *Hilchos Berachos* 11:15.

39. Rambam, *Hilchos Ma'asei HaKorbanos* 1:1, *Mishneh le-Melech*.

walked toward the Northeastern Corner of the *Mizbeach*(98) and splashed some of the blood against it, below the *Chut HaSikra*(102) [Red Line].[40] He then circled the *Mizbeach*, disappearing behind it. There he performed another splashing, this time onto the Southwestern Corner of the *Mizbeach*(100). He poured out the leftover blood onto the Southern Base(105) [*HaYesod HaDeromi*].

"The blood of the burnt-offering[41] is splashed twice so that all four sides of the *Mizbeach* are daubed," Naftali remembered. "That is to say, the Kohen splashes the blood once on the Northeastern Corner, and it adheres to both the northern and eastern sides. Then he splashes the blood on the Southwestern Corner and it adheres to both the southern and western sides."

The slaughtered animal was then taken to the *Nanasin*(79) [Low Pillars], to be flayed and cut up.[42]

Reb Shmuel signaled to the children to follow him.

"Would you like to visit *Lishkas HaGazis*(53) [Chamber of Hewn Stone], to see the drawing of the third *payis*?" he asked.

"Yes!" the excited children answered eagerly.

They started running down the steps, Reb Shmuel warning them worriedly, "Watch the steps! Be careful not to fall!"

They continued running, and Reb Shmuel walked quickly after them, praying to Hashem that his dear pupils not get hurt.

---

40. Mishnah *Tamid* 4:1.
41. *Zevachim* 53b.
42. Mishnah *Middos* 3:5.

The Kohen splashed some blood at the Northeastern Corner of the Mizbeach

Chapter Twenty-Six

In Lishkas HaGazis

The boys stopped at the bottom of the stairs and waited for Reb Shmuel, who arrived soon after. Then they all entered *Lishkas HaGazis*(53) through the entrance facing the *Cheil*(2),[1] which was now open. They saw a very large, mostly empty room.

"Here we can pick a good spot, from which we'll be able to see the two last *payis* drawings clearly," Reb Shmuel said and pointed to a certain corner.

Inside the *Azarah*, the Kohanim began cutting up the *korban Tamid*. First, they took the slaughtered sheep to the *Nanasin*(79). Usually, sheep brought as *korbanos* were hung on a lower hook;[2] but the enormous *Tamid*-offering needed to be hung on the highest one.

The Kohanim flayed the sheep and cut it up, whereupon they passed on its parts to the six Kohanim who had already won in the second *payis* the privilege of carrying the limbs and organs to the Ramp.[3]

---

1. *Yoma* 25a.

2. Mishnah *Tamid* 3:5.

3. Mishnah *Tamid* 4:2,3.

These six Kohanim were part of a group of nine who arranged themselves in a line. The first Kohen was carrying the head and the right hind leg of the *Tamid*. The second one had the honor of carrying the two forelegs. The third was carrying the tail in one hand and the left hind leg in the other. The fourth was carrying the chest and the *gerah* (throat, larynx with the windpipe, the lungs and the heart), and the fifth the two *defanos* (sides). The sixth Kohen was carrying a vessel with the *korban's* innards. The three other Kohanim were carrying the *minchas Tamid* (fine-quality wheat flour mixed with oil[4]), the *chavitin*, and the wine of *nisuch Tamid*, for pouring onto the *Mizbeach*.[5]

The Kohanim climbed the Ramp(92) and, before they reached its midpoint, put their loads down on its western half. Then they descended the Ramp and went to *Lishkas HaGazis* to recite *Kerias Shema*.

All this time the children had been waiting in *Lishkas HaGazis*. Their *rebbi* had decided to bring them in advance so they wouldn't miss the *payis*; consequently, they didn't see the cutting up of the *Tamid*-offering and its transport to the *Mizbeach*.

While they were waiting, Reb Shmuel taught them some very important *halachos*. "*Lishkas HaGazis* is the seat of the Great Sanhedrin [*HaSanhedrin HaGedolah*].[6] This is where the greatest Torah scholars of the generation conduct their deliberations and sit in judgment. The Sanhedrin numbers seventy-one great Sages of Yisrael,[7] corresponding to Moshe Rabbeinu and the Seventy Elders [*Shivim Zekeinim*]. The most difficult halachic issues and problems, which could not be resolved and ruled upon by other

---

4. *Bemidbar* 28:5.

5. Mishnah *Tamid* 4:3.

6. Mishnah *Middos* 5:4.

7. *Sanhedrin* 2a.

batei din (rabbinical courts), are discussed here.[8] Also, the Great Sanhedrin must rule in certain special cases, [9] such as to judge an *ir ha-nidachas* [a city whose population has worshiped idols and must, therefore, be annihilated, and the city burned], or decide whether to start a *milchemes reshus* [a war aimed at capturing spoils]. The Elders of the Sanhedrin sit in the northern half of the chamber, the part that opens to the *Cheil*(2).[10] This part does not have the sanctity of the *Azarah.*"

Gamliel interrupted Reb Shmuel's words with an expression of surprise on his face. "Wouldn't it be more fitting for the honorable Sanhedrin to hold sessions in a holier place?"

"Who thinks he knows why they do not sit in a place that has the *kedushah*, sanctity, of the *Azarah*?" Reb Shmuel answered with a question.

"Becasue only kings descended from King David are permitted to sit in the *Azarah*!" Bo'az shouted excitedly.

"Exactly," Reb Shmuel confirmed with a smile of satisfaction on his face. "The *dayanim*, judges, are forbidden to sit in a place that has the holiness of the *Azarah*. On the other hand, the *payis* drawings are held in the holier part of *Lishkas HaGazis.*"

"And why there in particular?" Reuven asked.

"The verse says, 'In the House of Hashem we shall walk with emotion.'[11] The emotional excitement and tumult accompanying the *payis* drawings must take place specifically in the House of Hashem — that is to say, in the most holy place."[12]

"Well, in that case, why not draw each *payis* in the *Azarah* it-

---

8. *Sanhedrin* 86b.

9. *Sanhedrin* 2a.

10. *Yoma* 25a.

11. *Tehillim* 55:15.

12. *Yoma* 25a.

self?" Naftali found it difficult to understand.

"There are two reasons why not,"[13] Reb Shmuel replied patiently. "The first reason is that, as we will see, the *memuneh* begins the *payis* by removing the *migba'as* [turban] from the head of one of the Kohanim. Standing in the *Azarah* bareheaded would be a disgrace. Another reason is that when a *payis* is drawn, the Kohanim stand in a circle. If they would be standing in the *Azarah*, some of them would have to turn their backs to the *Heichal*."

"Why can't all the participants of all the *avodos* of the morning service be determined in one *payis*? Why do you need four separate ones?" Bo'az was the one to pose a question this time.

Reb Shmuel answered well. "This halachah is also learned from the same verse: 'In the House of Hashem we shall walk with emotion.' How is it possible to increase the emotion? By having more than one *payis*. The more of them, the greater the excitement and tumult.[14] The excitement is for the sake of Hashem's glory and honor, because it is an expression of the Kohanim's great yearning to win the merit of performing an *avodah* during the Divine Service."

As they were talking, the chamber was filling up with crowds of Jews: Kohanim, Leviyim and Yisraelim.

"Before the *payis* takes place, the Kohanim and the rest of the people will recite *Kerias Shema* and say a few prayers. We'll join them," Reb Shmuel told his pupils. "We'll say *Kerias Shema* again later on,[15] when we can also say its first *berachah*—Yotzer or ('Who forms light')—which we can't say now because it's still before sunrise."[16]

---

13. Ibid., Tosafos (ד"ה והא בעינן).
14. *Yoma* 24b.
15. *Yoma* 37b.
16. *Berachos* 12a.

The voice of the *memuneh*[17] echoed in the room, declaring: "Make one *berachah*!" ["*Barechu berachah achas*!"]. A powerful mixture of voices burst out in the air and filled it with the pleasant sound of prayer. The voices mingled with each other, in a sweet tune, reciting *Ahavah rabbah*, the second *berachah* of *Kerias Shema*: "With abundant love have You loved us, Eternal, our God; You have been exceedingly compassionate toward us. Our Father, our King, in the merit of our forefathers who trusted in You, and whom You taught the laws of life, so too, favor us and teach us."

The voices grew in volume.

"Our Father, the merciful Father, Who acts compassionately, have compassion on us and inspire our heart to comprehend and discern, to listen, to learn and teach, to observe, perform and fulfill every detail of Your Torah's teaching with love!"

The prayer reached the height of fervor when both the Kohanim and the rest of those present pleaded with Hashem: "Illuminate our eyes in Your Torah, cause our heart to adhere to Your commandments, and unify our hearts to love and fear Your Name, so that we not be shamed forevermore."

The atmosphere in *Lishkas HaGazis* strongly resembled the *Ne'ilah* prayer of Yom Kippur. Naftali felt some moisture on his cheek. He passed his hand across his face, and discovered tears — to his own amazement.

"Am I crying?" he wondered to himself.

He had cried on many occasions — as all children do — but this was the first time he'd shed tears during prayer.

"O God," he prayed from deep within his soul, "please, help me! I want to grow into a *talmid chacham*! I want to have the *zechus* to learn Torah *lishmah*!" He felt his prayer emerging from the very depths of his heart and was sure Hashem would listen.

---

17. Mishnah *Tamid* 5:1.

After the congregation had finished the *Ahavah rabbah* bless-ing, they recited the Ten Commandments [*Aseres HaDibros*], which represent the essence of the Torah, and actually comprise it in its entirety, in condensed form.[18] This is hinted at by the fact that there are 613 letters in the Ten Commandments, correspond-ing to the 613 *mitzvos* in the Torah.[19]

Naftali pictured himself standing at the foot of Mount Sinai, receiving the Torah. It was so vivid in his imagination that he could actually feel himself standing there, squeezed among the millions of Jews, listening excitedly to the proclamation of *Aseres HaDibros*: "The sound of the shofar was becoming increasingly loud; Moshe would speak and the Eternal would respond with sound."[20]

The Kohanim recited *Kerias Shema*[21] and then said the morn-ing *berachah* recited afterwards, *Emes ve-yatziv*; however, they did not recite all of the *Shemoneh Esreh* prayer. They only said two blessings. The first one was the *Retzeh* blessing, and it went like this:[22]

רְצֵה ה' אֱלוֹקֵינוּ עֲבוֹדַת עַמְּךָ יִשְׂרָאֵל וְאִשֵּׁי יִשְׂרָאֵל וּתְפִילָתָם תְּקַבֵּל בְּרָצוֹן בָּרוּךְ אַתָּה ה' שֶׁאוֹתְךָ לְבַדְּךָ בְּיִרְאָה נַעֲבֹד.

"Take pleasure, Hashem our God, in the worship of Your people Yisrael, and accept favorably Yisrael's fire-offerings and their prayer. Blessed are You, Hashem, Who is the only One Whom we shall worship with fear."[23]

---

18. Mishnah *Tamid* 5:1, *Tiferes Yisrael* #3.

19. *Da'as Zekeinim MiBa'alei HaTosafos, Devarim* 17:20.

20. *Shemos* 19:19.

21. Mishnah *Tamid* 5:1.

22. *Berachos* 11b, Rashi (ד"ה ועבודה).

23. *Ezras Kohanim*'s ruling in accordance with the second opinion in Rashi, ibid.

Then the Kohanim recited the verses[24] of the priestly bless-ing.[25] They did not lift up their hands with their fingers spread in a special way (*nesiyas kapayim*). They would do that after the burning of the incense. The moving ceremony ended with the fi-nal blessing of the *Shemoneh Esreh, Sim shalom*.[26]

"For the first time in my life, I felt what real prayer is all about," Alexander admitted quietly. He saw in his friends' eyes that he had expressed everyone's feelings.

The *memuneh's* announcement interrupted their thoughts. "*Chadashim la-ketores, bo-u ve-hafisu!*" ["Those new to *ketores*, come and participate in the *payis!*"][27]

"This announcement means that only Kohanim who have never yet had the merit of burning the *ketores* may participate in this *payis*,"[28] Reb Shmuel explained the meaning of the proc-lamation. "The *ketores* has a special *segulah*:[29] it makes wealthy the one who burns it. Therefore, each Kohen is given a chance to attain wealth by burning the *ketores*. The Kohanim, who are the servants of Hashem, are especially in need of Hashem's blessing to become rich, so that they can dedicate all their time to serv-ing Him. This is also the reason why Hashem endowed them with the twenty-four priestly gifts [*matnos kehunah*], so they won't have to work for their sustenance and their time can be free for

---

24. *Bemidbar* 6:24–26.

25. Mishnah *Tamid* 5:1, Bartenura.

26. *Ezras Kohanim*, compromising between Tosafos' opinion in *Berachos* 11b (ד"ה וברכות) — according to which the Kohanim only recited the priestly blessing and did not say the *Sim shalom* prayer, and the Rambam's opinion in *Hilchos Temidin u'Musafin* 6:4, which maintains that they said *Sim shalom* but did not recite the priestly blessing.

27. Mishnah *Tamid* 5:2.

28. *Yoma* 26a.

29. *Segulah* — intrinsic feature, power, quality.

learning Torah and serving Hashem."[30]

Yonasan, who was so well versed in Tanach, immediately quoted, "He commanded the people... to give the portion of the Leviyim and the Kohanim, so that they could strengthen themselves in the Torah of Hashem."[31]

"I saw a *payis* once," Chananya whispered into Naftali's ear. "Pay attention to the old man sitting on the side. He is the overseer of the *payis*. He sees to it that everybody acts honestly."[32]

The Kohanim agreed that the *memuneh* would count until seventy-two.[33]

"Is there any special reason for this particular number?" Naftali asked Chananya.

Chananya showed great expertise. "No special reason really. The main thing is to choose a number larger than the number of the Kohanim participating in the *payis*."[34]

Fifteen Kohanim, who had never yet had the *zechus* to offer ketores, stood in a circle around the Kohen in charge of the *payis*, looking at him with eager eyes. Naftali recognized among them the Kohen who had pleaded with Hashem in the *Beis HaMoked*(56) to be given the privilege of carrying out an *avodah*. The Kohen-*memuneh* commanded the ones standing in the circle,

---

30. *Devarim* 18:5: "For the Eternal, your God, has chosen [both] him and his sons from all your tribes, to stand [and] serve in the name of the Eternal for all time."

31. *II Divrei HaYamim* 31:4.

32. *Yoma* 25a.

33. Rambam, *Hilchos Temidin u'Musafin* 4:3: "How was the *payis* carried out? They stood in a circle and agreed on a [certain] number, and [the *memuneh*] counted [fingers, going around the circle as many times as needed,] until...[he arrived at the] number that they had agreed on."

34. *Yoma* 22a, Rashi (ד"ה הצביעו).

"Hatzbi'u!" ("Stick your fingers out!")[35]

Each Kohen stuck out a finger.

"It is forbidden to count people; therefore, the fingers of the Kohanim are counted,"[36] Reb Shmuel explained.

The *memuneh* removed the *migba'as* from the head of one of the Kohanim,[37] in order to indicate that he would begin the count with this Kohen, and immediately returned it to him.[38] He then began counting the fingers that the Kohanim had stuck out, starting from the finger of the Kohen whose *migba'as* had been removed from his head.[39]

"The *memuneh* does not know which number the Kohanim have agreed upon, and the Kohanim do not know in advance whose *migba'as* will be removed, so the *payis* is going to be carried out with absolute fairness,"[40] Chananya whispered into Naftali's ear.

"The Kohanim who will not win the privilege of *ketores* today will not be able to do it during the next half a year either," Naftali thought to himself, "because each Kohen serves in the Beis HaMikdash only once every twenty-four weeks."[41]

The *memuneh* went around and around the circle of Kohanim, counting each one's finger, until he arrived at the number seventy-two. To Naftali's great surprise and satisfaction, the *memuneh*'s count landed on none other than the Kohen who had prayed so fervently in the *Beis HaMoked*. The Kohen was beside

---

35. *Yoma* 22a.

36. *Yoma* 22b.

37. *Yoma* 25a.

38. Rambam, *Hilchos Temidin u'Musafin* 4:3.

39. *Yoma* 25a.

40. Rambam, *Hilchos Temidin u'Musafin* 4:3, *Kesef Mishneh*.

41. *Ta'anis* 26a.

himself with joy, beaming and smiling from ear to ear. He turned to the Kohen who stood next to him on his right and told him: "*Zechei immi ba-machtah!*" ("Share the privilege [to do the *ketores*] with me by [using] the *machtah!*")[42]

"The Kohen who has won the *payis* will burn the *ketores*, and the second one will bring the *machtah*, the firepan with the burning coals, into the *Heichal*,"[43] Chananya said.

*   *   *

The news spread quickly from one person to another: The *Kohen Gadol* himself, Rabbi Yishmael ben Piyachi, was going to throw the parts of the *Tamid* onto the Great Pyre today, all by himself!

The fourth *payis*,[44] in which one Kohen would win the mitzvah of carrying the *eivarim* (limbs) and other parts of the *Tamid* from the Main Ramp(92) to the *Mizbeach*(7) and throwing them onto the Great Pyre(88),[45] had not yet been drawn. The *Kohen Gadol* could choose any type of *avodah* in the Beis HaMikdash himself, any time he wished, without participating in a *payis*.[46]

The children asked Reb Shmuel ardently, "Is the fourth *payis* going to be drawn? Wouldn't it be quite superfluous in view of the fact that the *payis*-winning Kohen won't be able to serve anyway, since the *Kohen Gadol* has expressed a desire to burn the *eivarim*?" A logical question, indeed.

Before Reb Shmuel could utter a word in reply, the Kohanim had already prepared themselves for the fourth *payis*. It was

---

42. *Yoma* 25b.
43. Ibid., Rashi.
44. Mishnah *Tamid* 5:2.
45. Mishnah *Tamid* 7:3, *Tiferes Yisrael, Bo'az* #1.
46. *Yoma* 14a.

drawn, and one of them won the privilege of lifting up the *eiv-arim* from the Ramp and carrying them to the *Mizbeach*.

On their way from *Lishkas HaGazis*(53), Reb Shmuel explained to the children, "The fourth *payis* is drawn anyhow, in spite of the fact that the *Kohen Gadol* will most probably burn the *eivarim*. The Kohen who wins the mitzvah will not be rejected and passed over for service in any case. No *payis* is drawn for the offering of the afternoon *Tamid*,[47] and the Kohen who wins the *zechus* to offer the early morning one offers the afternoon one as well, so that if he is deprived of his privilege to serve in the morning, he'll get a chance to serve in the afternoon."

The Kohanim and the rest of the people began to leave *Lishkas HaGazis*. The children streamed to the *Ezras Yisrael*(4) amid the crowd. Everyone was eager to secure a good spot for himself there, from where he could watch the *avodah*.

"I really want the *Kohen Gadol* to do the *avodah* today!" the candid wish escaped from Naftali's mouth. "No small thing—to watch the great *tzaddik*, Rabbi Yishmael ben Piyachi, worship his Creator with awe and trepidation!"

---

47. *Yoma* 26a.

Chapter Twenty-Seven

"And He Burned Spice Incense on It..."*

N aftali and the rest of the boys followed Reb Shmuel along the *Ezras Yisrael*(4). They occupied a comfortable spot next to *Lishkas HaMelach*(62) [Salt Chamber]. The Kohen who had won the *zechus* to burn the *ketores* hurried to *Lishkas Beis Avtinas*(65) [Avtinas Family Chamber] located above *Sha'ar HaMayim*(40) [Water Gate],[1] where the *ketores* was prepared[2] and stored.[3] He had already washed his hands and feet prior to climbing up the *Mizbeach* to prepare the Great Pyre together with other Kohanim.

The Kohen walked slowly and thoughtfully from *Lishkas Beis Avtinas*, with a serious expression on his face. This was going to be the first and last time in his life to have the *zechus* to burn the *ketores*. It was no trifling matter at all to gratify and please HaKadosh Baruch Hu by burning the *ketores* upon the Golden *Mizbeach*(83)! How thoroughly he had prepared himself, what a great number of prayers he had prayed until he finally attained

---

* *Shemos* 40:27.

1. Mishnah *Middos* 1:1, *Tiferes Yisrael* #2.

2. *Yoma* 18b, Rashi (ד"ה בית אבטינס).

3. *Yoma* 47a.

this lofty moment. Naftali saw the Kohen carry a large, golden ladle[4] whose capacity was three *kabin*.[5] The ladle had a piece of cloth on top of it serving as a decoration.[6]

"There is a small vessel, called *bazach*, inside the ladle.[7] It has a cover and is full of incense," Reb Shmuel explained to Naftali and Chananya, who were standing next to him. "The *bazach* is put into the bigger vessel on purpose:[8] it is not advisable to hold a *bazach* filled to the brim with *ketores* because some of it may fall out. On the other hand, to just put it in a bigger vessel, leaving the vessel half-empty, would not be regarded as sufficient honor of the Sanctuary."

The children nodded in understanding and continued watching, as the second Kohen's activity completely riveted their attention. He took a silver *machtah*[9] with the capacity of four *kabin*[10] and ascended the Main Ramp(92) with it in his hand. After he reached the top of the *Mizbeach*, he turned to the right[11] and walked around it along the *Kohanim*'s Footpath(91) until he reached the Second Pyre for incense(89), located next to the Southwestern Corner of the *Mizbeach*(100).[12] The Kohen shoved the dimmer and cooler outer coals to the sides and filled the firepan with burning coals.[13]

---

4. Mishnah *Tamid* 5:4; *Yoma* 26a.

5. *Kav*: approximately 2.9 pints or 1.4 liters.

6. Mishnah *Tamid* 5:4, Bartenura; Rambam, *Hilchos Temidin u'Musafin* 3:4.

7. Mishnah *Tamid* 5:4.

8. Ibid., Bartenura.

9. Mishnah *Tamid* 5:5.

10. *Yoma* 43b.

11. *Zevachim* 63a, Rashi on 63b (ד"ה ומקיפין).

12. Mishnah *Tamid* 2:5.

13. Mishnah *Tamid* 5:5.

After the Kohen had descended the Ramp he took a golden *machtah* with the capacity of three *kabin*,[14] and transferred the coals to it from the larger silver *machtah*. Some of the coals fell to the floor of the *Azarah*,[15] and the Kohen hurried to push them into the trough of water [*amas ha-mayim*] that flowed through the *Azarah*, to prevent the barefooted Kohanim from burning their feet.

Naftali remembered his *rebbi's* words concerning the reason for transferring the coals from one *machtah* to the other: a silver *machtah* is used in the beginning, to scoop out the burning coals, because the expensive golden *machtah* may get damaged if it is used for scooping.[16] It would be costly to replace it and the Torah is concerned not to overspend the money of Yisrael. Therefore, only afterwards are the coals transferred to the golden *machtah*, with which it is considered more honorable to enter the *Heichal*(11) in order to burn the incense.

During a lesson on the subject of the incense, Reb Shmuel had explained to his pupils why the golden *machtah* was smaller than the silver one: "We make a special effort to see to it that the *machtah* brought into the *Heichal* is full to capacity,[17] but when the coals are put into the silver *machtah* it doesn't always get filled to the brim. Therefore, the coals are transferred into the golden *machtah* that is one *kav* smaller than the silver one. This way it's bound to get filled right up to the top."

Reuven posed a question at this point. "We put the coals into a silver *machtah* because the Torah is careful with Jewish money.[18] But why don't we say, '*Ein aniyus be-makom ashirus*' ['There is

---

14. *Yoma* 43b.

15. Mishnah *Tamid* 5:5.

16. *Yoma* 44b.

17. Mishnah *Tamid* 5:5, Bartenura.

18. *Yoma* 44b.

The Kohen transferred the coals from the silver machtah into the golden one

no show of poverty in a place of wealth'] and use only the gold *machtah* anyway?"[19]

Bo'az suddenly had an inspiration. "The principle of '*Ein ani-yus be-makom ashirus*' is valid in cases similar to giving the sheep for the *Tamid*-offering to drink from a golden cup. This is where no financial loss is incurred — or only insignificant loss is incurred.[20] However, when there is the possibility that the financial loss will be great — such as damage caused to the golden *machtah* — we are bound to say, 'The Torah is concerned not to overspend the money of Yisrael.'"

*　　　　*　　　　*

The two Kohanim, who were carrying the incense and the *machtah* with the coals, reached the area Between the *Ulam* and the *Mizbeach*(9).[21] Then something interesting happened. One of the Kohanim grabbed a strange-looking vessel that looked like a rake, and threw it between the *Ulam* and the *Mizbeach*. It fell on the floor with a loud bang. The bang was heard in town, and it caused many people to interrupt their conversations for a moment. A minor commotion was heard in the *Azarah* immediately after the rake had been thrown. Many Kohanim who had heard the bang started running in the direction of the Entrance to the *Ulam*(41), so that they could manage to prostrate themselves in the *Heichal*(11) together with their fellow Kohanim. The Leviyim, for their own part, hurried to occupy their places on the *Duchan*(5) [Platform] in order to be ready to chant the *Shir shel Yom* [Psalm of the Day]. The musical instruments were taken out of *Lishkas Klei HaShir*(50)]Musical Instruments Chamber], and brought

---

19. *Menachos* 88b.

20. Mishnah *Shekalim* 8:5, *Tiferes Yisrael*, *Bo'az* #3.

21. Mishnah *Tamid* 5:6.

The Burning of the Incense

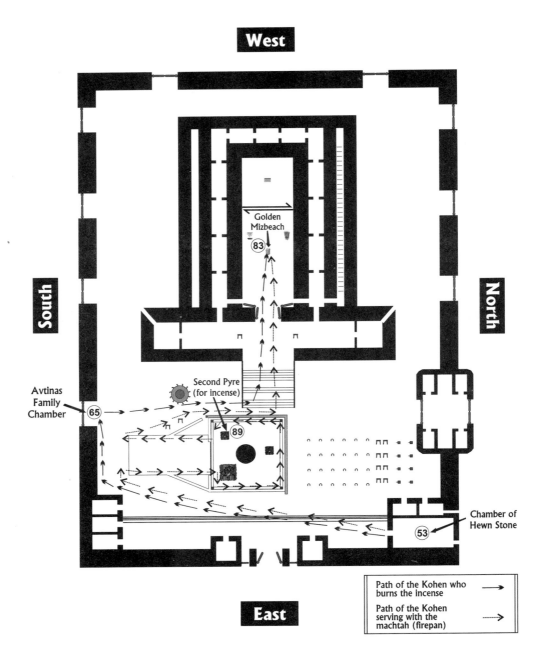

West

South

North

East

Golden Mizbeach
83

Second Pyre (for incense)
89

Avtinas Family Chamber
65

Chamber of Hewn Stone
53

Path of the Kohen who burns the incense →

Path of the Kohen serving with the machtah (firepan) ⇢

respectfully into the *Azarah*. All of this activity was initiated by the loud bang of the rake.

The Kohanim waited at the Entrance to the *Ulam* for the appearance of Rabbi Yishmael ben Piyachi, the *Kohen Gadol*. They could enter to prostrate themselves only after he had prostrated himself first.[22] A few minutes later the *Kohen Gadol* majestically appeared from his Chamber(54)[23] flanked by his deputy *Kohen Gadol [segan]* on his right.[24] He went up the Steps ascending to the *Ulam*(22), escorted by three Kohanim. The three Kohanim[25] entered the *Ulam*(10) together with the *Kohen Gadol*, and the *segan* remained waiting outside.[26] The *paroches* of the Entrance to the *Ulam*(41) that was usually raised in order to make it possible for the Kohanim to pass through,[27] was lowered in honor of the *Kohen Gadol* — to give him a chance to sequester himself with his Creator when he prostrated himself before Him.

Reb Shmuel whispered to Naftali and Chananya:

"When the *Kohen Gadol* prostrates himself he is supported by one *kohen hedyot* on his right and another one his left, while the third one supports him by holding on to the *ephod* stones on his shoulder."[28]

A few minutes passed, whereupon the sound of the *pa'amonim* [bells] attached to the hem of the *Kohen Gadol's me'il* [robe] heralded his approach to the *segan*.[29] The *segan* then lifted up the *paroches*

---

22. Mishnah *Tamid* 7:1.

23. Mishnah *Middos* 5:4.

24. Rambam, *Hilchos Klei HaMikdash* 4:16.

25. Mishnah *Tamid* 7:1.

26. Rambam, *Hilchos Klei HaMikdash* 5:11.

27. Mishnah *Tamid* 7:1, *Tosfos Yom Tov*.

28. Mishnah *Tamid* 7:1.

29. Ibid., *Tiferes Yisrael* #3.

> The cleaning out of the two lamps precedes the burning of the incense...

and the *Kohen Gadol* emerged from the *Ulam*. Naftali saw his face radiating holiness, as his eight garments gave him a unique, kingly appearance.

Dozens of Kohanim then entered the *Heichal* through the *Ulam* and prostrated themselves before the *Kodesh HaKodashim*, with their arms and feet outstretched on the floor.

The two Kohanim who had won the privilege of burning the incense slowly ascended the steps leading to the *Ulam*(22), carrying the incense and the coals.[30] The Kohanim who had won the privilege of removing the *deshen* (ashes) of the Golden *Mizbeach*(83) and cleaning out the Menorah(84) preceded them into the *Ulam*. The Kohen who had removed the *deshen* from the Golden *Mizbeach*(83) entered the *Heichal*(11). He lifted up the *teni* containing the *deshen* removed from the Golden *Mizbeach*, prostrated himself and went out. The Kohen who had cleaned out the five lamps of the Menorah entered the *Heichal* and cleaned out the last two lamps. On his way out of the *Heichal* he took the cup [*kuz*] that contained the remainders of the wicks, the *deshen* and the oil, prostrated himself in awe and fear, and left. The two Kohanim carried the *deshen*[31] and poured it out next to the Main Ramp, on its eastern side, at the spot where the *terumas ha-deshen* was placed.[32]

"This *deshen* is swallowed in this spot!"[33] Naftali remembered, as he shivered from awe.

The holy service continued. The two Kohanim who carried the ladle and the *machtah* passed through the *Ulam* on their way

---

30. Mishnah *Tamid* 6:1.
31. *Ezras Kohanim*.
32. Mishnah *Tamid* 1:4.
33. *Yoma* 21a.

to the *Heichal*. The *memuneh* and another Kohen accompanied them.[34] The Kohen who carried the *machtah* poured the coals in a pile onto the Golden *Mizbeach*(83), prostrated himself and went out.[35] The Kohen who had won the privilege of burning the *ketores* transferred the *ketores* into his hand with the assistance of the accompanying Kohen, who prostrated himself immediately afterwards and left the *Heichal*.[36]

"*Hakter!*" ["Burn the incense!"] the *memuneh* commanded. He then prostrated himself as the previous Kohen had done and left through the Entrance to the *Ulam*(41).

The Kohanim also left the area Between the *Ulam* and the *Mizbeach*(9),[37] whereupon the Kohen burning the incense remained alone in the *Heichal*. He stood still for a minute trembling from awe, whereupon he burned the incense with shaking hands, prostrated himself before his Creator and left the place perspiring heavily.

As soon as he had emerged from the *Heichal*, the Kohanim who had officiated in the Beis HaMikdash that morning went and stood on the Steps ascending to the *Ulam*(22). Five of them were holding the vessels they had used during their service.[38] The vessels were empty, which was a sign that the Kohanim had fully completed their *avodah*. The Kohen who had removed the

The Golden (Incense) Mizbeach

---

34. Mishnah *Tamid* 6:3.

35. Mishnah *Tamid* 6:2.

36. Mishnah *Tamid* 6:3.

37. *Yoma* 44a.

38. Mishnah *Tamid* 7:2. See also *Tiferes Yisrael* #8.

ashes from the Golden *Mizbeach* was holding the *teni* in his hand, and the Kohen who had cleaned out the lamps was holding the *kuz*. The Kohen who had brought in the coals was holding the *machtah*, and one of the two last Kohanim was holding the *bazach* for the incense. The last Kohen was holding the ladle into which the *bazach* had been placed, and the *bazach's* cover.

The five Kohanim were standing on the southern part of the Steps.[39] Their fellow Kohanim joined them and stood on the northern side. All the Kohanim waited silently to be joined by the Kohen who was to bring up the *eivarim* from the Main Ramp to be burned on the *Mizbeach*, whereupon they would say the priestly blessing [*Birkas Kohanim*] together.

Naftali heard people whisper to each other excitedly: the *Kohen Gadol* will offer the *eivarim* on the *Mizbeach* today!

---

39. Mishnah *Tamid* 7:2.

Chapter Twenty-Eight

Facing the Throne of Glory

Naftali stood on the side looking at the *Kohen Gadol* with adoring eyes. The *Kohen Gadol*, Rabbi Yishmael ben Piyachi, was one of the *bnei aliyah* (very distinguished), a saintly, righteous man.

His mother's name was Kimchis, a woman whose great modesty (*tzeniyus*) was widely known. In the merit of her modesty, she had the *zechus* to raise seven sons who became great Torah scholars and *tzaddikim*; all of them served as *Kohen Gadol*.[1] The Sages said about her that the verse in *Tehillim*, "All the glory of the king's daughter is within; greater than gold settings is her attire,"[2] meant a modest woman like her.[3] In reward for her deep modesty such a woman raises sons who wear garments with golden settings, i.e. the *choshen mishpat* and *ephod* of the *Kohen Gadol*.

It is told about Rabbi Yishmael ben Piyachi that once, on Yom Kippur, he went to the market and spoke to the heathen ruler (*hegmon*). As the *hegmon* spoke, some of his spittle fell onto the *Kohen Gadol's* garments, and the Sages feared that the *Kohen Gadol* might have become *tamei*. Because of this, his brother served in

---

1. *Yoma* 47a, Maharsha.
2. *Tehillim* 45:14.
3. *Yoma* 47a, Rashi (ד"ה לא ראו).

the Temple during the rest of the day instead of him. Thus Rabbi Yishmael's mother, Kimchis, had the *zechus* to see two of her sons officiating as High Priest that day![4]

Now this saintly and righteous man, Rabbi Yishmael, ascended the Main Ramp(92) flanked by his *segan* on his right.[5] He was followed by the six Kohanim who had previously brought up the *eivarim* to the Ramp. The *Kohen Gadol* covered half the length of the Ramp, whereupon his *segan* helped him climb up the rest of it, to the top. A Kohen approached, one of the winners in the second *payis*, who before had carried the head and leg of the *Tamid* to the middle of the Ramp. Now he lifted up the head and the leg and passed them on to the *Kohen Gadol*. Rabbi Yishmael stood with his eyes closed and rested his hands on the *eivarim*.

Reb Shmuel's whisper reached Naftali's and Chananya's ears. "Although the requirement of *semichah* (pressing one's hands on the *korban*'s head) is valid only when the sacrificial animal is still alive,[6] the *Kohen Gadol* performs *semichah* on the *eivarim* as well because of his high and honored position. Moreover, a *kohen hedyot* who brings the *eivarim* from the Main Ramp to the *Mizbeach* goes up and burns them all by himself. It is only the *Kohen Gadol* who is escorted by a *kohen hedyot* up the Ramp, and to whom the *eivarim* are respectfully handed, as a token of great honor and esteem."

> The incense offering precedes the burning of the eivarim...

Naftali looked attentively and saw how Rabbi Yishmael threw the head and the leg from the top of the Main Ramp(92) into the Great Pyre(88).[7] Now another Kohen walked

---

4. *Yoma* 47a.

5. Mishnah *Tamid* 7:3.

6. *Menachos* 94a.

7. Mishnah *Tamid* 7:3.

Rabbi Yishmael threw the head and the leg into the Great Pyre

forward from the middle of the Ramp carrying the two fore-legs, and passed them on to the first Kohen, and the first Kohen passed them on to the *Kohen Gadol*. He pressed his hands on them and threw them into the fire. The other Kohanim did the same with the other parts of the *Tamid*: the first Kohen received the *eivarim* from them and passed them on to the *Kohen Gadol*, who threw them into the fire.

When this part of the service was finished and all the parts of the *korban* were in the fire, Rabbi Yishmael and his assistants descended the Ramp. They stood on the Steps ascending to the *Ulam*(22) together with the other Kohanim who were standing there.[8] The meal-offering and wine libation of the *Tamid,* and the *Kohen Gadol*'s flour-offering, remained lying on the Ramp(92).

All of a sudden the silence was interrupted by a loud chorus of voices — both young and old — united in uttering the priestly blessing:

> Blessed are You, Hashem, our God, King of the world, Who sanctified us with the sanctity of Aharon and commanded us to bless His people Yisrael *be-ahavah* (with love)[9]

the Kohanim chanted fervently. Naftali could feel the Kohanim's great love for their brothers, Yisrael, permeating the powerful sound of the chorus.[10]

Naftali thought to himself, "This love causes HaKadosh Baruch Hu to look favorably on us, His children, and awakens His compassion for us. In this way the blessing of Heaven upon the people of Yisrael takes effect."

One of the Yisraelim, a tall and imposing man with a silver

---

8. Mishnah *Tamid* 7:2, *Tiferes Yisrael* #13.

9. *Sotah* 39a.

10. *Ma'or VaShemesh, Parashas Naso.*

beard, stood in front of the Kohanim and called out to them the words of the blessing,[11] one by one, and they repeated after him in a loud voice:[12]

"Yevarechecha" — *Yevarechecha.*

Now the older man uttered the Divine Name *beshem ha-meforash*,[13] i.e. the way it is spelled — *Yud-Hei-Vav-Hei* — and the Kohanim repeated it after him.

"Ve-yishmerecha" — *Ve-yishmerecha.*
"May Hashem bless you and protect you!"

The Kohanim recited the blessing with their hands raised above their heads. Only the *Kohen Gadol* was careful not to raise his hands higher than the *tzitz* (headband) that had the Name of Hashem engraved on it. A lofty atmosphere settled in the *Azarah*. The children felt as if the *Shechinah* was hovering above their heads. They had heard the priestly blessing before on many occasions but here, in this place that could only be called the gate of Heaven, the blessing seemed unlike any other blessing they had ever heard in their lives. At that very moment a *shefa gadol*, a great bounty, was bestowed from Heaven upon the people of Yisrael all over the world. The children were going to answer *Amen* after the first blessing, but Reb Shmuel motioned for them to be quiet.

Only after the Kohanim finished reciting all three priestly blessings[14] did the entire audience exclaim with great love for their Creator, "Blessed is Hashem, God of Yisrael, forever and

---

11. Rambam, *Hilchos Nesiyas Kapayim* 14:9.
12. *Sotah* 38a.
13. Mishnah *Tamid* 7:2.
14. *Sotah* 37b.

> The burning of the *eivarim* precedes the *Tamid* meal-offering, and the *Tamid* meal-offering precedes the offering of the *Kohen Gadol*'s flour-offering...

ever" [*Baruch Hashem, Elokei Yisrael, min ha-olam ve-ad ha-olam*"].[15] The children joined them with great fervor.

Naftali strained his neck and looked hard at the Kohanim. He could not look at them during the *berachah* because of the *Shechinah* that rested upon their fingers.[16] The face of the *Kohen Gadol* shone with an unearthly splendor, more radiant than ever.

"I heard from my father that during the priestly blessing the *Kohen Gadol* whispers the Divine Name consisting of twelve letters,"[17] Chananya whispered into Naftali's ear, as if sharing a secret with him.

The *Kohen Gadol* descended the Steps of the *Ulam*(22) and approached the Main Ramp(92) again. His deputy flanked him on the right and escorted him until they almost reached the top of the *Mizbeach*. There he received the vessel with the *Tamid* meal-offering and threw the fine-quality wheat flour [*soles*] mixed with oil into the Great Pyre(88).[18] He did the same with his *minchas ha-chavitin* (flour-offering).

Rabbi Yishmael walked up to the roof of the *Mizbeach*, turned right and went around it along the *Kohanim*'s Footpath(91). He passed the Southeastern Corner (97)[19] and the Northeastern Corner(98), and while there he turned over the parts of the *Tamid*-offering that were burning in the fire of the Great Pyre.[20] He used

---

15. Rambam, *Hilchos Nesiyas Kapayim* 14:9.
16. *Chagigah* 16a.
17. *Kiddushin* 71a.
18. Rambam, *Hilchos Temidin u'Musafin* 6:5.
19. Mishnah *Tamid* 7:3.
20. Ibid., Bartenura.

a tool called a *tzinora* to turn them over, so that they would get completely consumed by the fire.

"On Erev Pesach I saw a Kohen pouring the wine-offering onto the *Mizbeach*. He turned to the left, straight toward the Southwestern Corner(100) without circling the other three Corners.[21] Why doesn't the *Kohen Gadol* do the same now?" Naftali wondered.

"The *kohen hedyot* must turn straight[22] toward the Southwestern Corner in order that the wine will not get spoiled from the smoke of the Pyre, whereas the *Kohen Gadol* continues to follow the principle that all directional moves one makes in the Beis HaMikdash should favor the right side," explained Reb Shmuel. "His high-ranking position permits him to behave in the Beis Ha-Mikdash with less restriction and allows him to go the way he prefers.[23] So he circles from the right. The wine won't be spoiled because he doesn't take it with him past the smoke, and when he reaches the Southwestern Corner, the poured-offerings [*nesachim*] will be passed on to him by other Kohanim."

In the meantime, the Leviyim had finished their preparations for singing the *Shir shel Yom*. They stood ready on the *Duchan*(5), each one in his proper place. Some of them were holding musical instruments: lyres [*nevalim*], harps [*kinoros*], trumpets [*chatzotzros*] and flutes [*chalilim*].[24] Others were ready to start singing.

Two Kohanim stood on the western side of the *Mizbeach*, on the *chalavim* Table(80) holding trumpets.[25] The *segan* stood on the Southwestern Corner of the *Mizbeach* with a cloth [*sudar*] in his hand, and another Kohen stood next to him with a vessel full of the *nesachim*-wine. As soon as the *Kohen Gadol* approached them,

---

21. *Zevachim* 63b.
22. *Zevachim* 64b, Rashi (ד"ה הקפה).
23. Mishnah *Tamid* 7:3, Bartenura.
24. *Arachin* 10a,13a.
25. Mishnah *Tamid* 7:3.

Nisuch HaYayin
(The Poured-Offering of Wine)

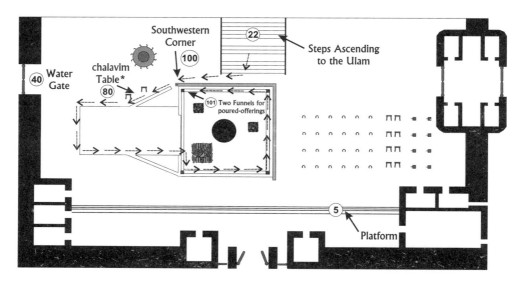

* The chalavim Table was made of marble. The other
  table here near the Mizbeach was made of silver.

the wine was passed on to him, and the two Kohanim blew their trumpets as follows:[26] "*tekiyah, teru'ah, tekiyah.*"[27] After they had finished blowing the trumpets they went down and stood on the *Duchan*(5) next to Ben Arza, who was the Levi in charge of music.[28] He held an instrument called a *tziltzal* (cymbals).

> And the *Kohen Gadol's* flour-offering precedes the poured-offering of wine.

There were Two Funnels next to the base of the Southwestern Corner. The *Kohen Gadol* bent down[29] and poured the wine into the eastern Funnel(101),[30] and the *segan* waved the cloth that he held.[31] Ben Arza banged the cymbals together and the Leviyim started singing the *Shir shel Yom*. Since it was a Thursday, the fifth day of the week, they sang Psalm 81.[32]

A heavenly singing seemed to have descended upon the Beis HaMikdash directly from the celestial realms of song. Naftali's eyes were filled with tears of emotion. Tens of Leviyim stood there, chanting the verses composed by King David, the sweet singer of Yisrael:

> Sing for joy unto God, our strength;
> shout for joy to the God of Yaakov.
> Lift up your voice in song, and sound the drum,
> the sweet harp with the lyre.[33]

---

26. Rambam, *Hilchos Temidin u'Musafin* 6:6.

27. Mishnah *Tamid* 7:3.

28. Mishnah *Shekalim* 5:1; *Tiferes Yisrael* #12.

29. Mishnah *Tamid* 7:3.

30. *Sukkah* 48b.

31. Mishnah *Tamid* 7:3.

32. Mishnah *Tamid* 7:4.

33. *Tehillim* 81:2–3.

The Leviyim interrupted their singing on two occasions, during which the Kohanim blew the trumpets,[34] and all those who stood in the *Azarah* prostrated themselves with their arms and legs outstretched.[35]

A lofty spirit filled the *Azarah* with the increasing power of the song. Jews stood there listening to the chanting with rapt attention. Their souls relished every sound of it.

> I am the Eternal, your God,
> Who brought you up from the land of Mitzrayim;
> open wide your mouth and I will fill it.[36]

The singing went on and on. Naftali wanted it to go on forever. He felt his soul rise from the sweetness of the tune. He was standing, **facing the Throne of Glory**, and his whole body trembled as tears rolled down his cheeks like little pearls.

"O Master of the world!" he whispered with great devotion, "I love You so much! I want to serve You truly and wholeheartedly! I want to please You! Please, Father in Heaven, help me escape from the *yetzer ha-ra*, who wants to catch me into his net and prevent me from doing Your will…"

As Naftali was praying and crying, one of the Sages' statements entered his mind: "No one ever slept overnight in Yerushalayim with a sin on his conscience. How was that possible? The *Tamid shel shachar* atoned for the sins committed at night, and the afternood *Tamid* atoned for the sins committed in the daytime."[37] Now he fully understood how these sacrifices were able to atone for sins.

---

34. Mishnah *Tamid* 7:3.

35. Ibid., *Tiferes Yisrael* #43.

36. *Tehillim* 81:11.

37. *Pesikta deRav Kahana*, par. 6.

Naftali was overcome by a spirit of *teshuvah* (repentance). He poured out his heart: "Woe is me; until now I haven't been careful to utter the *berachos* with proper *kavanah* (concentration) ...who knows how many *berachos* I may have made *le-vatalah* (in vain), God forbid! I have mentioned the holy Name of Hashem in vain! Please, Father in Heaven! Bring us back to Your Torah, and draw us near to Your Service, and make us do perfect *teshuvah* before You! Hashem, please forgive me. I hereby take upon myself to try with all my might to do Your will!"

When the song of the Leviyim ceased, Naftali felt that his heart was cleansed and purified. He thanked Hashem for having given him an opportunity to visit the Beis HaMikdash and for... having been born a Jew! He thanked Hashem for the opportunity to please his Creator, and for meriting such an abundance of *berachah* from Heaven.

*   *   *

A fervent prayer to our Father in Heaven bursts out from our yearning hearts, a prayer uttered with deep longing and hope: "O Master of the world, please have mercy on us, as a father has mercy on his sons! Aren't we Your children, and You — our Father? We want to see the Beis HaMikdash with our own eyes, and not only dream about it and learn about it from textbooks. We want not only to learn the *halachos* of *korbanos*, but also to physically participate in offering them. O Father in Heaven, we beg of you! Give us the *zechus* to prostrate ourselves **facing the Throne of Glory!**

> Appear from Your place,
> O King, and rule over us soon,
> for we are waiting for You...

Key to Reference Numbers, Charts, and Maps of Sites in the Beis HaMikdash

- *Most places and sites can be found on the main map in the back of the book.*
- *The Temple Mount Gates(24)(25)(26)(27) and the Minor Sanhedrin Chamber on the Temple Mount can be found on the map of the Temple Mount on p. 29.*
- *The Attic can be found in the diagram on p. 195.*
- *The Altar and its parts (nos. 87–106) can be found on the maps of the Altar on pp. 61 and 98.*
- *The locations of six chambers(71)(72)(73)(74)(75)(76) are unknown.*

Areas

		אֲזוֹרִים
(1)	*Har HaBayis* (Temple Mount)	(1) הַר הַבַּיִת
(2)	*Cheil*	(2) חֵיל
(3)	*Ezras Nashim* (Women's Courtyard)	(3) עֶזְרַת נָשִׁים
(4)	*Ezras Yisrael* (Israelites' Courtyard)	(4) עֶזְרַת יִשְׂרָאֵל
(5)	Platform (consisting of 4 steps)	(5) דּוּכָן (4 מַדְרֵגוֹת)
(6)	*Ezras Kohanim* (Kohanim's Courtyard)	(6) עֶזְרַת כֹּהֲנִים
(7)	*Mizbeach* (Altar)	(7) מִזְבֵּחַ
(8)	Beis HaMitbechayim (Slaughtering Area)	(8) בֵּית הַמִּטְבְּחַיִם
(9)	Between the *Ulam* and the *Mizbeach*	(9) בֵּין הָאוּלָם וְהַמִּזְבֵּחַ
(10)	*Ulam* (Antechamber)	(10) אוּלָם
(11)	*Heichal* (Temple Chamber)	(11) הֵיכָל
(12)	*Kodesh HaKodashim* (Holy of Holies)	(12) קֹדֶשׁ הַקֳּדָשִׁים

321

Walls and Partitons

(13) Temple Mount Wall

(14) *Soreg* (lattice fence)

(15) Wall of *Azarah*

(16) Wall of *Ulam*, Staircase, and Drainage Channel

(17) Wall of Compartments (*Ta'im*)

(18) Wall of *Heichal*

(19) Two Curtains and the one-cubit pasage between them, which divided the *Heichal* from the *Kodesh HaKodashim*

Steps

(20) 12 Steps ascending from *Cheil* to *Azarah*

(21) 15 Steps ascending from *Ezras Nashim* to *Ezras Yisrael*

(22) 12 Steps ascending to *Ulam*

(23) Staircase

(24) Drainage Channel

Gates

TEMPLE MOUNT GATES

(25) Two Chuldah Gates

(26) Shushan Gate

(27) Tadi Gate

(28) Kiphonus Gate

AZARAH GATES

(29) Eastern Gate (entrance to *Ezras Nashim*)

(30) Nikanor Gate (entrance to *Ezras Yisrael*)

(31) Two Side Doors on either side of Nikanor Gate

(32) Pyre Hall Gate (Music Gate)

חומות ומחיצות

(13) חוֹמַת הַר הַבַּיִת

(14) סוֹרֵג

(15) חוֹמַת הָעֲזָרָה

(16) כֹּתֶל הָאוּלָם, הַמְּסִבָּה וּבֵית הוֹרָדַת הַמַּיִם

(17) כֹּתֶל הַתָּא

(18) כֹּתֶל הַהֵיכָל

(19) אַמָּה טְרַקְסִין

מדרגות

(20) 12 הַמַּדְרֵגוֹת שֶׁבַּחֵיל

(21) 15 הַמַּעֲלוֹת

(22) 12 מַדְרֵגוֹת הָאוּלָם

(23) הַמְּסִבָּה

(24) בֵּית הוֹרָדַת הַמַּיִם

שְׁעָרִים

שַׁעֲרֵי הַר הַבַּיִת

(25) שְׁנֵי שַׁעֲרֵי חֻלְדָּה

(26) שַׁעַר שׁוּשָׁן

(27) שַׁעַר טָדִי

(28) שַׁעַר קִיפוֹנוֹס

שַׁעֲרֵי הָעֲזָרָה

(29) שַׁעַר הַמִּזְרָחִי

(30) שַׁעַר נִקָנוֹר

(31) שְׁנֵי הַפִּשְׁפְּשִׁים מִצִּדֵּי שַׁעַר נִקָנוֹר

(32) שַׁעַר בֵּית הַמּוֹקֵד(שַׁעַר הַשִּׁיר)

(33) The Women's Gate	(33) שַׁעַר הַנָּשִׁים
(34) Gate of the Sacrifice	(34) שַׁעַר הַקָּרְבָּן
(35) Gate of the Spark (Yechonyah Gate)	(35) שַׁעַר הַנִּיצוֹץ (שַׁעַר יְכָנְיָה)
(36) Two Western Gates	(36) שְׁנֵי הַשְּׁעָרִים בַּמַּעֲרָב
(37) Upper Gate	(37) שַׁעַר הָעֶלְיוֹן
(38) Gate of the Firewood	(38) שַׁעַר הַדֶּלֶק
(39) Gate of the Firstborn	(39) שַׁעַר הַבְּכוֹרוֹת
(40) Water Gate	(40) שַׁעַר הַמַּיִם

TEMPLE GATES	**שַׁעֲרֵי הַבִּנְיָן**
(41) Entrance to *Ulam*	(41) פֶּתַח הָאוּלָם
(42) Entrance to *Heichal*	(42) פֶּתַח הַהֵיכָל

Chambers

לְשָׁכוֹת

(43) Stone Chamber	(43) לִשְׁכַּת בֵּית הָאֶבֶן
(44) Minor Sanhedrin Chamber (on the Temple Mount)	(44) סַנְהֶדְרֵי קְטַנָּה — הַר הַבַּיִת
(45) Minor Sanhedrin Chamber (in the *Ezras Nashim*)	(45) סַנְהֶדְרֵי קְטַנָּה — עֶזְרַת נָשִׁים
(46) Nazirites' Chamber	(46) לִשְׁכַּת הַנְּזִירִים
(47) Wood Chamber	(47) לִשְׁכַּת הָעֵצִים
(48) *Metzora'im's* Chamber	(48) לִשְׁכַּת הַמְּצֹרָעִים
(49) Oil Chamber	(49) לִשְׁכַּת הַשְּׁמָנִים
(50) Musical Instruments Chambers	(50) לִשְׁכוֹת כְּלֵי הַשִּׁיר
(51) Chamber for the Preparation of the *Kohen Gadol's* flour-offering	(51) לִשְׁכַּת עוֹשֵׂי חֲבִיתִּין
(52) Chamber of Pinchas, Keeper of the Priestly Garments	(52) לִשְׁכַּת פִּנְחָס הַמַּלְבִּישׁ
(53) Chamber of Hewn Stone (seat of the Sanhedrin)	(53) לִשְׁכַּת הַגָּזִית
(54) Parhedrin Chamber (where the *Kohen Gadol* was sequestered for seven days before Yom Kippur)	(54) לִשְׁכַּת פַּרְהֶדְרִין
(55) Chamber of the Diaspora	(55) לִשְׁכַּת הַגּוֹלָה

(56) The Pyre Hall   בֵּית הַמּוֹקֵד (56)

(57) Chamber of Sacrificial Lambs   לִשְׁכַּת טְלָאֵי קָרְבָּן (57)

(58) Chamber for preparation of   לִשְׁכַּת עוֹשֵׂי לֶחֶם הַפָּנִים (58)
       Showbread (*Lechem HaPanim*)

(59) Chamber of the Receipts   לִשְׁכַּת הַחוֹתָמוֹת (59)

(60) Small Pyre Chamber   בֵּית הַמּוֹקֵד הַקָּטָן (60)

(61) Chamber of the Spark   בֵּית הַנִּיצוֹץ (61)

(62) Salt Chamber   לִשְׁכַּת הַמֶּלַח (62)

(63) *Parvah* Chamber   לִשְׁכַּת בֵּית הַפַּרְוָה (63)

(64) Rinsing Chamber   לִשְׁכַּת הַמַּדִּיחִין (64)

(65) Avtinas Family Chamber   לִשְׁכַּת בֵּית אַבְטִינָס (65)

(66) *Mikveh* of the *Kohen Gadol* above the   מִקְוֵה הַכֹּהֵן הַגָּדוֹל מֵעַל (66)
       Parvah Chamber   בֵּית הַפַּרְוָה

(67) *Mikveh* of the *Kohen Gadol* above the   מִקְוֵה הַכֹּהֵן הַגָּדוֹל מֵעַל (67)
       Water Gate   שַׁעַר הַמַּיִם

(68) Knives Chamber   בֵּית הַחֲלִיפוֹת (68)

(69) Compartments   תָּאִים (69)

(70) Attic   עֲלִיָּה (70)

(71) Chamber (*Shekels* Chamber)   לִשְׁכָּה (לִשְׁכַּת הַשְּׁקָלִים) (71)

(72) Chamber of Secrecy   לִשְׁכַּת חֲשָׁאִים (72)

(73) Vessels Chamber   לִשְׁכַּת הַכֵּלִים (73)

(74) Curtain Chamber   לִשְׁכַּת הַפָּרֹכֶת (74)

(75) Chamber of the Sacrifice   לִשְׁכַּת הַקָּרְבָּן (75)

(76) 13 Shofar-chests for storing the   שְׁלֹשׁ עֶשְׂרֵה הַשּׁוֹפָרוֹת (76)
       Temple moneys

Objects   חֲפָצִים

(77) Rings to secure the animals   טַבָּעוֹת (77)
       for slaughter

(78) Tables used for rinsing   שֻׁלְחָנוֹת בֵּית הַמִּטְבָּחַיִם (78)
       the flayed animals

(79) Low Pillars for flaying the   נַנָּסִין (79)
       slaughtered animals

(80) Two Tables near Altar   שְׁנֵי שֻׁלְחָנוֹת שֶׁלְּיַד הַמִּזְבֵּחַ (80)

(81) *Kiyor* (Washing Basin)   כִּיּוֹר (81)

(82) Two Tables in *Ulam*   שְׁנֵי שֻׁלְחֲנוֹת הָאוּלָם (82)

(83) The Golden Altar (Incense Altar)   מִזְבֵּחַ הַזָּהָב (הַקְּטֹרֶת) (83)

(84) Menorah   מְנוֹרָה (84)

(85) Showbread Table   שֻׁלְחַן לֶחֶם הַפָּנִים (85)

(86) *Ehven HaShesiyah* (Location of the Ark in the First Temple)   אֶבֶן הַשְּׁתִיָּה (מְקוֹם הָאָרוֹן) (86)

Mizbeach (Altar)   מִזְבֵּחַ

(87) (*Tapuach*) Pile of Ashes   תַּפּוּחַ (87)

(88) Great Pyre   מַעֲרָכָה גְדוֹלָה (88)

(89) Second Pyre (for incense)   מַעֲרָכָה שְׁנִיָּה שֶׁל קְטֹרֶת (89)

(90) Pyre for Sustaining the Fire   מַעֲרָכָה לְקִיּוּם הָאֵשׁ (90)

(91) Kohanim's Footpath   מְקוֹם הִלּוּךְ הַכֹּהֲנִים (91)

(92) Main Ramp   כֶּבֶשׁ גָּדוֹל (92)

(93) Small Ramp on the East   כֶּבֶשׁ קָטָן מִמִּזְרָח (93)

(94) Small Ramp on the West   כֶּבֶשׁ קָטָן מִמַּעֲרָב (94)

(95) Window, on the west side of Main Ramp, where disqualified burnt-offerings of birds were placed   חַלּוֹן (רְבוּבָה) (95)

(96) Circuit (*Sovev*)   סוֹבֵב (96)

(97) Southeastern Corner (Turret)   קֶרֶן דְּרוֹמִית-מִזְרָחִית (97)

(98) Northeastern Corner (Turret)   קֶרֶן מִזְרָחִית-צְפוֹנִית (98)

(99) Northwestern Corner (Turret)   קֶרֶן צְפוֹנִית-מַעֲרָבִית (99)

(100) Southwestern Corner (Turret)   קֶרֶן מַעֲרָבִית-דְּרוֹמִית (100)

(101) 2 Funnels for poured-offerings   שְׁנֵי הַסְּפָלִים (101)

(102) Red Line (*Chut HaSikra*)   חוּט הַסִּקְרָא (102)

(103) Northern Base   יְסוֹד צְפוֹנִי (103)

(104) Western Base   יְסוֹד מַעֲרָבִי (104)

(105) Southern Base   יְסוֹד דְּרוֹמִי (105)

(106) Passageway between Main Ramp and Altar leading under the Altar   לוּל (106)

Glossary

The following glossary provides a partial explanation of some of the Hebrew and Aramaic (A.) words and phrases used in this book. The spellings
and explanations reflect the way the specific word is used herein. Often,
there are alternate spellings and meanings for the words.

AKEIDAS YITZCHAK: the Binding of Isaac (see *Genesis/Bereishis* 22).

ALIYAH LE-REGEL: the mitzvah of making a pilgrimage to Jerusalem for
the three festivals — PESACH, SHAVUOS, and SUKKOS — during the time
of the BEIS HAMIKDASH.

AMAH (pl. AMOS): a cubit; a measure of approximately 21.5 inches, or 54
centimeters.

ANSHEI KNESSES HAGEDOLAH: the Men of the Great Assembly (circa
355-273 B.C.E.).

ARON (HAKODESH): the Holy Ark.

ASHAM: see KORBAN ASHAM.

ASHAM TALUY: see KORBAN ASHAM-TALUY.

AVEIRAH: a sin.

AVNET: the belt that a KOHEN wears when performing the Temple service.

AVODAH: service; the service performed in the BEIS HAMIKDASH.

AVOS: forefathers.

AVRAHAM: our forefather Abraham.

AZARAH: the Temple courtyard.

B'EZRAS HASHEM: "With God's help."

BARUCH DAYAN HAEMES: lit., "Blessed is the True Judge," a blessing recited upon hearing bad tidings.

BAZACH: a small, covered vessel filled with KETORES used in the KORBAN TAMID service.

BEIS DIN (pl. BATEI DIN): a Jewish court of law.

BEIS HABECHIRAH: lit., the Chosen House, i.e., the BEIS HAMIKDASH.

BEIS HAMIKDASH: the Holy Temple in YERUSHALAYIM.

BEMIDBAR: the Book of Numbers.

BERACHAH (pl. BERACHOS): a blessing.

BIGDEI KEHUNAH: the garments KOHANIM wear when performing the Temple service.

BLI NEDER: a phrase that changes a firm promise into an intention.

CHACHAMIM: Sages.

CHAGIGAH: see KORBAN CHAGIGAH.

CHALILAH: "God forbid!"

CHAMETZ: leavened food, prohibited during Passover.

CHAS VE-SHALOM: "God forbid!"

CHATAS: see KORBAN CHATAS.

CHAVURAH (pl. CHAVUROS): a group of Jews who bring and eat the Pesach-offering together.

CHEIL: the narrow area between the *Soreg* (lattice fence) and the wall that surrounds the AZARAH.

CHELEV (pl. CHALAVIM): layers of fat from some of the internal organs of animals. Some of these can be EMURIM.

CHILUL SHABBOS BE-SHOGEG: desecrating the Sabbath unintentionally.

CHOL HAMO'ED: the intermediate days of the Festivals of PESACH and SUKKOS.

CHOSHEN MISHPAT: the breastplate worn by the KOHEN GADOL.

CHUMRAH (pl.CHUMROS): a stringent ruling.

CHUTZ LA'ARETZ: outside the Land of Israel.

DAYAN (pl. DAYANIM): a judge.

EIFAH: a measurement of solid volume, equaling 18 KAV.

EIVARIM: limbs.

EIZOV: hyssop.

EMURIM: sacrificial portions.

EPHOD: an apron-like garment worn by the KOHEN GADOL.

ERETZ YISRAEL: the Land of Israel.

EREV PESACH: the day before Passover, i.e., the fourteenth of the Hebrew month of Nisan.

EREV SHABBOS: the day before the Sabbath, i.e., Friday.

ETZBA: lit., finger; the measurement of a thumb-width: about .9 inches, or 2.25 centimeters.

GEMATRIA: (A.) the numerical equivalent of a Hebrew word.

HALACHAH (pl. HALACHOS): Jewish law.

HALLEL: a song of praise (TEHILLIM 113-118) recited on ROSH CHODESH and Festivals.

HAR HABAYIS: the Temple Mount.

HAR HAZEISIM: the Mount of Olives.

HASHEM: God.

HEICHAL: the inner Temple chamber where the Menorah, Golden MIZBEACH, and Showbread Table are kept.

HIN: an ancient measurement of liquid volume, equivalent to 3 LOG.

IM YIRTZEH HASHEM: "God willing."

ISH HAR HABAYIS: an officer of the Temple Mount.

ISSUR: a prohibition.

ISSUR VADAY: something definitely prohibited (see SAFEK ISSUR).

IYOV: the Book of Job.

KAL VA-CHOMER: One of the thirteen rules for learning HALACHOS in the Torah: If a strict law applies to a lenient case, it certainly must apply to a more strict case.

KARES: the death penalty executed by Heaven.

KAV (pl. KABIN): an ancient measurement of volume, approximately 2.9 pints or 1.4 liters.

KEREN (pl. KRANOS): a corner of the MIZBEACH.

KERIAS SHEMA: the recital of *Shema*, the fundamental prayer which proclaims the unity of God.

KETORES: the incense used in the BEIS HAMIKDASH.

KIPPAH (pl. KIPPOS): a dome-like roof.

KLAL YISRAEL: the Jewish Nation.

KODASHIM: sacrifices.

KODASHIM KALIM: sacrifices of lesser sanctity.

KODESH HAKODASHIM: the Holy of Holies; the most inner room of the BEIS HAMIKDASH.

KODSHEI KODASHIM: sacrifices of the highest sanctity.

KOHEN (pl. KOHANIM): a member of the priestly tribe; a descendant of Aaron.

KOHEN GADOL: a high priest.

KOHEN HEDYOT: a regular priest (i.e., not the KOHEN GADOL).

KORBAN (pl. KORBANOS): a sacrifice or offering.

KORBAN ASHAM: a guilt-offering.

KORBAN CHAGIGAH: a Festival-offering.

KORBAN CHATAS: a sin-offering.

KORBAN HAOMER: the *Omer*-offering, brought on the 16th of the Hebrew month of Nisan (i.e. the day after the first day of Pesach).

KORBAN OLAH: a burnt-offering.

KORBAN PESACH: the Pesach-offering.

KORBAN TAMID: the daily or "continuous" offering, brought twice a day in the BEIS HAMIKDASH.

KORBAN TAMID SHEL SHACHAR: the daily morning sacrifice.

KORBAN TZIBUR: a KORBAN brought on behalf of the entire Jewish People.

KUTONES: the garment worn by a KOHEN serving in the BEIS HAMIKDASH.

LASHON HA-RA: malicious gossip; speaking badly about another person.

LEVI (pl. LEVIYIM): a Levite; a member of the tribe of Levi.

LISHKAH: a chamber in the BEIS HAMIKDASH.

LISHMAH: for its own sake; usually refers to learning Torah.

LOG: a measurement of liquid volume, equaling approximately .7 pints, or .3 liters.

MA'ARACHOS: the special fires arranged on the MIZBEACH.

MACHTAH: the firepan used for holding burning coals during the service in the BEIS HAMIKDASH.

MAHN: manna.

MAYIM: water.

MAYIM CHAYIM: lit., "living water," i.e., water from a spring.

MECHUSAR KIPPURIM (pl. MECHUSAREI KIPPURIM): someone who has already immersed in a MIKVEH but has not sacrificed his obligatory KORBAN to atone for his TUM'AH completely.

MEGILLAS ESTHER: the Scroll of Esther.

MEI CHATAS: special water mixed with the ashes of the PARAH ADUMAH, used to purify someone with TUM'AS MEIS.

MEI NIDDAH: another word for MEI CHATAS.

MEIS: a corpse.

MELACHIM: the Book of Kings.

MELAMED: a teacher of Torah.

MEMUNEH: the official in charge of the SHOMRIM. Either he, or one of the men he supervises, patrols the guard posts on HAR HABAYIS and the BEIS HAMIKDASH at night.

METZORA (pl. METZORA'IM): someone afflicted with TZARA'AS.

MICHNASAYIM: the pants worn by a KOHEN serving in the BEIS HAMIK-DASH.

MIGBA'AS: the turban worn by a KOHEN serving in the BEIS HAMIKDASH.

MIKVEH: a pool of water for ritual immersion and purification.

MISHNAH (pl. MISHNAYOS): the codified Oral Law redacted by Rabbi Yehudah HaNasi; a specific paragraph of the Oral Law.

MITZVAH (pl. MITZVOS): a commandment.

MIZBEACH: Altar.

MUSSAR: Torah ethics and values aimed at character improvement.

NACHAS: pleasure, satisfaction.

NE'ILAH: the closing service on Yom Kippur.

NEGA (pl. NEGA'IM): a mark of TZARA'AS that brings on TUM'AH.

NESECH (pl. NESACHIM): a poured-offering upon the MIZBEACH.

NEVI'AH: a female prophet.

NEZIRIM: people who accept upon themselves the status of Nazirite.

NISUCH HAMAYIM: the water-offering poured on the MIZBEACH each day of the Festival of SUKKOS.

NISUCH HAYAYIN: the wine-offering poured on the MIZBEACH.

NISUCH TAMID: the NISUCH HAYAYIN for the KORBAN TAMID.

OHEL MO'ED: the Tent of Meeting in the desert Tabernacle, equivalent to the HEICHAL in the BEIS HAMIKDASH.

OLAH (pl. OLOS): see KORBAN OLAH.

OLEH REGEL (pl. OLEI REGEL): one who makes a pilgrimage to YERUSHA-LAYIM for one of the three Festivals (PESACH, SHAVUOS, and SUKKOS). See ALIYAH LE-REGEL.

PARAH ADUMAH: the Red Heifer (Cow), whose ashes are burned and used for ritual purification.

PASUL: unfit; invalid; disqualified.

PAYIS: lottery.

PAYOS: sidelocks.

PESACH: the Festival of Passover; the name of the Pesach sacrifice.

PESACH SHEINI: lit., a "second Pesach," the 14th of the Hebrew month of Iyar, when those who were unable to offer the KORBAN PESACH a month previously have a second chance to bring the offering.

REBBI: a Torah teacher.

RECHILUS: talebearing; gossip which causes discord.

REVI'IS: lit., "one fourth," a liquid volume measure, equivalent to ¼ LOG.

ROSH CHODESH: the first day of the Hebrew month.

RU'ACH HA-KODESH: lit., "the holy spirit," a lower degree of prophesy; Divine inspiration.

SANHEDRIN: the high/supreme court in the time of the BEIS HAMIKDASH.

SE'AH: a grain measure equaling 8.2 liters, slightly less than ¼ bushel.

SEGAN: deputy.

SEMICHAH: pressing one's weight with his hands on the KORBAN's head.

SHABBOS: the Sabbath.

SHAVUOS: lit., "weeks," the Festival celebrated seven weeks after PESACH, when firstfruits may begin to be brought to the BEIS HAMIKDASH.

SHE'EILAH: a halachic question.

SHECHINAH: the Divine Presence of God.

SHECHITAH: ritual slaughter.

SHELAMIM: peace offerings.

SHEMIRAH: guarding; guard duty around HAR HABAYIS and the BEIS HA-MIKDASH.

SHEMONEH ESREH: lit., "eighteen," the blessings of the *Amidah* prayer, which forms the main part of the prayer service.

SHERETZ: a low-creeping creature, which is spiritually impure. An example of this would be a mouse.

SHIR SHEL YOM: the Psalm of the Day.

SHIUR: a Torah class; a specified amount.

SHOCHET: a ritual slaughterer.

SHOFAROS: trumpets made of rams' horns.

SHOMER (pl. SHOMRIM): a guard.

SHULCHAN (pl. SHULCHANOS): a table.

SHUMAN: permitted fat of an animal.

SIMCHAH: happiness.

SIYATA DISHMAYA: (A.) Heavenly assistance.

SUKKOS: the Festival of Tabernacles.

TAHARAH: ritual purity.

TAHARAS HA-METZORA: purification of the METZORA.

TAHOR: ritually pure.

TALLIS: a prayer shawl.

TALMID CHACHAM (pl. TALMIDEI CHACHAMIM): a Torah scholar.

TAMEI (pl. TEMEI'IM): ritually impure.

TAMID: see KORBAN TAMID.

TAMID SHEL SHACHAR: see KORBAN TAMID SHEL SHACHAR.

TEFACH (pl. TEFACHIM): a handbreadth — about 3.5 inches, or 9 centimeters.

TEHILLIM: the Book of Psalms.

TEMEI MEIS (pl. TEME'EI MEIS): someone who is TAMEI from a corpse.

TERUMAH: an especially holy tithe, separated from produce and given to a KOHEN.

TESHUVAH: repentance.

TUM'AH: ritual impurity.

TUM'AS HA-NEGA'IM: ritual impurity from a NEGA.

TUM'AS MEIS: ritual impurity from a corpse.

TZADDIK (pl. TZADDIKIM): a righteous person.

TZARA'AS: a disease meted out as Divine punishment for certain transgressions (see NEGA).

TZEDAKAH: charity.

ULAM: the antechamber to the HEICHAL in the BEIS HAMIKDASH.

VIDUY: confession of sins.

YAAKOV: our forefather Jacob.

YERUSHALAYIM: Jerusalem.

YESOD: the base of the MIZBEACH.

YETZER HA-RA: the evil inclination.

YIRAS SHAMAYIM: fear of Heaven.

YISRAEL: Israel; the Jewish People.

YITZCHAK: our forefather Isaac.

YOM TOV: lit., "a good day," a Jewish Festival.

ZECHUS: merit.

West

60 32 59
56
57 58

35 34 33 15
61

79

36

78

68
8
16
23
17
69 69 69 69 69
18
82
86 12 19 85 83 11 41 22
84 42
7
69
69 82
69 18 10
69 69 69 69 69 9
17
24 81 80
16
68

37 38 39 67 65
15 40